T0301550

Institutional Reform, Regulation and Privatization

Institutional Reform, Regulation and Privatization

Process and Outcomes in Infrastructure Industries

Edited by

Rolf W. Künneke
Associate Professor, Delft University of Technology,
The Netherlands

Aad F. Correljé
Associate Professor, Delft University of Technology,
The Netherlands

John P.M. Groenewegen
Professor, Delft University of Technology,
The Netherlands

BELGIAN–DUTCH ASSOCIATION FOR INSTITUTIONAL AND
POLITICAL ECONOMY

Edward Elgar
Cheltenham, UK • Northampton, MA, USA

Published by
Edward Elgar Publishing Limited
Glensanda House
Montpellier Parade
Cheltenham
Glos GL50 1UA
UK

Edward Elgar Publishing, Inc.
136 West Street
Suite 202
Northampton
Massachusetts 01060
USA

A catalogue record for this book
is available from the British Library

ISBN 1 84542 276 7

Printed and bound in Great Britain by MPG Books Ltd, Bodmin, Cornwall

Contents

Figures

Tables

Contributors

Pablo Arocena Garro is Associate Professor of Business Economics and Strategic Management in the Faculty of Economics and Business Administration at the Universidad Pública de Navarra, Spain. He has research interests in the economic analysis of firms and markets, the regulation and privatization of utilities and the measurement of efficiency and productivity. Among his publications are articles in the *International Journal of Industrial Organization, Kyklos, Energy Policy, European Journal of Operational Research and International Journal of Production Economics.*

Johannes M. Bauer is a Professor in the Department of Telecommunication, Information Studies and Media at Michigan State University. He is also the Executive Director of the Quello Center for Telecommunication Management and Law at Michigan State University. He joined Michigan State University in 1990 after receiving his doctorate in economics from the Vienna University of Economics and Business Administration, Vienna, Austria. From 1993 until 1998 he directed the Institute of Public Utilities and Network Industries at the Eli Broad Graduate School of Management at Michigan State University. Dr Bauer taught and researched as a visiting professor at the Delft University of Technology, the Netherlands (2000–2001) and in Beijing, China (2002). His research covers a wide range of issues related to the evolution of telecommunications and information industries, in particular the design and effect of public policies towards these industries, and business strategies in network industries.

Peter A.G. van Bergeijk is a member of the Economic Council of the Netherlands Competition Authority (NMa) in The Hague and affiliated to the Research Center for Economic Policy (OCFEB) of the University of Rotterdam. He held professorships in economics at Zurich University and Erasmus University Rotterdam.

Ignacio Contín Pilart is Associate Professor of Business Economics and Operations Management in the Faculty of Economics and Business Administration at the Universidad Pública de Navarra, Spain. He has research interests in energy economics, the regulation of utilities and entrepreneurship. Among his publications are articles in *Energy Journal* and *Energy Policy*.

Aad F. Correljé is an Associate Professor in the Section Economics of Infrastructures at the Faculty Technology, Policy and Management, Delft University of Technology. He also is an associate fellow at the Clingendael International Energy Programme (CIEP) of the Netherlands Institute for International Affairs, Clingendael. In 1994, he graduated from Political Sciences (International Relations and European Law) at the University of Amsterdam. Combining Political Sciences and Energy Economics, he wrote a PhD thesis entitled, 'The Spanish Oil Industry: Structural Change and Modernisation', at the Centre for International Energy Studies (EURICES) and the Tinbergen Institute of the Erasmus University in Rotterdam, supervised by Prof. P.R. Odell. His current fascination lies with the theoretical and empirical analysis of decision-making processes in respect of public policy and private strategy development, focussing on challenges to the development of infrastructure-bound sectors (particularly oil, gas and water).

John P.M. Groenewegen is Professor in the Economics of Infrastructures, Faculty of Technology, Policy and Management, Delft University of Technology and of Institutional Economics at Erasmus University Rotterdam. He graduated in economics at the Erasmus University Rotterdam. Prof. Groenewegen received his PhD at the University of Maastricht in 1989.

In addition to his chairs he is a research fellow of the Tinbergen Institute (TI) of the Erasmus University Rotterdam and he is General Secretary of the council of the European Association for Evolutionary

Political Economy (EAEPE), member of the board of trustees of the Association for Evolutionary Economics and president of the Board of the Dutch–Belgian Association of Political and Institutional Economics (APIE).

Jacco R. Hakfoort holds a PhD degree in economics. He is currently working for the Dutch Ministry of Economic Affairs dealing with market structure issues.

Erik J. Kloosterhuis is Deputy Director Merger Control of the Netherlands Competition Authority (NMa).

Rolf W. Künneke is Associate Professor in the Economics of Infrastructures at the Faculty of Technology, Policy and Management of Delft University of Technology, The Netherlands. He holds a masters degree in economics (University of Dortmund, Germany) and received his PhD degree from Twente University, The Netherlands. He has a long record of research on the restructuring of infrastructure industries, with a special focus on the energy sector. Recent research includes: innovations in energy networks; national reforms in European gas, convergence of infrastructures; business strategies of energy firms in liberalized markets, regulation and governance of liberalized infrastructure industries.

Atle Midttun is Professor at the Norwegian School of Management, Co-Director of The Centre for Energy and Environment and Director of The Centre for Corporate Citizenship. He received his PhD from the University of Uppsala, Sweden and his Magister Artium from the University of Oslo. His fields of interest include economic organization, regulation theory, organization theory, innovation theory, corporate social responsibility, political and institutional economics, and methodology. His numerous publications address topics in energy and environmental policy/economics, corporate social responsibility, industrial policy, innovation policy, business strategy, and public sector management.

Tony Prosser has been Professor of Public Law, University of Bristol since 2002, and was previously John Millar Professor of Law, University of Glasgow, 1992–2002. His books include *Test Cases for the Poor* (1983),

Nationalized Industries and Public Control (1986), *Privatizing Public Enterprises*, with Cosmo Graham (1991), *Judicial Review in Scotland*, with T. Mullen and K. Pick (1996), *Law and the Regulators* (1997). He has also published over 90 articles and research reports on issues of privatization, regulation, constitutional law, media regulation etc. He has made over 100 invited presentations and lectures in the UK and abroad. His current research interest is public service and the limits to competition law, and his new book *The Limits of Competition Law: Markets and Public Services* was published in early 2005 by Oxford University Press.

Laurens J. de Vries studied Mechanical Engineering in Delft, specializing in environmental and energy technology. After graduating in 1991, he moved to the USA. In Olympia (Washington State) he studied at The Evergreen State College, where he finished his Master of Environmental Studies Degree in 1996. In his studies there, he focussed on environmental economics. In 1997 he left the USA, travelling through Asia for about nine months before returning to the Netherlands. He worked for one year at an environmental consulting company before rejoining Delft University of Technology, this time at the Faculty of Technology, Policy and Management, where he obtained his PhD degree in June, 2004. His dissertation concerned the design of wholesale electricity markets and focused upon the question of generation adequacy. Since obtaining his PhD he has been conducting research and lecturing on the design of electricity markets.

Acknowledgements

The editors would like to thank Amy Mahan, Françoise Dunant, Crista Drost, Fleur Hinse and Wouter Jonker for assisting in delivering the manuscript of this book.

1. Process and Outcomes of the Infrastructure Reform: An Evolutionary Perspective

John P.M. Groenewegen and Rolf W. Künneke

1   INTRODUCTION

Over the past two decades, infrastructure-based industries like telecom, public transport, water management and energy, have been increasingly exposed to the dynamism of the market. Traditionally in Europe these public services were provided by publicly owned monopolies. In many countries these sectors are now in the process of being opened up to new entrants, competing with the incumbent public firms that are often privatized. Thus, the private initiative is stimulated to undertake the further development of these sectors fundamental to society within a competitive market context. The main objectives of this process of liberalization are the stimulation of short-term efficiency and long-term innovativeness.

ECD statistics illustrate that these expectations are realistic, by and large. Infrastructure firms have become much more sensitive to customers' preferences (OECD 2000). Prices have fallen in many cases and the services' quality and choice have substantially improved. This may suggest that the former public utility infrastructures have evolved towards ordinary industrial sectors, the operation and management of which can be left to the private sector, checked by the market. Sometimes it is even argued that tight regulation of the access conditions and the use of the network infrastructures may become redundant in the future. Competition expectation, however, seems overly optimistic. Recent experiences with liberalized infrastructures, notably the Californian energy crisis, the railway accidents in the UK and the increasing concerns about the long-term security of supply in energy have made politicians and public opinion increasingly sensitive to the possibility of destructive effects over the longer term. Gradually, it is being acknowledged that shifts in the governance structures, caused by liberalization and privatization, have a fundamental impact upon the evolution of the network industries. This not only changes the economic performance of these sectors; it also alters firms' preferences regarding technologies and strategies to provide essential social and economic needs – i.e. the formerly public services. Traditionally, the *public* element in these services was characterized by objectives in terms of: safety, long-term security of supply, politically acceptable pricing strategies especially for low-income users and specific industrial and agricultural sectors, regional development and – more recently – sustainability and environmental protection. How are these public objectives addressed in liberalized infrastructures? Should they still be treated as public interests? If yes, what are the policy instruments or economic incentives to safeguard them under the new institutional framework?

A new balance is sought between various institutional arrangements, including markets, public sector involvement, and private initiatives. The various chapters of this book provide deeper analyses into specific aspects of institutional change in various infrastructures. The focus is on the process and the outcome of the restructuring of infrastructure industries from a theoretical and empirical perspective.

This chapter develops a framework for the process of institutional change that is often labelled as 'liberalization of infrastructures'. How does this process develop, what are the driving forces and where does it possibly end? Will there be a new institutional equilibrium after a process of gradual change, or are we in a situation of a radical reform? To what degree is this process predictable or to be influenced by government or private actors? We mainly refer to the field of institutional economics that has potential to provide some understanding of the evolution of institutions in infrastructure industries.[1]

This chapter is structured as follows. In the next paragraph we present some theoretical considerations on the evolution of institutions. Based on a model by Williamson (1998) we provide a short overview of the various perspectives that economic theory provides on institutions. Using this as a starting point, we elaborate on two different approaches to institutional change, i.e. equilibrium- and process- based. This results in a simple model of institutional change that is presented in the third section. Section 4 uses this model to pinpoint the significance of the various contributions in this book. Some concluding remarks finalize the chapter.

2   THE EVOLUTION OF INSTITUTIONS: SOME THEORETICAL CONSIDERATIONS

A useful starting point for the analysis of institutions in a broad sense is the so-called four-layer model of Williamson (1998). These four consecutive layers show the relevance of various economic perspectives on institutions, ranging from a broad socio-economic perspective of Original Institutional Economics (OIE) via New Institutional Economics (NIE) to Neoclassical Economics (NCE).

Level 1 refers to the informal institutions like values, norms, traditions and customs that influence the behaviour of managers and government. It is the level of 'embeddedness'; the domain of social sciences like anthropology, history and sociology. The formation and influence of informal institutions (and the interaction with formal institutions) is often referred to as 'Original Institutional Economics' of which Veblen and Commons belong to the founding fathers.[2] This work elaborates on the embeddedness of economic and social behaviour in informal institutions, customs, norms and even religion. This complex field of research is necessarily quite descriptive by nature.

Level 2 refers to the formal institutions such as the legal rules, like property rights and the public organizations, like bureaucracies. These 'economics of property rights' theories provide important insights into how formal rules influence economic behaviour (Furubotn and Pejovich 1974). The focus is on economic incentives and costs of the enforcement of formal rules.

Figure 1.1   The four-layer model of Williamson (1998)

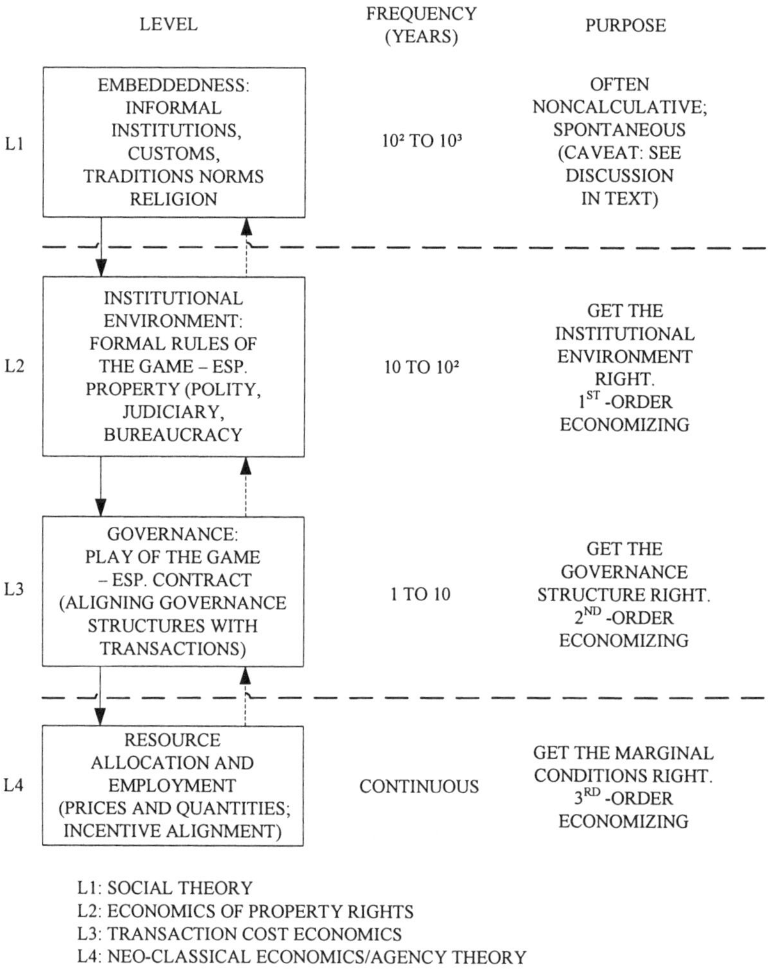

	LEVEL	FREQUENCY (YEARS)	PURPOSE
L1	EMBEDDEDNESS: INFORMAL INSTITUTIONS, CUSTOMS, TRADITIONS NORMS RELIGION	10^2 TO 10^3	OFTEN NONCALCULATIVE; SPONTANEOUS (CAVEAT: SEE DISCUSSION IN TEXT)
L2	INSTITUTIONAL ENVIRONMENT: FORMAL RULES OF THE GAME – ESP. PROPERTY (POLITY, JUDICIARY, BUREAUCRACY	10 TO 10^2	GET THE INSTITUTIONAL ENVIRONMENT RIGHT. 1ST-ORDER ECONOMIZING
L3	GOVERNANCE: PLAY OF THE GAME – ESP. CONTRACT (ALIGNING GOVERNANCE STRUCTURES WITH TRANSACTIONS)	1 TO 10	GET THE GOVERNANCE STRUCTURE RIGHT. 2ND-ORDER ECONOMIZING
L4	RESOURCE ALLOCATION AND EMPLOYMENT (PRICES AND QUANTITIES; INCENTIVE ALIGNMENT)	CONTINUOUS	GET THE MARGINAL CONDITIONS RIGHT. 3RD-ORDER ECONOMIZING

L1: SOCIAL THEORY
L2: ECONOMICS OF PROPERTY RIGHTS
L3: TRANSACTION COST ECONOMICS
L4: NEO-CLASSICAL ECONOMICS/AGENCY THEORY

The third level is dedicated to 'governance structures' of organizations and contracts that coordinate economic transactions that is often referred to as transaction costs economics (Williamson 1985, 1996). The economic rationale of various contractual arrangements and organizational structures of firms are explained. The positive agency theory and transaction cost economics are located at level 3. Together with the theory of property rights of level 2, they form the New Institutional Economics (NIE).

At the fourth level the neoclassical resource allocation is located: the level of the markets and prices as presented in the marginal mainstream neoclassical economic (NCE) analysis. Also the normative branch of agency theory is situated at this level (see Douma and Schreuder 1998).

Williamson uses two main criteria to distinguish the layers. One of them is the frequency (in years) of change. This might range from hundreds or thousands of years of layer 1, to continuous change in layer 4. The other is the 'purpose' of change: noncalculative and spontaneous in layer 1 to getting the marginal conditions right in layer 4.

In the following we use this four-layer scheme as a point of departure for the discussion on the conceptualization of the evolution of institutions. We will briefly discuss two different approaches: (a) Equilibrium focussed approaches as used in NCE and NIE. This is the mainstream economics approach in which the evolution is modelled in terms of equilibrium end states. (b) Approaches oriented on the process of institutional change that refers to 'original institutional economics'. The process itself is analysed resulting in a fundamentally different conceptualisation of the evolution of institutions.

2.1 Equilibrium-Focused Approaches

Central in NCE and NIE is the concept of efficiency. Products and services are produced and transacted in such a way that costs are minimized. Competition is the driver behind the selection process. NCE offers insights into 'economies of scale and scope'. Typically these approaches use the ceteris paribus clause to reflect on the optimal resource allocation: Given the technology, given the institutional structure, given preferences, and assuming effective competition, what is for instance the optimal combination of production factors?

NIE focuses on issues of efficient coordination of transactions. There are certain costs associated with transactions, labelled as transaction costs or agency costs. They refer to the costs of collecting information or handling information asymmetry, monitoring and bonding, or costs associated with *ex post* control of transactions. Insights are provided into efficient incentive structures, safeguards against opportunism and costs of coordination. Given the technology, given the structures of (in)formal institutions, and given preferences: what is the cost-minimizing governance structure? In other words: in NCE and NIE equilibrium is central; when exogenous variables change (technology, preferences, institutional environments), then the new equilibrium can be calculated (*ex ante*) or is assumed to emerge *ex post* out of a competitive selection process. According to mainstream economics one best governance system will eventually survive the selection process as the most efficient one, and consequently also one theory will turn out to be relevant (monism). With increasing globalization also a standardization and unification of institutions will take place because in a competitive environment only the most efficient one will survive.[3]

Williamson introduced the role of the institutional environment. How can cases be explained in which identical transactions are differently coordinated in similar infrastructures, for example UK and France? The 'institutional environment' was modelled as an exogenous variable to shift in time and place. Governance structures then differ between, for instance, electricity sectors in the US and Europe for the coordination for exactly the same transaction, not because actors react differently when transaction costs rise due to increasing asset specificity, but only because the (in)formal institutions differ.

Applying NIE to the liberalization of infrastructures results in the expectation that ultimately one most efficient institutional structure will emerge, because it is assumed that in a globalizing world also the institutional environments will converge and competition will force actors then to select the only worldwide uniform most efficient structure. Because there is one single equilibrium, there will ultimately be one most efficient institutional structure that will dominate all others. The European Union seems to follow this reasoning, because it promotes liberalization as an instrument to unify the national infrastructure markets into one single market. There is an expectation that eventually a new equilibrium will emerge with unified institutional structures and efficient uniform pricing schemes.

However, it appears that in reality there is a variety of different institutional arrangements that are far from converging towards a unified equilibrium. Specific national or cultural features seem to make a difference. Even within the European Union, regulation and governance is quite different in France than in the UK. The UK belonged to the pioneers in liberalizing infrastructure industries, among others, because there is a public preference for a free market. On the contrary, the French have a long tradition of cherishing 'national champions' that are protected from competition in exchange for providing certain public services. Also from a theoretical perspective there are serious doubts. Even certain neoclassical approaches consider multiple equilibriums in network industries as a realistic option (see for example Economides 1997). Focussing on another branch of institutional economics, we will now discuss the approach of Original Institutional Economics[4] that analyses the embeddedness of institutions.

2.2 The Process of Institutional Change

Two facets of the process of institutional change are of interest for our analysis: the embeddedness of institutions that results in multiple equilibria and the perceptions and mental maps that are important drivers for evolutionary change.

2.2.1 The embeddedness of institutions

The arrows in Figure 1.1 suggest an interaction between the layers. Williamson (1998, p. 26) recognizes the interdependencies, but does not really take them on board:

> Although in the fullness of time, the system is fully interconnected, for my purposes here, these feedbacks are largely neglected.

However, for our purpose to develop a framework to understand institutional change in infrastructure-based industries, we cannot isolate the layers in that way. The role of the first layer is mentioned, but as in Williamson's earlier work only as a 'shift parameter'. Anthropologists, historians and sociologists ('social theory' in Williamson's terminology), who analyse the embeddedness of institutions, explicitly analyse the interactions between the layers in order to get an understanding of the process of institutionalization. Recently also in economics more attention is paid to the importance of embeddedness and attempts are made to incorporate embeddedness and processes of institutionalization in the economic analysis. Aoki for instance stresses the importance of historical specificities. Analysing the development of concrete industries provides the insight that reality is not and will not be uniform, but that different systems evolve and continue to exist with different characteristics and different efficiencies. Or as Aoki (2000) puts it:

> Rather we ought to admit the diversity in economic systems and analyse their sources and evolution, the comparative advantages and disadvantages of different systems, and the possible gains from diversity. In doing so it will not be sufficient to analyse market institutions alone, but it will be necessary also to analyse the interdependencies of institutions mutually interwoven in complex ways. Because of the variance in historical conditions among economies and the need for structural consistency between regulations and other institutions, a convergence towards a universal model would be difficult.

Aoki explains that institutions can be considered as equilibrium outcomes of a process to be analysed with evolutionary game theory. Individuals have limited information processing capabilities and the existing institutional structure and organizational modes influence the strategy of individuals. In evolutionary game theory each economic agent will strategically choose a skill type that optimizes his payoffs given the constraints of his bounded rationality.

> Under Darwinian dynamics, the situation in which the expected payoffs of every member of the population are equal, that is, the situation in which the possibility of changing strategies through imitation of the fittest no longer exists, is called an 'equilibrium'. (Aoki, 2000)

> If the dynamics of an economy that starts out with a fixed set of historical conditions reinforces the complementarity between specific strategies and approaches the corresponding equilibrium situation, establishing rules to enforce the adoption of those strategies will serve to reduce social and individual costs. (Aoki, 2000)

Accordingly, cost efficiency is the explanatory variable, and in particular information costs for agents will reduce because expectations converge. The social cost of rule enforcement will be relatively low for agents close to the equilibrium. 'Institutionalization' can then be conceptualized as 'the codification of evolution equilibrium strategies'. Aoki is clear about the need for a complementary approach to game theory in which the historical specificities are analysed:

> we cannot predict endogenously which of those equilibria will be chosen without some other information, such as history, or institutional environments surrounding the domain of the game (institutions existing in surrounding domains). This implies that, in spite of the development of the game theory on which institutional analysis relies, game theory alone cannot provide a complete, closed frame for institutional analysis. The analysis of historical and comparative information must be essentially complementary. (Aoki, 2000)

The upshot of the approach of Aoki is the opening of the economic analysis to the explanation of several equilibria each with its own path of development in the explanation of which initial historical conditions play an important role. In the meantime, Aoki claims to maintain the rigorous economic analysis as presented in the game theoretic modelling. However, the question arises whether and how the two can be combined. Contributions of Douglass North and especially Denzau and North (1994) might offer valuable insights to analyse the process of institutional changes deeper and to show that things are probably more complicated then suggested above.

2.2.2 Perceptions and mental maps

Political scientists like Lindberg, Campbell and Hollingsworth (1976) and Campbell (1997), have shown what a process of 'the evolution of governance structures' might look like. Especially Campbell discussed the 'interaction, interpretation and bricolage' in which the preferences and cognitions of actors become endogenized. In economics Douglass North in particular has made important steps in recent years in that direction. In Denzau and North (1994) the 'intimate relationship' between mental models and institutions is discussed. With mental models (internal) individuals interpret the environment, whereas institutions (external) are created by individuals to structure and order the environment. The conceptualization of time is important: logical, or discrete time is used in neoclassical and new institutional economics, whereas 'real', historical time is used in Denzau and North, which implies a fundamental change in conceptualizing the evolution of institutions. Mostly changes in historical time are incremental: over time elements are added to the existing structure in such a way that there is continuity. The new system that results from that adding of elements beholds the possibilities of changes in the future. In situations of incremental change there certainly is change, but the nature of change is a specific one. Also in situations of incremental change the system as a whole can fundamentally change over time. Incremental change can only be understood in relation to what preceded, while such a change implies the possibilities for the future.

According to North institutions are 'humanly devised constraints that shape human interaction'. However, this should not be understood in the way mainstream economics conceptualizes the construction of institutions (optimalization under constraints). In North there is room for interaction: institutions constrain, but are also 'devised'. In the terminology of the agent-structure literature: 'agents and structures are mutually constituted'. In that constitutive process learning takes place, which 'represents' and 're-describes' the 'priors', such as the initial structure of ideologies, habits and so on (Giddens 1984). The world of Denzau and North is a world of procedural rationality, perceptions, historical time, and re-description of the past. The priors generate the 'event space', the past that is recalled, but at the same time it is 'represented', it is again newly re-described.

This perspective has large implications for the relations between the layers in Figure 1.1. Actors cannot be presented any more as agents with 'attributes', but preferences and mental maps are endogenous. Actors interact and interpret, while their interpretation scheme evolves. The institutional environment of formal and informal institutions is not objective, but interpreted; the world is socially 'constructed'. Evolution, incremental change, is the 'normal' kind of development due to the switching costs involved and the difficulties in fundamentally changing the related mental maps of actors. The relation between mental maps and institutions make actors change institutions, actors 'represent' and 're-describe' them. Institutions then are a 'reflection', 'the inter-subjective manifestation of perceptive frames' (North 1990, p 26). At the same time the institutions constrain the mental maps.

The question now arises how this incremental change takes place. What is the driver, what about power and control by vested interests, what about the efficiency of the evolution? Moreover, how to understand more fundamental changes in which one can identity a rupture with existing practices?

3   TOWARDS A FRAMEWORK OF THE EVOLUTION OF INSTITUTIONS

Both in the work of Aoki and North incremental change and processes of institutionalization dominate the picture. Or as Aoki puts it: 'the analysis up to now worked with short sighted economic agents who choose strategies that assure them the best payoff in the present. 'In that case the selection from among multiple equilibriums is entirely path dependent' (Aoki 2000, p 53). But what about agents that operate under different conditions and have different interpretations of reality and perceptions for the future? Suppose a portion of the population has the same future expectations. Suppose that their expectations for payoffs from each skill type do not merely project future payoffs that are equal to current average payoffs, but project to changing future payoffs (capital gains). Under specific conditions the equilibrium path can then bifurcate. In case of sufficient people possessing an entrepreneurial spirit and considering a different skill better fitting future conditions, 'there may be cases in which organizational diversity is ultimately realized' (Aoki 2000, p 54). Consequently, path dependent processes in which institutionalization reinforces the complementarity between a specific set of institutions can then be replaced by a more fundamental change in which actors are able through collective action to change the path. The analysis of institutional change seems to demand a different kind of theoretical framework that digs deeper into the causalities. We do this along two dimensions:

(a) The process of change: evolutionary versus revolutionary;
(b) The outcome: on path versus off path.

First we elaborate on these two dimensions, and in a second step we identify different cases of institutional change.

3.1 The Process of Change

In contrast to historical institutionalism and path dependence, institutional frameworks can also be conceptualized as more open systems. First of all institutions are no longer considered to be constraints and filters that determine outcomes of behaviour of actors, but under certain conditions institutions can erode and discontinue (Oliver 1992) and offer actors opportunities to change institutions. The emergence of contractions that are then not considered to be exceptions, but are part and parcel of institutional systems, is important. In processes of institutional change equilibrium and stability are considered to be the exception and contradiction and change are the rule. Actors are conceptualized as free, creative and able to reconstruct institutions on the basis of reasoned analysis of both the limits and the potentials of present institutions.

To understand more precisely under what conditions incremental or revolutionary change occurs, we need to dig deeper into how individual actors are able to turn the desired change into collective action (Seo and Douglass Creed 2002). An important aspect is the emergence of potential change agents. In the existing institutional system the interests of certain individuals or groups are not always well served. Misaligned interests create potential change agents. The number of agents and the degree of misalignment are important. Whether an incremental change or a more radial change will take place after participants are aware of the misalignments and resulting inefficiencies depends among other things on the kind of relationships inside the system. The relations between the different levels and sectors can be loosely or tightly coupled, which has large implications for the nature and potential of institutional change. It is generally hypothesized that tightly coupled systems do not change gradually, but reproduce behaviour. Loosely coupled systems allow for incremental institutional change. However, when external shocks confront tightly coupled systems with complete new scarcities, institutional change comes about through a revolution and an institutional crisis (Greenwood and Hinings 1996).

When institutions are deeply embedded and tightly coupled, the system is not considered to be able to adapt smoothly because alternative behaviour is not accepted. In those cases when the inefficiencies and misalignment continue, it is hypothesized that in the end the system will collapse after a severe crisis. In cases of gradual change, a process from individual change agents will bring about an awareness of inefficiencies, therefore resulting in collective action to achieve improvement. For collective action to create a new institutional setting it is crucial that alternatives are available that fit into the existing mindset of actors. The 'art of gradual institutionalization' is to stay close to the existing societal systems of belief. When sufficient actors are mobilized, collective action can create an institutional change. This will almost never take place without struggle. Vested interests will try to block institutional change; various frames and cognitive schema will then result in 'institutional war'.

3.2 The Outcome of Change

We differentiate between two kinds of outcomes of institutional change, i.e. on-path and off-path. An on-path outcome stays within the overall logic of the initial institutional arrangement. The logic of the system refers to the degree of alignment between the four layers of the Williamson model. The logic of the system is assumed to be strong if the values, formal rules and governance structures fit well together. In the case of an on-path outcome, the nature of the relationship between the four layers of the Williamson model is essentially unchanged. This does not imply that no change is possible; the specific informal and formal rules and the governance can change without changing the overall logic. An example illustrates this case. Traditionally the organization of the French energy sector strongly relies on the norms and values of providing social services and serving national objectives. Initially this sector was organized as a regulated monopoly with state ownership. In the course of the EU liberalization policy, this sector had to be reorganized in order to allow for competition. Networks had to be opened for third party access, allowing for new market entrance. Gas and electricity firms were obliged to unbundle network-related activities from production and supply. Although these changes resulted in different institutional arrangements, the overall logic still remained the same. Even under the new conditions, there are strong institutional safeguards to guarantee public services and national interests, among others by the still prevailing state ownership rights.

3.3 Different Cases of Institutional Change

In this section we analyse three different processes of institutional change:

– Stability
– Evolutionary change;
– Revolutionary change.

The case of stability serves as reference and will not be deeply analysed. The process and outcomes are stable and unchanged per definition. Evolutionary and revolutionary change can have both on path and off path outcomes. This results in four cases as illustrated in Figure 1.2.

Figure 1.2   Processes and outcomes of change

		Process of change	
		Evolutionary	Revolutionary
Outcome	On path		
	Off path		

3.3.1   Stability

The four-layer model of Williamson (Figure 1.1) can be considered to imply that all institutional arrangements throughout the four layers are consistent in their relation to each other, and hence there is no incentive for change. This describes a situation of stability, of reproduction, of a 'circular flow' (see Figure 1.3). There is a strong prevailing logic that does not allow for any change at all. When nothing changes exogenously (technology for instance) then the system reproduces itself. The case of institutional stability is not very likely to occur in modern industrial societies in which economic growth strongly depends on innovation and change. But it might be found in isolated natural-oriented living communities or religious groups in which there is a clear dominance of customs, norms, traditions or religious principles.

Figure 1.3   Equilibrium model of evolution

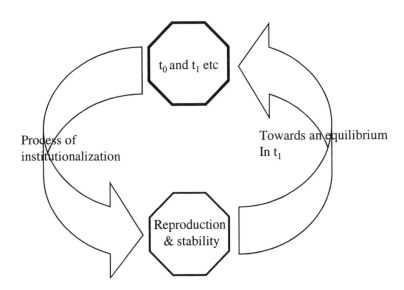

3.3.2   Evolutionary change

Within the framework of institutional economics, evolutionary change is explained by changing arrangements within and between the four layers of the Williamson model (see Figure 1.4). Different internal or external drivers can induce changes. Evolutionary change depends on internal drivers and is perceived as the result of continuous processes of learning and adaptation. Most likely the outcomes are on-path, and under certain conditions even off-path, i.e. many small changes can eventually lead to a change in the logic of the system itself.

3.3.2.1 On-path outcome Evolutionary change is characterized by path dependence and relatively loosely coupled relations between the four layers. The process of institutionalization is characterized by incremental changes of the institutional arrangements due to experiences from the past, expectations and learning processes, increasing returns and lock-in effects (North 1990).

Figure 1.4   Evolutionary change

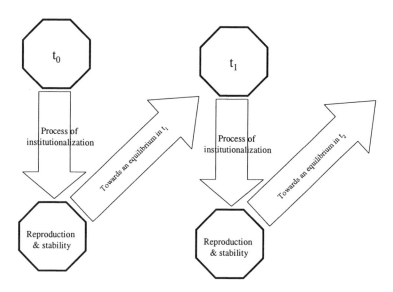

This is a self-reinforcing process with predictable outcomes. The process itself can be characterized as equilibrium oriented, since it maintains a certain stable logic between the various institutional arrangements. Existing structures largely determine the behaviour of actors; institutions first of all constrain and guide behaviour in a specific direction. This approach to institutionalization draws from the literature that is often labelled as 'historical institutionalism'. Path dependence is characterized as a self-reinforcing sequence of events with its own logic (North 1990). A path has a distinct pattern of institutionally rooted constraints and incentives that create typical strategies, routine approaches to problems and shared decisions and rules that produce predictable patterns of behaviour. A path constructs the mental maps of actors, determines the problems actors perceive and the solutions available. Path dependence is often analysed in terms of efficiency and rent seeking. According to this reasoning it is efficient for economic actors to maintain a specific institutional setting because a switch to an alternative (and possibly societally more efficient) structure would be too costly due to sunk costs, complementarities and the like. Moreover, power relations can prevent the switch to more efficient institutions when the benefits for those in power are reduced in the new setting.

3.3.2.2 Off-path outcome Gradual change can also lead to off-path results. As a consequence of evolutionary learning and adaptation, actors might gradually develop new insights into an alternative logic of institutional arrangements. This results in changing preferences, stimulating the development of a new logic of institutional arrangements. Actors acquire new norms and values that are successively translated into different formal rules and governance structures that reflect this new logic. For example, in infrastructure industries the logic of 'providing public services and protecting national interests' can be amended over time into 'serving the interests of the firm in a competitive environment'. Both logics require different institutional arrangements.

3.3.3   Revolutionary change

Revolutionary change might be caused by an external shock that confronts a tightly coupled system with completely new conditions for economic allocation. Institutional change then comes about through a revolution and an institutional crisis. Change agents have an important role in initiating collective action to promote new institutional arrangements. These new arrangements might also suffer from misalignments, and as a consequence new collective action is initiated, resulting in a new institutional arrangement. This process might continue, or end up in a new equilibrium. Most likely the underlying logic of the institutional arrangements changes, which gives rise to an off-path outcome. However, under certain conditions on-path results are not unlikely.

3.3.3.1 Off-path outcome   The case of revolutionary institutional change involves the change of institutional arrangements as well as changing interrelations between the four layers in such a way that the process is not incremental, but revolutionary (see Figure 5.1). The process is characterized by structural contradictions, incompatibilities and misalignments between the layers. A process starts in which actors become increasingly aware of the inconsistencies between the different institutional arrangements. Actors experience the disadvantages of conflicting institutional arrangements and develop perspectives for improvements that contribute to their individual objectives. Actors start to reshape institutional settings through initiating collective action resulting in new institutional arrangements and/or new formal institutions. The result of the revolutionary, conflicting process will often be of an off-path nature, changing the logic of the system.

Figure 1.5   Revolutionary change

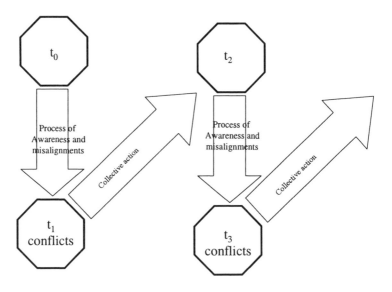

3.3.3.2 On path outcome However, institutional lock-ins and strong positions of powerful interest groups can prevent an 'off path' development. After a radical change, a process towards a stable equilibrium might develop, but also the emergence of new contradictions is possible, giving rise to new changes in the formal institutions and arrangements.

3.4 Conclusion

This framework aims to provide an evolutionary perspective on the reform of infrastructure industries. Starting from the four-layer model of Williamson, we elaborated three different cases for the evolution of institutions: stability, evolutionary change and revolutionary change, all of which are characterized by specific processes and features. The outcomes are characterized as on–path or off–path, depending on whether the overall logic of the institutional arrangements is stable or changes. In the case of stability the relations between the four layers are tightly coupled with a strong dominance of informal institutions, customs and norms. The logic of the institutional arrangements is deeply incorporated into individuals and society. If incidentally there are misalignments, they will be corrected at the initial stage and the equilibrium will be restored. This type of equilibrium is not very likely to appear in the ongoing liberalization of infrastructure industries. It is generally recognized that this process is not reversible.

Evolutionary change is characterized by path dependence and relatively loose relations between the four layers. The process of institutionalization is characterized by incremental changes of the institutional arrangements that are based on experiences from the past, expectations and learning processes, increasing returns and lock-in effects. This is a self-reinforcing process with predictable outcomes that are most probably on–path. The process itself can be characterized as equilibrium oriented, since it maintains a certain stable logic between the various institutional arrangements. Infrastructure industries inhibit important features that foster path dependent developments, including increasing returns characteristics as a result of high initial investments and network effects. However, it is argued that under certain circumstances off–path results can occur.

Revolutionary change develops as a consequence of an external shock that confronts a tightly coupled system with complete new conditions for economic allocation. Institutional change comes about through a revolution and an institutional crisis. Change agents have an important role in initiating collective action promoting new institutional arrangements. These new arrangements might also suffer from misalignments, and as a consequence new collective action is initiated, resulting in a new institutional arrangement. This process might continue, or result in another equilibrium. Most probably the outcomes are off–path. In case interest groups are very strong and/or a high degree of technological or institutional path dependence exists, on–path results can also occur.

4 THE INSTITUTIONAL REFORM OF INFRASTRUCTURE INDUSTRIES

The chapters of this book highlight different aspects of the institutional reform of various infrastructure industries and the ongoing processes of change. According to our framework, the book is divided into two parts; i.e. the process and the outcome of the infrastructure reform. Both parts consist of two theoretical and two empirically oriented contributions.

The following sections highlight the importance of the various chapters in relation to different aspects of the process and outcome of the restructuring process. Although a strict delineation is not possible, four chapters are more oriented towards the process, and the others to the outcome of the reform.

4.1 Part One: Process

4.1.1 Deregulation from a static and dynamic perspective
In Chapter 2 (Deregulation: Design, Learning and Legitimacy) Midttun reflects on the process of restructuring of infrastructure industries, especially the electricity sector. In general he distinguishes three different perspectives:

1) Static efficiency. 'This position is characterized by a dominant deductive orientation. The market is constructed with a clear theoretical anchoring, which in principle makes it possible to impute strong a priori optimization logic into the regulatory design and to specify predictable outcomes.' In terms of our model, this approach assumes that the final result of the reform can be planned beforehand in some 'economic engineering approach'. The process of institutionalization is in the best case completely managed, and results in t_1 in a new stable equilibrium. This is the case of gradual

evolutionary change with only one period of iteration. Under softer rationality assumptions, more iterations are likely, resulting from incomplete information of the 'policy planner' and hence unexpected outcomes that create a need for new interventions.

2) Dynamic efficiency. 'This perspective suggests that rather than being designed up front, markets evolve over time through discovery and creative participating actors.' This perception is mainly based on Austrian economic theory. Like the 'process of creative destruction' between industry competitors, regulation is interpreted as a learning process with essentially unpredictable outcomes. The process might be evolutionary as well as radical. The occurrence of an equilibrium is very unlikely, because of continuously changing economic circumstances and conditions. As a characterizing feature of this perspective, the process of change as well as the intermediate states of the system in t_n are perceived as a consequence of various economic incentives.

3) Institutional legitimacy, 'Combined with "Austrian" notions of learning and entrepreneurial discovery, the institutional perspective focuses on how not only market processes, but also market design and institutionalization faces ambiguities, uncertainties and experimentation.' This approach focuses on social processes of institutional change. Political influence and social-economic power serve as explanatory variables for institutional change. Confronted with changing political and economic circumstances, actors re-adjust their activities and interests. They try to influence the process of institutionalization in order to promote outcomes in t_{n+1} that are advantageous for them. Legitimacy turns out to be a major criterion for the stability and acceptability of certain outcomes in t_{n+i}. This is a remarkable difference from the first two perspectives in which economic efficiency was a dominant criterion and driver.

Midttun exemplifies these different perspectives for the case of the restructuring of the electricity industry. He identifies different national approaches to this reform process and its consequences with respect to market outcomes and political acceptability and legitimacy. Given the low level of institutional coordination and the limited institutional acceptance of many simple first-best regulatory designs, Midttun states that the stage is set for extensive learning both for governmental regulation and industry. As a result, a dual equilibrium might develop, which satisfies political legitimacy as well as economic efficiency.

Midttun identifies three levels of institutional transformation that potentially bridge the gap between the static and dynamic worlds. The first level of competitive iteration is a reform of the market structure in order to provide more effective or efficient services. Examples include the abolishing of barriers to entry or structural monopolies. On a second level partial structural transformation can take place. Within a stable institutional and technological framework certain aspects of the sector are changed. For example, there might be experiments with new technologies, or consumer participation. The transformation is limited to certain niches. Transformation takes a modular form allowing sector–specific reforms according to general design rules. This modularization reduces the complexity of the change process and allows for variation and flexibility. The third level of radical transformation encompasses structural changes of institutions and/or technologies in unstable regimes. In this case government can only structure this process on a very high institutional level. The restructuring of infrastructure industries in the EU can be viewed from this perspective. Midttun argues that soft, negotiated regulation needs more iteration and thus a longer period of time to make it effective as compared to strong regulation. However, the final results might be more favourable for soft, negotiated regulations as they are based on a dual equilibrium that satisfies legitimacy and economic efficiency.

4.1.2   Challenges for competition policy

Chapter 3 addresses competition law as a specific instrument to stimulate innovation, especially in markets where virtual and physical networks play a fundamental role. When referring to our framework that is outlined in the first part of this chapter, the contribution of Bergeijk and Kloosterhuis deals with the second layer of the Williamson scheme (formal rules). Promotion of innovation is assumed to be an important objective to governmental intervention. Given processes of evolutionary or revolutionary change, how can competition policy support or stimulate the occurrence of welfare enhancing-innovations? In relating competition policy to network based-markets, the authors address three important questions: (1) What is the relevance of competition law for (virtual and physical) network industries?

(2) How does competition law deal with intellectual property rights that are often the basis for innovation and constitute virtual networks? (3) What makes the application of competition law to network-based markets different from other markets?

Competition law mainly deals with three aspects of the economic behaviour of firms that potentially restrict the working of markets: restrictive agreements, bundling of economic power by mergers and acquisition, and abuse of economic power. The authors argue that there are sufficient legal opportunities to adapt these rules and regulations promoting innovative co-operations between firms. Restrictive agreements between companies are often desirable in order to allow sharing of expertise and funding to develop innovations. The existence of virtual or physical networks is not per se an indication for intervention. Networks might serve different markets and there might be alternatives.

Intellectual property rights are often the basis of virtual networks. Examples include operating systems for computers, specific norms, standards or technologies. The owner of these intellectual property rights has the possibility to assert some influence on the users. He might even be able to gain extraordinary economic profits. Is this a signal for abuse of market power, which needs intervention by the competition authority? Or is the Schumpeterian view applicable, that this is the reward for innovation and sooner or later the process of creative destruction will bring up another firm with an even better innovation? Under these circumstances the market is doing its work very well, and hence no intervention is warranted. The answer to this fundamental question depends on the way in which these intellectual property rights are exercised and whether they are considered as an 'essential facility'.

Network-based markets differ form others in at least two respects: the existence of economies of scale and network externalities. Both can have huge impacts on the nature of competitions, since in both cases there tends to be only one supplier that can produce goods or services at minimum costs or for the greatest benefits to the consumers. Competition is possible *for the market* but obviously not *on the market*. Among several competitors there will be only one winning party that serves the market. Whether this creates a problem for the competitive functioning of markets depends on three aspects:

(1) The actual definition and delineation of the relevant market, with respect to the customers' functionality, region, and time period.
(2) The assessment of market power. Is there a 'public utility' or a contestable market?
(3) The monopolizing behaviour. Is there an abuse of monopoly power, or is the monopoly just the result of a healthy competitive process in which 'the winner takes it all'?

Bergeijk and Kloosterhuis summarize the present legal rulings and regulations and the difficulties of proper demarcation between abuse of monopoly power and the Schumpeterian reward of the 'process of creative destruction'. They argue that these problems are not new for competition authorities as they occur not only in network–related markets but also in other sectors. Network industries are only special where aspects of natural monopolies and public utilities come into play.

This chapter provides a good illustration of how a specific policy instrument (in casu competition policy) has developed over time to support dynamic innovation in network-related markets. Originally competition policy was mainly based on the static 'structure–conduct–performance paradigm' in which monopolies by definition resulted in allocative inefficiency. This chapter provides a quite different view.

4.1.3   California electricity crises

Chapter 4 provides an example of process of revolutionary change that resulted in a crisis and severe malfunctioning, which is illustrated by the case of the California energy sector. De Vries investigates the causes and some consequences of the California electricity crisis. This crisis received ample publicity and became a metaphor for failures in infrastructure reforms. The design for a liberalized energy market turned out to have major shortcomings in providing unexpected adverse incentives, which resulted in the partial technical and financial breakdown of the system. The consecutive re-reform established strong governmental involvement, among others in the procurement of energy for the state of California.

By the end of the 1990s, California restructured its power sector in which the incumbent utilities divested much of their generation assets and all purchases by the utility distribution companies were made in a mandatory power pool in which only spot contracts were allowed, while retail prices were fixed for small consumers. In the summer of 2000, two years after the restructuring, wholesale prices started to rise. In January 2001 the crisis reached a new climax, when the independent system operator was forced to impose rolling blackouts throughout significant portions of the state for two consecutive days. As the crisis unfolded, a heated debate developed with respect to its causes and potential remedies. Opponents of deregulation were quick to claim the crisis as proof that a market in electricity was impossible. Proponents of deregulation countered that the way California had restructured was highly flawed so that it could not be considered proper deregulation, etc. Through an analysis of several basic trends, like demand, installed generator capacity, generator outages and imports, de Vries explains the development of the crisis. The image that emerges from these trends is that the reserve margins (the difference between generation capacity and imports on the one hand and demand for electricity on the other hand) steadily shrank throughout the 1990s. Demand did not grow exceptionally fast (neither peak nor average demand), but it did grow. The fundamental problem of California's electricity market was a lack of investment in generating capacity. The shortage of generation capacity was aggravated by a number of circumstances such as drought (which reduced the available hydropower), heat (which temporarily increased demand), generator failures and transmission capacity constraints. Moreover, by withholding generation capacity, generating companies increased prices far above their competitive levels and contributed to the power outages. The pattern of under-investment predated the restructuring law. However, the new market structure did fail to send the necessary signals for the need for new generation capacity in time. The most likely cause of the lack of investment within California is regulatory uncertainty during the time leading up to the restructuring of the market, exacerbated by a flawed market design. The distribution companies had to purchase electricity at prices much higher than the regulated retail tariffs for which they had to sell much of their electricity. They incurred high losses, forcing them into severe financial difficulties, bankrupting one of them and forcing another to sell off a substantial part of its assets.

De Vries draws a number of lessons: First, it is essential for the long-term stability of the system that there are adequate incentives for investment. A second lesson is that in electricity markets with a low demand price-elasticity, even generating companies with a small market share have market power during periods of scarce supply. Finally, the crisis demonstrated the high social cost of consumers being completely isolated from the market. The fact that consumers did not respond to high wholesale prices (because consumer prices were fixed) contributed substantially to the crisis, as demand was not reduced when supplies were tight. The high response to the call for voluntary conservation and load shifting to off-peak hours during the crisis demonstrated that demand price-elasticity could be significant.

4.1.4   The Dutch gas industry: learning processes in regulation

The fifth chapter 'Dilemmas in Network Regulation: The Dutch Gas Industry', elaborates more deeply on different aspects of learning in the process of institutionalization. Correljé argues that the design, the implementation and the maintenance of regulatory systems are a dynamic process, evolving over time. This process is partly driven by exogenous pressures. Yet, the evolution of regulation is inseparable from a process of endogenous, sectorial, collective learning, in which the main actors, i.e. the firms in the industry, the regulator and the political realm, gain new insights time and again. An evolutionary perspective on regulation implies that both the regulator's actions, as well as the firm's responses to these actions and the perception of what constitute public values, are the products of a process of discovery.

An analysis of the post-1990 development of the Dutch regulatory framework for the gas market yields an illustrative application of the evolutionary perspective on regulation. The emergence of the regulatory framework from the mid-1990s can be interpreted as a series of discoveries, in which step by step the importance and complexity of the set of technical and economic functionalities of the gas supply system were unravelled. Until the process of restructuring took off in the mid-1990 these functionalities had been embedded, or internalized, within the overall gas supply structure of the NAM/Gasunie public-private partnership. Yet, once the Dutch government, motivated by a diverse set of factors, began to dismantle this structure, they began to 'escape' from the framework, as externalities. Of course, the plight of the Dutch regulatory office (Dte) became to re-internalize these functionalities in a newly established framework, based on the paradigm of free market coordination. What this chapter argues is that this process of re-internalization is inherently a difficult process, for reasons of lack of information, information asymmetry and strategic behaviour. It also shows that any *ex ante* choice for a market and ownership structure and the regulatory approach may prove inconsistent in later stages. Overtly simplistic interpretations of the *structure–conduct–performance* paradigm take no notice of the process of discovery and learning. Instead of promising voters and customers a performance of low prices and innovation, as a result of an instant regulatory system, it should be made clear that regulators by definition face challenges and dilemmas in restructuring markets and introducing competition. Moreover, the industry itself including the incumbent will be drawn into a process of learning and discovery in respect of its new business practices and strategies. Finally, public authorities will have to reformulate and rediscover the content and form of the public values they aim to secure and the way to do that.

4.2 Part Two: Outcome

4.2.1   The dual role of the state as owner and regulator

In chapter 6 Bauer examines the dual role of states as owners and regulators of infrastructure industries. In many countries infrastructure liberalization proceeded faster than the privatization of former state monopolies. Regulatory agencies, established to oversee the transition and safeguard the preconditions for competition, therefore monitor state-owned firms in addition to privately-owned firms. In liberalized telecom markets in the EU this was the case in 9 out of 15 member states in the year 2000. Thus, this is a significant phenomenon at least for this specific case. This mixed ownership developed partly as a consequence of deliberate policy to detain governmental control over telecom networks. In other cases capital markets proved to be unfavourable, thus privatization was postponed.

Bauer examines two aspects that are related to the outcome of the restructuring process. First, the nature of the relation between the regulator and the publicly-owned firm; is the regulatory practise in favour of these enterprises, or overly stringent, or neutral? Second, is there a specific role for publicly-owned firms in competitive markets, or do they just behave as their private competitors? A particular role for public ownership might be justified by the realization of specific tasks that are not fulfilled by private firms.

In terms of our model, Bauer clearly focuses on the formal arrangements (more specifically the property rights structures) in the liberalized EU telecom market. As the consequence of the restructuring process, these property rights are newly defined by the privatization of state–owned firms and the assignment of regulatory responsibilities to newly established public bodies. The chapter examines the internal logic and consistency of these evolving property rights regimes.

In a literature review Bauer summarizes the main findings on the performance of regulated private, public and mixed firms, which have both public and private owners. In the case of public and mixed ownership, the incentive structures might be muddled. Regulation might serve other objectives and thus provide other incentives than ownership rights. On the other hand there might also be opportunities to realize specific public goals through ownership rights that would be unattainable in a completely privately–owned industry. Publicly-owned firms might provide unprofitable social services or engage in politically desirable investments.

The incentive structures under public and private ownership are reviewed, concluding that potentially private ownership tends to promote a higher degree of efficiency, although there are also circumstances under which public ownership performs comparably. Mixed firms fall between the cases of public and private ownership. However this general picture can be influenced by regulation and market structure. Bauer concludes that 'competition is generally considered a more powerful mechanism than the specification of property rights'. Consequently empirical research is needed to gain specific insights into the nature of these complex incentive structures.

Bauer finds hints of tensions between state ownership and government regulation, but not any systematic bias. This, what Bauer calls a 'surprising ownership neutrality of regulation', is a consequence of the mature legal and institutional framework in the EU with its 'high degree of regulatory pragmatism and enforcement by a stable court system'. The importance of competition with respect to the incentive structure of firms is confirmed.

There is a strong potential to use public ownership as an instrument to pursue social objectives without harming competition. However, given the diminished trust in the abilities of governmental regulation, Bauer finds this choice presently quite unlikely. There are some limited clues but not strong evidence that state ownership is used to pursue public interest goals that could not be achieved by private regulated firms.

4.2.2   Limits of Law as a Planning Mechanism

In chapter 7 Prosser explores the limits of law as a planning mechanism in infrastructure industries for the case of the privatization of various UK utilities. He focuses on the second and third layer of the Williamson scheme of institutional arrangements; i.e. formal rules and governance structures. Prosser primarily focuses on the question to what degree new institutional arrangements that developed as a consequence of the restructuring process have been successful in maintaining or enhancing various infrastructure services. He provides an interesting description of how the regulatory instruments have been adjusted over time as a consequence of crises, unexpected outcomes or changing political objectives. This chapter illustrates the outcomes of the restructuring process that took place in the UK. In most cases the outcome was on-path, but there is also an interesting example of an off-path outcome.

The restructured infrastructure industries have been quite successful in safeguarding public goals. This is mainly due to the work of the regulatory authorities, which can be perceived as important change agents. Next to the promotion of competition they also treated some elements of social regulation as part of their duties. Among others, licence agreements with the operators addressed specific issues of public concern, for example, the availability of telephone boxes and public transport in rural areas, social acceptable disconnection policies for energy and water and affordable tariffs for essential services for the old and disabled. Prosser concludes: 'What we saw, ... was a change from consumer protection being based on the goodwill of an industry, or on very ineffective political controls, to rules enforceable by regulators in the form of statute or licence conditions.' As a consequence public goals are better protected under the new regulatory regime. This was an unexpected result, because critics of the reform were warning that public goals could not be sufficiently safeguarded in liberalized infrastructures.

Prosser elaborates more specifically on the reforms of the electricity and railroad sectors. The restructuring of the electricity sector proved quite successful, although there are problems especially with respect to electricity production. The wholesale power pool, where all producers had to bid in their supply, was a failure. There have been concerns about the security of supply and diversity of primary energy sources. An unexpected rush for gas–fired power plants raised concerns about an overdependence on this power source with a limited availability in the UK. As a consequence, a long–term strategic plan for energy supply was developed by the British Government. This was quite a revolutionary policy change, because it 'is now accepted that the future of energy in the UK cannot be left to the decentralized contracting between private parties in the marketplace; government has a legitimate long-term planning role'. For the UK this is a complete new approach, which has some taste of the French energy policy. Is this a change of the embedded norms and values in British policy, i.e. the first Williamson layer of institutional arrangements?

The reform of the railroad sector resulted in a major crisis and needed some fundamental reorientation on the initial plans. The sector was strongly fragmented vertically as well as horizontally into over one hundred companies. Private contractual relations proved not to be able to sufficiently coordinate the activities in this sector. Incentives provided by law, contractual relations and the regulatory office resulted into unexpected behaviour of market parties. There was a lack of investment in infrastructures and a weak maintenance of the physical equipment, especially the railroad tracks. As a consequence, major accidents occurred with a considerable loss of life. Public pressure and political concern made major re-adjustments unavoidable to restore the security of the system. Prosser concludes that 'rather than attempting to create incentives through contractual specification, it should be accepted that sometimes hierarchical organizations will work better through having cultures of co-operation embedded in them. These cultures may facilitate the achievement of safety goals, for example, through an acceptance that some types of conduct are simply unacceptable thus simplifying monitoring. They may reduce transaction costs through keeping lawyers out and providing simpler means of resolving disputes than litigation. The challenge is to combine such cultural expectations with a degree of transparency which is similar to that which may be required by independent regulation.' These cultural expectations exemplify the importance of 'embeddedness of norms and values' (the first layer of Williamson's scheme) into the regulatory reform. Formal rules and governance are only part of the institutional regime, as this contribution of Prosser clearly illustrates.

4.2.3   Energy network regulation

Chapter 8 provides interesting empirical insights into the effects of network regulation and the revealed behaviour of regulatory authorities. Which interests do these regulators actually serve: consumers, network operators, or are they neutral? The authors suggest a method to test the possible consumer or industry bias of the regulatory system in place. This method is applied for the access tariff regulation for the Spanish national electric transmission network, operated by Red Eléctrica de España (REE), and the pipeline distribution system for oil products, operated by La Compañía Logística de Hidrocarburos (CLH). Both network companies, as essential facilities, have undergone major regulatory reforms to promote the liberalization of the oil and power market. It is argued that in the process of setting the access tariffs to such essential facilities the regulator faces a conflict of interests. For example, an increase in the access charges simultaneously implies a decrease of the users' surplus and an increase in the regulated firm's revenues. The question, thus, arises as to what extent these networks' access-pricing strategies have resulted in either a pro-users or a pro-network bias. To answer this question, the evolution of the average tariffs of CLH and REE, their levels of productivity and the input price differentials of these network companies are compared with the general development in competitive industries in Spain. To this end, three price benchmarks are constructed. One benchmark represents the best practice from the point of view of the users. Competitive price adjustment suggests that the regulator sets prices to maintain breakeven operation over time. Another benchmark represents an evolution of tariffs that includes an input price reduction, while the essential facilities absorb the total amount of productivity changes. The third alternative may be considered the most attractive from the perspective of the essential facility: price increases allow it to keep all cost reductions and pass all cost increases on to the users.

The results show that the successive adjustments of access tariffs of REE and CLH have generally protected consumers from an excessive monopolistic abuse. Yet, this has not precluded the companies from securing higher and more stable profitability rates than those achieved on average in the Spanish manufacturing sector. This suggests that the restraint on prices was not very tight. Obviously, both industry and consumers could take some profit from the regulatory system. In this sense it might be interpreted as neutral. As Bauer puts forward in Chapter 6, this is probably a consequence of the mature legal institutional framework of the EU with a high degree of regulatory pragmatism that enables a relatively neutral position of regulators.

4.2.4   Airport privatization

Chapter 9 elaborates on the liberalization of international aviation. Hakfoort analyses how the changes in (European) aviation policy affect the opportunities for government intervention to cope with various market failures, especially with respect to the privatization of airports. Amsterdam Schiphol airport is taken as an example.

Hakfoort provides a brief overview of the history of aviation regulation. The Paris Convention in 1919 is recognized as the major starting point of governmental intervention in international air traffic. This resulted in a system of bilateral contracts between national governments, regulating the access to their national air territory. Price regulation was accomplished by the IATA cartel. This regulatory regime remained quite stable until 1978, when the USA government introduced the Airline Deregulation Act for its internal market. The US opened up various bilateral contracts and replaced them with so-called 'open sky agreements' that allowed for more international competition between airlines. This was the starting point for an international liberalization of the airport sector. The EU followed in 1988 with a directive that liberalized its internal market in three steps in 1990, 1992 and finally 1997. A comparable development also took place in other parts of the world, like Australia, Asia, and New Zealand.

Airlines reacted to these developments in several ways. Among others they established international alliances that took the control of the international aviation flows away from national governments. The configuration of network routes also changed from point-to-point traffic to hub-and-spoke systems. This allowed considerable cost savings through a more efficient use of the existing capacity.

For the airports the income stream changed quite significantly. As a consequence of the growing degree of competition, profit margins shrank considerably, and, there was no longer the security of long-term agreements between governments that guaranteed the use of the airport facilities. Looking for new business opportunities, airports engaged strongly in non-aviation activities, which nowadays cover in some cases even more than 50 per cent of the revenues. The exploitation of airports developed towards predominantly commercial activity. Consequently airport privatization seems a logical next step in this process of drawing back of governmental influence in this sector. Hakfoort elaborates more deeply on this aspect.

The author identifies market failures and public interests that might justify governmental intervention even under these changing circumstances. He addresses positive and negative externalities of airport-related investments, the possibilities for abuse of market power, opportunities to re-allocate ownership rights, and different managerial incentives under a privatized regime. No fundamental arguments against privatization appear. However, there are some concrete aspects that need special attention. The regulatory regime should be put in place before the privatization process, the government should think of the possibility of auctioning slots in the future, the term of concession for the airport operator should not be unlimited and an independent aviation regulator should be set up before the privatization process.

5 CONCLUSION

This book aims to provide an evolutionary perspective on the reform of infrastructure industries. This process started in the 1970s and 1980s in a few sectors in a few countries, and is now a global phenomenon encompassing all infrastructure sectors. Core ingredients include stimulation of competition (liberalization), changing of ownership structure in favour of private actors (privatization) and reducing the direct governmental control and intervention (deregulation). This is a very fundamental regime change. A new balance is sought between various institutional arrangements, including markets, public sector involvement, and private initiatives. The various chapters of this book provide deeper analyses into specific aspects of institutional changes in various infrastructures.

This first chapter addresses three topics. Section 2 gives a limited overview of some literature on the evolution of institutions, concentrating on the field of institutional economics. Based on a model by Williamson, four different levels of institutional research are identified, ranging from embedded informal norms and standards, formal rules, actual 'rules of the games' (governance structures) to market allocation. Taking this as a starting point, section 3 proposes a theoretical framework on the process and outcome of institutional change. In a simple model five different cases for evolutionary change are analysed: stability, on-path and off-path evolutionary change, and on-path and off-path revolutionary change. Section 4 provides an overview of the various chapters in relating them to different aspects of the process and outcome of the restructuring process.

NOTES

1. Traditional economics does not really address issues of change; the analysis is mainly of a comparative static type. Moreover, the theoretical insights are presented as universal. Basically there is no room for variety and no analysis of the processes of change. Nevertheless mainstream economics might be helpful for understanding drivers and constraints on institutional changes as long as they are approached in a static setting

2. See Rutherford (1994) for a thorough comparison between New and Original (or Old) Institutional Economics.

3. NCE and NIE constitute the mainstream in economic theory: the analysis is of a deductive nature based on methodological individualism in which equilibrium is central. The world out there is to be explored by social scientists in an objective way: put more energy and time in scientific research and the objective world will be revealed for mankind. This holds for nature, but also for economic institutions.

4. Rutherford (1994) compares the two schools in institutional economics extensively; like other he refers to Original Institutional Economics as 'Old

Institutional Economics'. See also Bush and Tool (2001, chapter 1) for an introduction into OIE.

REFERENCES

Aoki, M. (2000), *Information, Corporate Governance, and Institutional Diversity,Competitiveness in Japan, the USA, and the Transitional Economies,* Oxford, UK: Oxford University Press, 48–57.

Bush, P.D. and M.R. Tool (2001), 'Foundational Concepts for Institutionalist Policy Making', in *Institutional Economics and Policy Making,* Boston, US/Dordrecht, NL: Kluwer Academic Publishers.

Campbell, J.L. (1991), 'Mechanisms of Evolutionary Change in Economic Governance: Interaction, Interpretation and Bricolage', in L. Magnusson and J.Ottoson (eds), *Evolutionary Economics and Path Dependence,* Cheltenham, UK: Edward Elgar Publishing Company, pp. 10–32.

Denzau A.T. and D.C. North (1994), 'Shared Mental Models: Ideologies and Institutions', *Kyklo,,* 47, 3–31.

Douma, S. and H. Schreuder (1998), *Economic Approaches to Organizations,* Hertfordshire, US: Prentice Hall.

Economides, N. (1997), 'The Economics of Networks', *International Journal of Industrial Organization,*14 (6), 673–700.

Furubotn, E. and S. Pejovich,. (eds) (1974), *The Economics of Property Rights,* Cambridge, US: Ballinger.

Greenwood, R. and C.R. Hinings (1996), 'Understanding Radical Organizational Change: Bringing together the Old and the New Institutionalism', *Academy of Management Review,* 21 (4), 1022–54.

Giddens, A. (1984), *The Constitution of Society: Outline of the Theory of Structuration,* Cambridge, US: Polity Press

Lindberg, L.N., J.L. Campbell and J.R. Hollingsworth (1976), 'Economic Governance and the Analysis of Structural Change in the American Economy', *Governance of the American Econom,,* Cambridge, US: Cambridge University Press, pp. 3–34.

North, D.C. (1990), *Institutions, Institutional Change and Performance,* New York, US: Cambridge University Press.

OECD (2000) *Economic Outlook 67,* Paris: OECD.

Oliver, C. (1992), 'The Antecedents of Deinstitutionalization', *Organization Studies,* 13 (4), 563-88

Rutherford, M.H. (1994), *Institutions in Economics: The Old and the New Institutionalism,* Cambridge, US: Cambridge University Press.

Seo, M and D. Creed (2002), 'Institutional Contradictions, Praxis, and Institutional Change: A Dialectical Perspective', *Academy of Management Review*, 27 (2), 222-47.

Williamson, O.E. (1985), *The Economic Institutions of Capitalism*, New York, US: The Free Press.

Williamson, O.E. (1996), 'Efficiency, Power, Authority and Economic Organization', in J. Groenewegen, *Transaction Cost Economics and Beyond*, Dordrecht, NL / Boston, US; Kluwer Academic Publishers.

Williamson, O.E. (1998), 'Transaction Cost Economics: How it Works: Where it is Headed', *De Economis,,*146 (1), 23-58.

PART ONE

Process

2. Deregulation: Design, Learning and Legitimacy

Atle Midttun

1 INTRODUCTION

The late 1980s and 1990s have seen a massive move towards the deregulation of infrastructure industries. Both the public service model in Europe and the regulated monopoly model in the US have come under attack. The argumentation for deregulation is most often phrased in static efficiency terms and competitive exposure is seen as a means to improved resource allocation under known technological conditions and proven organizational models. It is also thought possible to correct undesired market behaviour with well-defined market designs, which provide the 'right' incentive structures to the market actors. The vision is that a sectoral public service approach may be substituted by a consistent regulatory regime where regulators have sufficient knowledge to specify efficient rules and workable procedures and also have sufficient control to implement them.

However, many elements of this vision can be questioned: one typically finds that competitive exposure creates its own dynamics, which includes new modes of economic organization and changes that also transcends the premises for the new market design. This entails a need to reformulate an understanding of deregulation and market competition also in dynamic terms, where structural and technological transformation is explicitly included.

Furthermore deregulation, particularly in complex infrastructure industries such as telecommunication, electricity and gas, may transcend regulatory domains and sectoral boundaries. Deregulation may therefore unleash complex interaction in a series of interrelated regulatory fields.

This chapter explores the challenges to the 'rational' deregulation and market design approaches confronting the static efficiency premises with a dynamic efficiency approach. It also brings in the question of institutionalization and political legitimacy as a critical challenge to deregulation and market design. Due to such considerations, market designs may have to be forsaken to the advantage of second or third best solutions upon which vested interests can agree.

The chapter is organized in three sections: the first elaborates on the three analytical perspectives: static efficiency, dynamic efficiency and institutional legitimacy. The second section provides some examples of regulatory challenges from European deregulation of energy markets. The third section presents a discussion and draws some analytical conclusions.

2   THREE PERSPECTIVES ON DEREGULATION AND MARKET DESIGN

Deregulation generally implies a move towards a more open platform for industrial configuration than the public service or regulated monopolies that it replaces. This is achieved by setting more general design rules that allow flexibility and freer recombination of competencies (Table 2.1).

In economic terms deregulation typically *implies* a move from sector specific regulation to general competition, patent and commercial regulation. This again enables the commodification and commercialization of infrastructure industry.

In political terms deregulation implies a move from operative public management of sector services in Europe, or from special public service regulation of monopoly providers in the US towards more general formulation of the public service goals. This allows public service obligations to be maintained while opening up for competitive market-based implementation.

In technological terms, deregulation entails a move from direct specification of operative solutions to specification of the general technical performance   criteria.   This   leaves   more   room   for   competitive experimentation with new technological combinations, but may also weaken long-term, large-scale technological development based on 'patient' public budgets.

Table 2.1   Deregulation as a more general platform for commercial, political and technological experimentation

	Economics	Political	Technological
Second order	General competition, patent, commercial law regulation	General public service and implementation of public policies	General performance criteria
First order	Sector specific regulation	Operative public management sector services	Specific operative solutions

The open design of deregulation can be supported both from a static and a dynamic perspective, as the two positions potentially share a common critique against monopolistic infrastructure governance. However, opinions differ as to how the new deregulation strategies are to be shaped.

On the one hand, a mainstream static efficiency–oriented tradition seeks to substitute public service and monopoly regulation with a fairly comprehensive set of competitive market and quasi-market designs, usually under strong explicit or implicit rationality assumptions.

On the other hand, a dynamic efficiency–and innovation–oriented tradition tends to emphasize the value of openness and experimentation and therefore takes a more critical attitude to comprehensive market design. A basic premise for this position is that the strong rationality criteria from the static efficiency perspective cannot be met when dynamic efficiency is considered. Furthermore, an institutional perspective brings in distributive issues and the question of power and legitimacy.

2.1 Static Efficiency

A mainstream approach to deregulation and market design opens up for competitive forces in infrastructure industries, while at the same time developing fairly detailed market designs that provide incentives for the firms to work in the 'right' direction. This position is characterized by a dominant deductive orientation. The market is constructed with a clear theoretical anchoring, which in principle makes it possible to impute strong a priori optimization logic into the regulatory design and to specify the predictability of outcomes.

The analytical legitimacy for this approach comes from an emerging literature in economics that, on the basis of game-theoretical reasoning, has provided a basis for policy intervention by targeted market design (Roth 1999; McMillan 2003; Milgrom 2003). Game-theoretic consulting, which until recently has focused largely on giving strategic advice for behaviour in existing markets, has more recently started to offer advice on the design of economic institutions and markets.

This has allowed governments to move from introducing a new mechanism into an already existing market to constructing totally new markets by political design. The strong rationality embedded in the static efficiency assumptions commonly made in this tradition, allows it to take an 'economic engineering approach' and to establish fairly elaborate governance through market design (Roth; 2002, Blumstein et al. 2000).

To maintain the strong deductive logic necessary for rational market design, integrated infrastructure systems have been divided into functional components that are subsequently subjected to specialized market or quasi-market rule (Savas ,1987, and Midttun and Svindland, 2001). In some cases such decoupled functions may be directly market exposed. In other cases the market design approach has developed a repertoire of quasi-market solutions where public authorities auction out specific functions under a well-designed incentive regime. In either case, the market designers must be able to:

- design and implement a venue for buyers and sellers, with a relevant format for transactions;
- map the market development;
- measure the deviance from an optimal state and, if necessary ;
- specify corrective measures.

A central assumption in static efficiency-orientated regulation is that the commercial effects of options are in principle calculable, and that government may shape market design that unleashes optimal welfare-enhancing strategies at the micro level. The strong rationality orientation thus assumes knowledge about alternative production possibilities as explicit, freely transmissible and easily encapsulated in what Joan Robinson (1956) calls 'blueprints' that can be systematically furthered by market design.

2.2 Softer Rationality Assumptions

Even within the rationalist market design position it is recognized, however, that operative market design entails considerable complexity, as deductive design has to be blended with empirical detailing. This introduces elements that modify the deductive logic and thereby reduce the strong rationalist position towards a softer, more judgemental market design.

Roth, for instance, notes that practical design carries with it a responsibility for detail and that, for this reason, the simple models and deductive analytical methods that characterize most game-theoretic analysis in the economic literature need to be supplemented with the complexity of the strategic environment itself, and to the complexity of participants' behaviour (Roth 1999).

McMillan (2003) also cautions about exaggerating the expectations tof traditional, theoretically-deductively based market design. He notes that the state firm privatizations in the 1980s and 1990s mostly had little input from theory and that in economy-wide reform, economic theorists have had still less impact than in state firm privatization. The most successful of the transition countries, measured by economic growth, he notes, is China, where reform policies were pragmatic and adaptive.

2.3 Dynamic Efficiency, the Learning Perspective

The strong, deductive and weaker blended deductive inductive distinction treats the theoretical design capability as a question of degree and blending of a priori theoretical and substantive knowledge. The rationalist market design position may, however, also be challenged more in principle by a competing dynamic learning perspective. Such a perspective can be theoretically anchored both in the Austrian tradition in economics and in innovation theory. This perspective suggests that rather than being designed up front, markets evolve over time through discovery and creative participating actors.

As pointed out by Roth (1999), one fact that stands out from both experimental and field data is that behaviour in markets evolves, as people learn about the environment by interacting with it. He notes that in new markets, what people learn initially is about the behaviour of other inexperienced players, so that an analysis that focuses only on equilibrium behaviour may miss the importance of a market's initial history.

This insight corroborates Hayek's view of markets and competition as a process, emphasizing the nature of competition as a 'discovery procedure'. For Hayek (1948, p. 94) 'competition is essentially a process of the formation of opinion. a process which involves a continuous change in the data and whose significance must therefore be completely missed by any theory which treats these data as constant' (Kirzner 1997).

The learning perspective differs essentially from the rational market design where a chosen course of action is determined by deductive theoretical analysis, even if blended with substantive knowledge. In the market-process world of entrepreneurial discovery, on the other hand, one would expect the initial plans for deregulation and active market design to be at least partially flawed. Deficiency in market design would subsequently be adjusted through the responsiveness of alert, imaginative entrepreneurs to the opportunities revealed.

The perhaps most radical anti-rationalist position, in the Austrian tradition, is taken by Ludwig Lachmann (1976) who sees the market process in a ceaseless motion in which at no time is there any assurance that the equilibrative forces are stronger than the disequilibrative forces. Following on the later work of George Shackle (Lachmann 1976) this group of Austrians has questioned the very meaningfulness of any equilibrium concept at all and thereby undermines much of the basis for neoclassical market design.

Joseph Schumpeter is perhaps the clearest proponent of a dynamic innovation perspective in economics (1989). Schumpeter pointed out that entrepreneurs innovate, not just by figuring out how to use inventions, but also by introducing new means of production, new products, and new forms of organization. These innovations, he argued, were at the core of market–based wealth creation.

Schumpeter saw perfect (static) competition as relatively unimportant. Instead he saw from the new commodity, the new technology, the new source of supply, the new type of organization... as the core element of dynamic wealth creation of a dynamic market development with limited room for rational design. The question, as Schumpeter saw it, was not 'how capitalism administers existing structures,... [but] how it creates and destroys them.' This creative destruction, he believed, caused continuous progress and improved standards of living for everyone.

This, however, creates little room for the calculation implied in the rational market design, and the role of the regulator is limited to systematically stimulating market opening and stimulating innovation. Concepts such as disruptive technologies (Christensen 1997) have continued to emphasize the unforeseen and creative destructive sides of markets and to delegate market design more to procedural than to substantive rationality.

2.4 The Institutional Challenge

While the Austrian market process perspective and innovation theory challenges the actor assumptions in the rational design model, the institutional perspective challenges its structural/institutional assumptions. Combined with 'Austrian' notions of learning and entrepreneurial discovery, the institutional perspective focuses on how not only market processes, but also market designs and institutionalization, face ambiguities, uncertainties and experimentation. The notion of entrepreneurship is lifted up here to the institutional level, where entrepreneurs can support or oppose processes of socialization of actors and the mobilization of 'subsidiary actors' within the organizational field as strategies for institutional change (DiMaggio and Powell 1991). The recognition of multiple, and in some instances competing, institutional frameworks opens up for the development of a more complex perspective of social action and structure than under the rationalist model.

Institutionalized rules are brought into question if some actors become aware of more attractive alternative institutional solutions. The deviation from institutionalized forms of behaviour simultaneously increases uncertainty in subsequent rounds of interaction. Hence, the market design itself becomes contested and subject to strategic agency which can have destructive consequences for existing institutional regulations, even to the point of deconstructing the basis for a rational assessment of means–ends relationships. Only through renewed processes of institutionalization is it then possible to reduce uncertainty and recreate preconditions for strategic agency.

The consequence of this position is that successful market design not only must succeed in providing an adequate context for desired competitive behaviour, but also succeed in justifing the design on the political arena as well. Stabilisation of an institutional framework, such as a given market design, thus, does not only rely on the efficiency of the market design, but also on the ability to legitimate the design *vis-à-vis* vested interests (Beckert 2003)

2.5 Transition Management: from Substantive to Procedural Rationality

Insights such as the learning perspective and the institutional critique have led some researchers and policy-makers to replace the rationalist market design concept with a more process-oriented approach to policy formation. Under the term 'transition management' institutional design is staged as an innovation process, where market practices and the market institutions co-evolve (Kemp and Loorbach 2003).

In line with March and Olsen (1995) this perspective takes as its point of departure that political institutions must cope with problems of intelligent change: (1) ignorance: uncertainties about the future and causal structure of experience; (2) conflict: inconsistencies in preferences and interests, and (3) ambiguity: lack of clarity, instability and endogenity in preferences and interests.

Transitions, like major sectoral deregulation, therefore, in this perspective cannot be managed in a controlling sense, but are the result of the interplay of many different processes, several of which are beyond the scope of control. What the policy designer can do is to influence the direction and speed of a transition and change the odds that a transition will occur (Kemp and Loorbach 2003). In this process, the transition management literature calls attention to the following points:

- One should be careful not to get locked into suboptimal solutions, which again generally calls for the use of markets for coordination and context control instead of planning.
- One should embed transition policy into existing decision-making frameworks and legitimize transition management.
- One should ascertain a dynamic mechanism of change, making sure that the process does not come to a halt.
- One should engage in multi-level coordination: coordinate top-down policies with bottom-up initiatives.

3 CHALLENGES FROM THE ELECTRICITY INDUSTRY

Can one of the major deregulation and market reforms in Europe, the electricity market, be said to be rational in the strong deductive sense, or has it reflected a learning process where business models and market structures have emerged in dynamic interplay. How, if at all, have institutional factors shaped the deregulation trajectory?

Taking selected elements from this sector as an example, we shall investigate the interfaces between the three perspectives and how they are operative in the European electricity market case. We do not pretend to be comprehensive. Rather, elements from the complex story of European electricity market deregulation are collected to illustrate the analytical points, and to highlight how challenges to rational design may play (themselves) out in practice.

3.1 The Challenge of Shaping a Unitary Design Across National Borders

The rational market design model assumes the possibility of strong means-ends calculability traditionally formulated in terms of causal effects from structure–conduct–performance (Bain 1968). However, the European electricity deregulation and market design process has been highly diverse and tainted by national variation. Rather than one common design, we have seen multiple designs, clearly tainted by national regulatory styles. The European market space has become an arena for competition among business systems (Whitley 1992; Finon and Midttun 2004) just as much as between companies. This seems to have extensive elements of learning and muddling through both the commercial and institutional levels.

Deductive rational design elements have become highly blended with nation-specific institutional factors. It is debated to what extent the sum of this development has been rational in any strong sense. It could be complementarily interpreted as an iterative learning process, where national and industry-specific factors play out against each other in a new strategic possibility space.

Within the fairly heterogeneous European energy markets governments have pursued highly diverse structural policies and that industry has developed strategies with highly different structural effects indicating the strong influence of national style on the predominant market design.

On the one hand, certain countries, such as the UK, have launched strong structural fragmentation and de-verticalization policies, while prioritizing competition policy over industrial policy. Other countries, such as Norway, have inherited a decentralized municipalistic structure and adopted the radical third party access and end user market opening in the electricity sector, thereby not only furthering competition in wholesale, but also in end user markets.

On the other hand, countries such as France and Germany have allowed their industry to exploit scale and scope economies, to assume the risk of investment in large operations of capital-intensive electric equipment and gas infrastructures, thereby clearly prioritizing industrial policy over competition policy.

While the former group of countries has tended to emphasize the neoclassical virtues of decentralized competition, the latter group has emphasized contestability theory and international negotiation power to control price risk in the contractual gas purchase. This was presumably the German government's rationale for accepting the acquisition of Ruhrgas by E.ON. Pro-centralization policies are also self-reinforcing as they are promoted to allow national champions to compete, in an equitable way, with the other European giants in their respective markets and to be rivals in the European capital market for company acquisitions.

Central elements of the de facto evolving market design in the West European electricity market may be schematically represented in a two-dimensional matrix as in Figure 2.1, with the degree of effective competition along the horizontal axis and geographic expansion of the market along the vertical axis.

Developments in dominant Continental European markets such as France and Germany point to a trajectory away from national and monopolistic planned economies (quadrant III) towards a European semi-competitive and semi-integrated market system (between quadrants I and III), characterized in line with the contestable market theory rather than the liberal free-trade model. Other countries, such as England and Norway, have made unilateral moves into deregulated positions (in quadrant IV). In the Nordic case, a further expansion into quadrant II has taken place, but this position is challenged by the scaling up of companies as well as weak regulatory control at the EU level.

From a market design perspective one may ascertain that the European electricity market features fairly soft design criteria, allowing flexible adaptation to multiple national and industrial interests.

While each national position draws heavily on national institutional tradition within an emerging commercial context, the interfaces between the national configurations remains highly experimental and open to learning and innovation. The free trade competitive market design specifies competitive conditions in quadrant II that yet remain to be realized. A possible option for the EU electricity market, therefore, is that stabilization because of the institutional strength of major European players remains in the interface between I and II.

Figure 2.1 Regulatory patterns in EU electricity markets

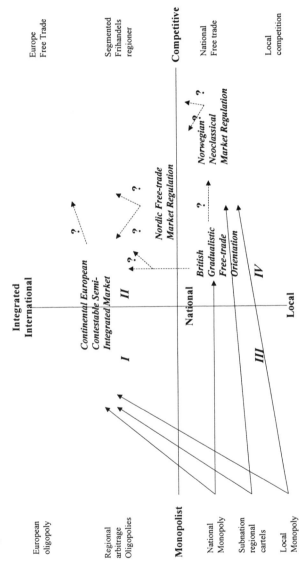

3.2 The Challenge of Multi-sectoral and Multifunctional Configuration

The deductive theoretical strength of the strong market design relies on the ability to delineate analytically discernable partial elements of the market system and apply specific market design to each of them

However, industrial practices are complex and typically involve multi-sectoral and multifunctional configuration. The variety of configuration and regulatory models creates complex interfaces within one sector that multiply across several sectors. This makes the total configuration highly complex and difficult to specify up front. It can be argued that the process of multifunctional business strategies and of regulatory approaches to an evolving multi-sectoral market space seems more appropriately described by a learning model at both levels. Given a matrix of relevant sectors and functions market configuration can involve both horizontal sectoral and vertical functional recombination (Figure 2.2)

Deregulation, in this perspective, allows vertically integrated sectoral systems to be decomposed into functionally integrated vertical systems. This implies substituting an integrated sectoral regulation regime with multiple functional regimes referring to elements of the sectoral value chain. On the other hand, it could also imply a more unitary management of similar functional issues across industrial sectors. However, to achieve this one would need multi-sectoral competency and awareness in market design, which is not often present in practical regulation.

As indicated in Figure 2.2, some of the regulatory concerns may be related to specific parts of the value chain (depicted by the horizontal ovals), where different arenas with their specific 'logics' typically represent complementary functional elements that can be subject to specific regulatory/market design, such as grid access and tariffing regimes; wholesale and retail trading regimes; regimes for balancing power etc.

However, regulatory concerns may also overlap, and tradeoffs may have to be developed between less complementary and potentially more competing regulatory concerns, such as competition policy, innovation policy and environmental policy. Given limited social acceptability of simple market compatible taxation instruments, some of the environmental policy regulation has questionable impacts on the electricity market.

Similarly, national champion-oriented industrial policy may also, under certain circumstances, impinge on both competition policy and environmental policy.

The functional differentiation of infrastructure regulation may also accommodate different and seemingly contradictory normative positions. While grid regulation and access regimes typically have a static efficiency focus, at least as far as we are talking about stable, mature technologies, innovation policy by definition must take a dynamic efficiency view.

The fact that European companies have been repositioning themselves dynamically across multi-sectoral and multifunctional engagements illustrates that the regulatory design challenges spelled out above are indeed encountered in practice (Midttun and Omland 2004)

Starting out, in many cases from mono-sectoral engagements either in gas/petroleum or in electricity, a number of European companies moved into wider multi-energy and multi-utility positions.

The two major German electricity players, as well as the Belgo French Suez group and its Tractebel subsidiary covering Electrabel and Distrigaz, on the other hand, were already at the outset of deregulation conglomerates with extensive engagements across a wide range of industries. Commercial adaptation to the market economy therefore came to signify an opposite process towards stronger focus, in E.ON's case towards a multi-energy position, and in RWE's case towards a multi-utility position. Ruhrgas, which was focused on the consolidation of a mono-energy strategy, has been integrated into E.ON's multi-energy portfolio. Suez has continued to manage complex multi-utility engagements, with a refocusing on energy, water and environmental services.

The restrictive regulation, which forces French public energy companies to abide by the 'principle of spécialité', precludes the French publicly owned energy companies from broader configuration. Both EDF and GDF thereby have remained locked into sectoral specialist positions in the domestic market up to 2004, but they have compensated that restriction by broad diversification.

The UK industry, following the politically orchestrated de-verticalization at the outset of the electricity market reform, has engaged in vertical reintegration as soon as restrictions were taken away. From positions of specialists in production, distribution or wire businesses, the

Figure 2.2 Vertical decomposition and horizontal integration of value chains

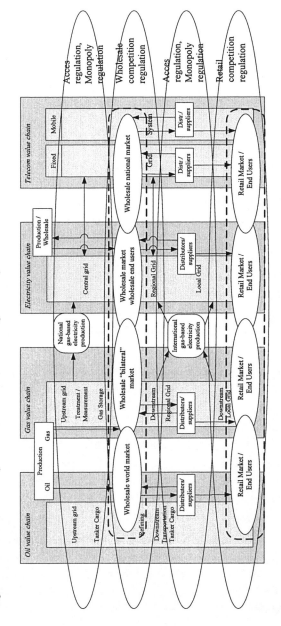

UK companies have also sought broader multi-energy engagements in particular in dual fuel competition.

In the Iberian market, companies like Iberdrola, Endesa, Union Fenosa and Natural Gas positioned themselves as 'global service operators' or 'customer focused multi-utility companies' in the first phase of deregulation only to retreat to more consolidated multi-energy positions following the economic downturn in Latin America in the early 2000s.

The large Nordic companies have followed both broader and specialized functional strategies. The merger of petroleum and electricity in Fortum in 1998 clearly signals a strong commitment to a multi-energy strategy from the largest Finnish market actor. However, the two Norwegian state companies, Statoil and Statkraft have, with only small exceptions, upheld 'French style' mono-sectoral energy strategies.

The plethora of industrial configurations in the European energy and infrastructure market space indicates that there is indeed a demand for both cross-sectoral and cross-national consistency. Given the low level of institutional coordination and the limited institutional acceptance of many simple first-best regulatory designs, this sets the stage for extensive learning.

3.3 The Institutional Challenge of Social Equilibrium

Market designs are generally developed with allocative efficiency in focus and also potentially with a supplementary innovation focus. From a distributive point of view, however, some of the market solutions, while efficient in economic terms, may run up against social limitations. Given the prominence of the energy sectors as general infrastructure, price formation and availability potentially figure high on the political agenda.

The difficulty posed by the deregulated electricity market, particularly as the market reaches scarcity, is that the economic and political equilibria may not always overlap. The market process may generate prices that politicians find unacceptable, while such prices may be necessary to trigger new investment. There may be, in other words, a set of economic equilibria that fall outside of the socio-political domain and a set of socio-political equilibria that fall outside of the economic domain (Figure 2.3) (Finon, Johnsen and Midttun 2004).

Figure 2.3   Social and market equilibria

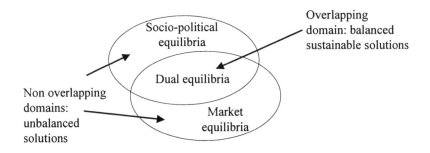

Source: Finon, Johnsen and Midttun (2004)

Some pure economic market solutions with a high degree of economic efficiency may imply socially unacceptable distributive effects and not qualify on the social criteria. On the other hand, solutions where the economic realities are neglected would be examples of unilateral socio-political equilibria where economic efficiency conditions are not met.

The concept of socio-political acceptability/equilibrium poses a challenge to deregulation and market design as it implies that such design, if conducted within the traditional strong rationality model, would potentially jeopardize the institutional legitimacy of design solutions. This could be done by addressing them at the political level, where distributive issues are both relevant and carry importance. Important market design elements could then be overrun by political decisions, and result in design modifications that could undermine the economic logic of the basic design, and even cause severe efficiency losses. The politically introduced price cap in the California power market was one of the reasons behind the California market collapse. Similar reactions were on the political agenda in Norway, following the winter 2002 price hike.

However, including the social dimension as a design criterion would create a setback for at least the strong deductive position. In this way, the market designers might get caught up in a difficult choice between strong deductive, but potentially socially disruptive designs on the one hand, and 'softer' but more socially inclusive designs, however with less room for deductive optimization.

3.4 Investment Challenges

The social and political constraints on market solutions is increasingly being recognized as a major challenge to the deregulated electricity industry when it comes to investment in new generation and transmission capacity. Many of the continental European electricity markets are still in the grace period, as they were liberalized in a situation of large overcapacity. However, some of them have met short periods of price spikes – the Scandinavian peninsula in the winters of 1996 and 2002–2003, The Netherlands during some periods for reasons of transitory rules, Spain during the winter of 2001–2002 for hydro reasons, Germany in December 2001 and France and Germany during the heat episode of summer 2003.

The worry is, among some market designers, that the price range and the duration of high prices necessary to stimulate new investments will be socially impeded and the market thereby will remain short (Finon, Johnsen and Midttun 2004).

However, coming out of the Nordic price hike is an experience, especially from Norway, of a potential for flexible decentralization, indicating that the answer to the price-hike challenge may not only come from the market design of the centralized energy system itself, but also from alternative approaches. In attempts to opt out of the high-price electricity market, Norwegians have extensively increased bio-fuelled heating, and have also taken increased interest in energy-saving technologies such as heat pumps. A wave of investment in small-scale local hydros has also emerged as a decentralized alternative to traditional, centralized large-scale supply sources. Finally, rental of mobile oil- or gas-fired back-up power turbines was high on the agenda last winter. There is an international lease market for such equipment, which may limit price spikes if applied. Clearly, these elements were not previously part of the electricity market design and must be interpreted as input of market learning.

3.5 The Challenge of Environmental Policy

The intriguing regulatory complexity and the interfacing between various regulatory domains is also demonstrated in the interfacing between environmental and energy policy/regulation. Environmental policy-motivated support for new renewable technologies has, under an innovation perspective, been justified as a learning curve investment to close the gap between immature technologies and the market's willingness to pay (Wene 2003).

This could, however, have spillover effects in the regular energy markets, as it could lead to surplus capacity and price fall which could postpone price hikes, but also obviously postpone investments from ordinary market players. The large environmental externalities, as well as international coordination already achieved on investment in new renewable resources, would seem to make this strategy more attractive than publicly-financed conventional investments in generation capacity. However, it would represent a semi-planned intervention into the regular market not foreseen in the regular market design

Not only is the attempt to green Europe through innovative quasi-market practices a highly experimental learning game, but also the ramifications of these new practices on the regular electricity markets represent highly challenging regulatory innovations, thus transcending the premises for the static efficiency model and pointing to a more dynamic learning design.

4 DISCUSSION

The case examples from the electricity industry demonstrate that, although there are European ambitions in the development of 'rational' market designs, there is a high level of configurational, institutional and technological complexity which plays itself out in unforeseen ways. This forces us, in many ways, to include a dynamic dimension in the regulatory design.

The problem that then arises, however, is how to bridge the two rather analytically diverse conceptual worlds. In the first, 'rational design' case, there is a belief in developing fairly detailed market designs with incentives to stimulate efficient resource allocation. In the second, dynamic innovation case, there is an orientation towards wider configurational and technological freedom to foster exploration of new technologies and business models.

A distinction between the three levels of transformation may, however, provide a possible bridge between the static and the dynamic worlds:

- At a first level, deregulation can be seen as the opening up of monopolistic governance with commercial adjustment and commodification within existing technological/organizational boundaries but with competitive exposure.
- At a second level, deregulation may be seen as structural experimentation with modularization and transformative exposure of elements. This is a semi-dynamic state with bounded structural/technological/organizational transformation within an over all rationally designed structural platform.
- At a third level, deregulation may be seen as fundamental transformation implying dramatic dynamic change with radical structural and technological transformation.

Taking the first level perspective as a point of departure, transformation basically allows a 'rational' design approach as described within mainstream static efficiency-oriented deregulation theory. Bringing infrastructure services on a commodity form, and opening up for competitive iteration against consumer interests should unleash cost-efficiency and consumer-oriented service provision. The advantage of the static efficiency perspective is that it carries with it a programme with a relatively well-developed set of remedies and operative procedures to meet regulatory challenges.

Given the fairly well-defined analytical premises for the static efficiency perspective and our focus on dynamic aspects of regulation as well as the interface between static and dynamic efficiency, we shall focus mainly on the second- and third- level perspectives.

4.1 Modularization: Deregulation as Structural Experimentation

Taking the second-level perspective as a point of departure allows us to see deregulation and market design as partial structural transformation, within a context of stable institutional and technological design. Transformation therefore takes a modular form, where technological and/or institutional platforms serve as anchors for lower level innovative restructuring. Modularization thus allows combinations of lower level processes of both a static and dynamic nature

In the case of the electricity market deregulation, one could see the split-up into various functional regulatory specialities such as natural monopoly regulation, competition regulation etc. as regulatory modularization. The overall regulatory design then becomes a structural platform for the integration of functionally specialized regulation. The design rules set by the regulatory architecture then guarantee that the various cases of modular experimentation fit together and that the static efficiency-oriented and dynamic-oriented modular development can co-exist side by side.

As argued by Baldwin and Clark (2000), modularity is a structural means of achieving functional integration in a complex system where the options embedded in the design are simultaneously multiplied and decentralized (Figure 2.4). Through well-developed design rules modularity helps simplify complex systems and partitions complex tasks so that individuals and companies can focus their efforts productively on a manageable set of objectives.

Modularity makes complexity manageable, it decentralizes organization and enables parallel work. The tolerance for uncertainty in subsystems allows for greater variation, and the competitive exposure of several supplies to the specific supply chain interface. As argued by Baldwin and Clark (2000) for each module it is possible to conduct a number of parallel, uncoordinated experiments and many parallel experiments imply many independent work groups with a greater potential for variety creation.

Interpreted as a regulation strategy, modularization implies that regulatory authorities are able to establish an overall structural stability at some level, which may be used as a platform to specify fitness parameters for the decentralized combination of both static efficiency and dynamic experimentation. The premise for this regulatory strategy is therefore that the regulatory regime actually allows full freedom within modular experimentation while at the same time securing fit within the overall regulatory design.

Figure 2.4   Modularity and design options

Modularity Creates Design Options

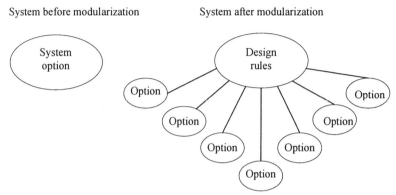

Source: Carliss and Baldwin (2001).

4.2 Temporal Sequencing: Deregulation as Transformation

Taking the third level perspective as a point of departure allows us to conceptualize radical transformation also at higher levels of industrial organization, leaving design possibilities only at a very high, constitutional level. Specific industrial structuring, both in terms of company structure, industrial combinations and institutional configuration is up for dramatic change. Deregulation, in this case, unleashes dynamic forces that basically cannot be controlled at least not within a sector-specific regulatory design, and therefore invites a more extensive *laissez-faire* policy.

In the case of deregulation–induced radical transformation, therefore, it is only possible to stabilize fairly general constitutional rules, whereas more selective modular experimentation remains difficult to delineate and specific designs with detailed incentive structures remain obviously misplaced in a dynamic transformation setting.

While the modular solution, therefore, constitutes a workable solution to the static–dynamic interface under stable conditions over all regimes, it will not work when this precondition is not met. Such conditions may arise following unforeseen spillover from regulatory innovation in one domain to another, which undermines established modular architecture. They may also arise, however, from institutional constraints such as social acceptability of market outcomes or national diversity in institutionalising functional demands that trigger complex development in new directions.

To cope with similar dynamic transformation at the firm level, Bart Nooteboom (1999), in his dynamic theory of industrial organization, allows both static and dynamic efficiency-oriented configurations to be sequenced over time. Conceiving innovation as a learning and implementation process, Nooteboom notes that this process has both an exploration and an exploitation phase (Figure 2.5). In the early invention/exploration phase, the managerial design needs to be open and flexible, to allow novel combinations, while in the ensuing exploitation phase, the novelty needs to become standardized in a 'dominant design' as Abernathy and Utterback (1975/2000) have put it, indicating that at this stage what is needed is an organizational design aimed at consolidation.

Figure 2.5   Cyclical theory of industrial organization applied to regulation (Nooteboom 1999)

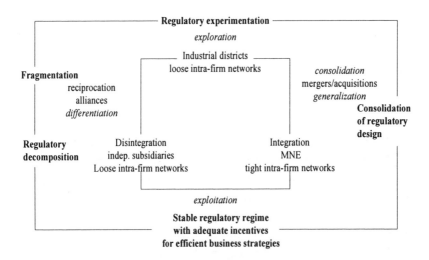

Disintegrated, open configurations have a comparative advantage in the early stages of experimentation and invention. In the later stages of consolidation and generalization winning designs may be integrated into more tightly governed contractual structures, or fully integrated hierarchy.

Transferred to the field of regulation and market design, the cyclical model suggests phases of dynamic reconfiguration followed by phases of static efficiency-oriented consolidation of regulatory design. The model of industrial configuration can be transposed to equivalent stages of regulatory design. Starting with the old regulatory regime, one can distinguish a process of regulatory decomposition (parallel to the decomposition of the industrial structure into loose networks); then an opening up and fragmentation leading to regulatory experimentation. Winning designs may subsequently be consolidated into new possibly modularized regimes, which establishes a stable new generation of regulatory design.

The European market deregulation process could, as a whole, be fruitfully seen in this perspective. Decomposition of the planned economy under deregulation unleashes commercial experimentation that again consolidates new business models and market designs.

4.3 Institutional Legitimacy and Distributive Challenge

Besides the need to face the challenge of dynamic configuration, deregulation and market design also faces the need for legitimacy. Societal acceptance for the distributive outcomes among vested interests resulting from new regimes may prove vital to their implementation and stability. In the case of electricity deregulation the price hike experiences in the Californian and Norwegian markets indicate that certain market outcomes in the electricity markets are highly controversial. The case also shows that there is rivalry around national regulatory designs in the European market space, with strong political 'competition' around preferred market designs.

In situations where deregulation and radical change in market design are seen to affect strong vested interests, therefore, distributive issues may translate into institutional barriers to 'rational' market design. Taking a transition management perspective, however, radical change might become institutionally feasible through stepwise transformation.

More systematically, the sequential impact of even soft regulatory intervention can be schematically presented in a game tree, where the implications of regulatory choices and their consequences are displayed in a sequential order (Midttun and Koefoed 2001) (Figure 2.6).

Figure 2.6   Dynamic aspects of regulation

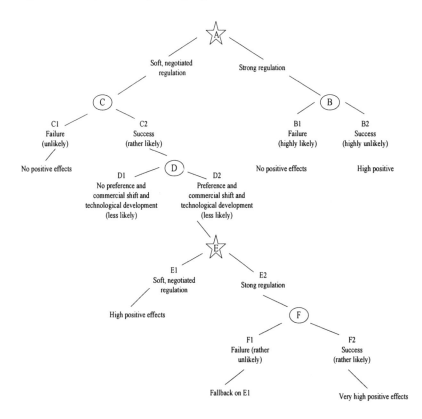

The game tree has two kinds of nodes: nodes where choices are being made (represented by a star) and nodes where nature chooses its moves as consequences of regulatory choices (designated by circles). Assuming that strong regulation, due to problems of legitimacy, is highly improbable in the short run, insistence on direct strong regulatory action is likely to lead to failure (b1), which means that we forsake the high positive effects that such a strategy might have if successful (b2). Choice of softer negotiated regulation might be more likely to succeed (c2), but would in turn yield smaller yet considerable positive effects (dl). However, in the next round, the soft regulatory intervention might trigger preference shifts or technological shifts, or both, and thereby create a new basis for the next round regulation. At the next decision point (E), strong regulation has a far larger chance of being implemented (f2), as industrial interests might have prepared themselves already, or may be compelled by the marker forces to adjust their policies. Furthermore, leading firms that have already adapted to the coming regime might welcome strong regulation at this point to secure compliance from smaller firms. It is, therefore, possible that we might end up with strong regulation (f2) bur only through the initial soft regulation path (C-D-E-F).

As shown in the game tree exposition, temporary suboptimal market design solutions may, in a long-term perspective, contribute to moving primary commercial interests in the 'right' direction. We may thereby come to see a shift in direction of the new policy target in steps over time.

However, even with active transition management there is no guarantee that rational design ambitions will be reached, even in a long-term perspective. As we have seen in the European case, whether the European liberalization project may in the longer run lead to fuller integration, open trade and competitive markets still remains a fairly open question. The new 2003 gas and electricity directives and the so-called Florence and Madrid processes indicate stronger competitive market policy in Europe. However, at the same time major European companies have kept growing at a spectacular rate and the European countries strike very different balances between internationalization and competition.

At the end of the day, therefore, 'rational' market design or 'rational' regulatory models, even in the long run, may be highly contested. A large business system literature (Whitley 1992) and a system of innovation literature (Edquist and McKelvey 2000; Lundvall 2002) argue that efficient and innovative economic activity may take place in numerous ways, drawing on specific routines, capabilities and resources. Given the European project of economic integration under limited policy consensus, market–based models stand out as attractive regulatory options. However, markets come in a variety of fashions, with different institutional designs. Institutional fit must therefore clearly be an important design criterion besides efficiency and innovative capability.

REFERENCES

Abernathy, W.J.and J.M. Utterback (1975/ 2000), 'A Dynamic Model of Process and Product Innovation', *The Political Economy of Science, Technology and Innovation*, Elgar Reference Collection. *International Library of critical Writings in Economics,* vol. 116. Cheltenham, UK and Northampton, US: Edward Elgar.

Baldwin, C. Y. and K.B. Clark (2000), *Design Rules: the Power of Modularity*, Cambridge US: MIT Press.

Bain, J.S (1968), *Industrial Organization*, New York, US: John Wiley.

Beckert, J. (2003), 'Economic Sociology and Embeddedness: How Shall We Conceptualize Economic Action?', *Journal of Economic Issues*, September, 37 (3).

Blumstein, C., S. Goldstone and L. Lutzenhiser (2000), 'A Theory-based Approach to Market Transformation', Energy Policy, February.

Christensen, C.M. (1997), *The Innovator's Dilemma. When New Technologies Cause Great Firms to Fail*, Boston, US: Harvard Business School Press.

DiMaggio, P. and W. Powell (1991), *Introduction in The New Institutionalism in Organizational Analysis*, Chicago US and London UK: Chicago University Press.

Edquist, C. and M. McKelvey (2000), *Systems of Innovation: Growth, Competitiveness and Employment*, Vol. II. Cheltenham, UK and Northampton, US: Edward Elgar.

Finon, D. and A. Midttun (2004), *Reshaping European Electricity and Gas Industry*, London, UK: Elsevier Science.

Finon, D., T. A. Johnsen and A. Midttun (2004), 'Challenges when Electricity Markets Face the Investment Phase', *Energy Policy*, 32.

Hayek, F. (1948), *Individualism and economic order,* London: Routledge and Kegan Paul.

Kemp, R. and D. Loorbach (2003), 'Governance for Sustainability Through Transition Management', Paper for EAEPE 2003 Conference November 7-10 2003 Maastricht, The Netherlands.

Kirzner, I.M. (1997), 'Entrepreneurial Discovery and the Competitive Market Process: An Austrian Approach', *Journal of Economic Literature*, 35 (1).

Lachmann, L.M. (1976), 'From Mises to Shackle: An Essay on Austrian Economics and the Kaleidic Society', *Journal of Economic Literature*, March 14.

Lundvall, B.Å. (2002), *Innovation Growth and Social Cohesion*, Cheltenham, UK and Northampton, US: Edward Elgar.

March, J.G. and J.P. Olsen (1995), *Democratic Governance*, New York, US: Free Press.

McMillan, J. (2003), 'Market Design: The Policy Uses of Theory', *AEA Papers and Proceedings*. http://iis-db.stanford.edu/pubs/20656/Market_Design-McMillan.pdf

Midttun A. and A.L. Koefoed (2001), 'The Effectiveness and Negotiability of Environmental Regulation', *International Journal of Regulation and Governance*, 1 (1), 79-111.

Midttun, A. and T. Omland (2004), 'Configuration and Performance of Large European Energy Companies: A Statistical Analysis', in D. Finon and A. Midttun, *Reshaping European Electricity and Gas Industry*, London, UK: Elsevier Science.

Midttun, A. and E. Svindland (2001), *Approaches and Dilemmas in Economic Regulation*, Chippenham: Palgrave.

Milgrom, P. (2003), *Putting Auction Theory to Work*, Cambridge, UK: Cambridge University Press.

Nooteboom, B. (1999), 'Innovation, Learning and Industrial Organization', *Cambridge Journal of Economics*, March 23, 2.

Robinson, J. (1956), *The Accumulation of Capital*, London, UK: Macmillan.

Roth A.E. (1999), 'Game Theory as a Tool for Market Design', Paper 5/6/99 Harvard University, Department of Economics and Graduate School of Business Administration

Roth, A. E. (2002), 'The Economist as Engineer: Game Theory, Experimentation and Computation as Tools for Design Economics', *Econometrica*, July.

Schumpeter J.A. edited by Clemence R.V. (1989), *Essays: On Entrepreneurs, Innovations, Business Cycles, and the Evolution of Capitalism*, New Brunswick, US: Transaction Publishers.

Savas, E.E. (1987), *Privatization: the Key to Better Government*, Chatham, NJ, US: Chatham House Publishers.

Wene, C.O. (2003), 'Learning Curves, Tools, Energy Policy Analysis and Implementation', Presentation at the Norwegian School of Management, February 11th.

Whitley, R. (1992), *European Business Systems:Ffirms and Markets in their National Contexts*, London UK: Sage.

3. Competition Policy, Networks and the 'New Economy'[1]

Erik J. Kloosterhuis and Peter A.G. van Bergeijk

1 INTRODUCTION

From a competition policy perspective, network industries are presently characterized by three global trends. First, the role of private parties in infrastructure industries is clearly growing. Second, a dominant policy preference appears to have emerged: 'use markets if possible, regulate if necessary'. Third, customer preferences are increasingly becoming important determinants of infrastructure investment decisions. The groundwork for this emerging policy landscape was laid down in the 1990s when many industrialized countries embarked on the road to structural reform such as the deregulation and re-regulation of network industries, the strengthening of competition policy and privatization of public monopolies and semi-monopolies. Essentially, structural reforms aim at an increase of potential output and the quality of that output by improving the functioning of markets and institutions. Privatization, deregulation and competition policy became important issues on the policy agenda because economic studies indicated that substantial benefits could derive from structural reforms, including higher productivity, lower inflation and (potentially) more employment (van Bergeijk, van Sinderen and Vollaard 1999). For example, the Organization for Economic Co-operation and Development (OECD 1997) produced estimates based on an in-depth analysis of the electricity and telecom sectors. Figure 3.1 summarizes some of the results reported in the OECD study, which are in line with results generally found in other studies that deal with regulatory reform in network industries in individual countries.

Figure 3.1   Predicted consequences of regulatory reform (OECD 1997)

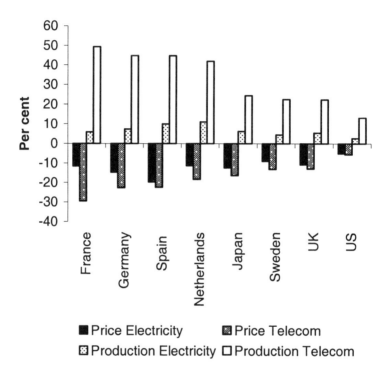

The expected benefits of deregulation and re-regulation according to the OECD study show up in both substantial increases in production and reductions in prices.[2] Interestingly, and possibly due to the fact that technological change is less important in the electricity sector, relatively strong price and quantity effects occur in the telecom sector.

These changes in prices and quantities translate easily into welfare consequences that are the natural focus of most economic analyses (i.e. the so-called Harberger triangle or efficiency loss[3]). However, these efficiency losses, large as they may be, are dwarfed by the consumer loss that results from the fact that the existing quantity is bought at too high a price level (Figure 3.2). Indeed, it is the consumer loss that in most cases motivates the political interest in deregulating or re-regulating a network industry.

Figure 3.2   Welfare and efficiency losses due to sub-optimal regulation (per cent of business GDP)

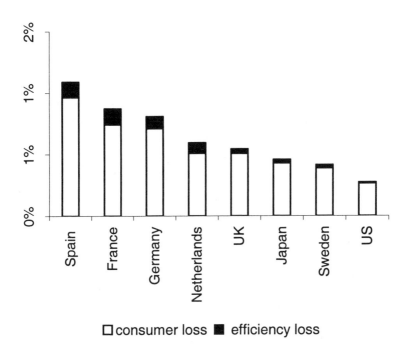

□ consumer loss ■ efficiency loss

It is a truism that the economic gains were only one side of the coin. In Europe, for example, political and legal aspects were key determinants in reshaping the regulatory perspective on a great many network industries (Pelkmans 2001). Moreover, in addition to the expected economic benefits from regulatory reform and the regional prerequisites of the completion of the European internal market other – essentially global – factors were relevant as well.

Policy makers were, so to say, forced to reconsider regulatory practices because of unprecedented trends towards globalization, individualization and exceptionally rapid technological change (Summers 2001). Production of goods and services increasingly became knowledge-based, footloose and driven by creative destruction, that is to say the dynamic Schumpeterian process in which new combinations of products, distribution and production techniques emerge in order to replace existing ones. But no a priori reason exists why regulatory activities and competition policy would be exempted from the, as Schumpeter (1976) called it, 'perennial gale of creative destruction'. Indeed it is not farfetched to argue that economic, technological and social opportunities have led to the quest for the principles that might govern the New Regulation of the New Economy.

In this chapter we will focus on the proper role of competition and competition policy in a dynamic environment. It is important for our discussion to recognize that a number of characteristics of deregulated network industries are by no means unique (Määttä and Virtanen 2001). This is true for the most obvious issue at stake, namely the fact that scale effects can be reaped on the demand side (since the value of the services provided by a network increases with the number of users of that network). This problem, however, is not new for a competition authority (White 1998). Indeed, scale effects on the supply side of the market are part of its toolbox. Moreover, modern network industries are part and parcel of the so-called New Economy. Thus, many competition (policy) problems have to be dealt as well in sectors where network effects are absent. Examples of factors that complicate the analysis are very high rates of innovation, decreasing costs and capital abundance (see for example Posner 2001). The upshot is that network industries are only 'special' where (natural) monopoly aspects come into play.

The remainder of this chapter is structured as follows. First we discuss the general principles of competition law and offer some examples of specific applications of these principles to co-operation and unilateral behaviour of firms in high-tech and network industries. This will amongst others show that the competition law does not *per se* prohibit co-operation between firms in these sectors. Moreover, this is especially true in the field of innovation (and for good reasons). Next we focus on two issues that are of particular relevance from the perspective of the application of competition policy in the new economy: We take a look at knowledge-intensive production and the interface between intellectual property rights and competition law. In addition, the issue of networks and (natural) monopoly comes to the fore. In section 4 we reverse the perspective discussing the consequences that the specificity of new economy activities may have on the way competition policy should be applied. The final section draws some conclusions.

2   ON THE RELEVANCE OF COMPETITION LAW FOR KNOWLEDGE-BASED AND NETWORK INDUSTRIES

In most jurisdictions, competition law rests on three pillars, as it comprises policies with respect to

- restrictive agreements,
- the bundling of economic power by mergers and acquisition, and
- abuse of economic power, respectively.

In both the formal and the legal sense these three pillars are always quite differently structured but their economic purpose is very similar. The ultimate policy goal is to keep markets open for competition and to protect the customers from unfair exploitation. At the same time competition policy wants to preserve the positive effects of co-operation and scale.

2.1 Restrictive Agreements between Companies

The first pillar of competition law deals with restrictive agreements between companies. These agreements can be 'naked' cartels or agreements that are linked to some kind of co-operative arrangement. The first point to note is that co-operation between partners that are neither competitors nor potential competitors will not often create problems under European competition law or its national pendants. When competition law does apply because co-operation takes place between (potential) competitors, such co-operation can also be allowable. Especially the EC regulation (a so–called 'block exemption') for R&D co-operation makes apparent that such co-operation is possible.[4] One could say that as long as the partners stay within the limits of the regulation, an 'efficiency presumption' exists and no further proof of conformity of a given agreement with EC competition rules is necessary. The regulation covers joint R&D as well as the joint exploitation thereof. The regulation has recently been revised and is now much less the juridical straitjacket than its predecessors were perceived to be. The main points of the regulation are as follows. Co-operation between competitors falls within the scope of the regulation as long as the joint market share of the firms concerned does not exceed 25 per cent of the relevant market. The exemption is, however, subject to further conditions. *Inter alia*, the regulation does not allow for agreements that may lead to quantity restrictions or price fixing.

It should, however, be noted that also licensing and distribution agreements could bring about restrictions that fall within the scope of competition law. This is, for example, the case for exclusive dealing and agreements to restrict the quantity of production, to divide the market or to fix prices. For our discussion it is especially relevant that competition law is applicable on exclusive licensing of IP rights ('know how' included). Another EC block exemption for technology transfer agreements, however, offers the appropriate room for agreements that, although restricting competition, on balance can be considered to yield positive results for society.[5] This exemption deserves to be scrutinized in case licenses with territorial restrictions or with exclusivity rights are to be granted. The same holds for the obligatory use of trademarks of the licensor by the licensee and/or restrictions of the quantity that the licensee is allowed to produce. The exemption is conditional: field-of-use restrictions are, for example, allowed, whereas customer allocation between licensor and licensee within the same technical field of use is not. Many additional dos and don'ts are spelled out in the regulation.

2.2 Mergers and Acquisitions

The second pillar of competition law deals with structural changes in the control of undertakings. The issue at stake is to prevent that mergers, acquisitions or the formation of full-fledged joint ventures will give rise to anti-competitive market structures. Actually, only very seldom do problems arise in technology sectors, probably because these markets tend to be very dynamic. But it can happen of course. For example, in the case

Shell/Montecatini a joint venture was established that would be in control of the two technologies that enable the production of polypropylene.[6] According to the European Commission, the company would acquire market power on this 'technology market' to the detriment of the customers. Also, concentration of knowledge or IP rights may stifle innovation and obstruct the dissemination of knowledge in a particular sector. Consequentially, this might create a situation in which a merger would not be acceptable for competition authorities.

It is more likely that mergers between competing networks will raise competition concerns if considerable scale effects and sunk costs are present. The same may even be true in the case of the integration of complementary networks. Quite another situation arises in the case of the structural linking of infrastructure and the provision of 'content'. Also this will sometimes receive the critical attention of competition authorities because it may enable a firm to discriminate against independent suppliers and dictate what content the customer will receive. In the case *MSG/Media Service* the European Commission concluded:

> 'the foreseeable effects of the proposed concentration suggests that it will lead to the sealing-off of and early creation of a dominant position on the future markets for technical and administrative services and to a substantial hindering of effective competition on the future market for pay-TV.'[7]

Consequently, the merger was blocked. A similar case was the proposed RTL/Veronica/Endemol merger that was only accepted after Endemol withdrew from the project.[8]

2.3 Abuse of Economic Dominance and Monopolisation

The third pillar applies when a situation of economic dominance already exists. Competition laws within the EU forbid the abuse of a dominant position, while the United States apply the similar notion of (abusive) monopolization (Gifford 2001). These legal standards relate to unilateral company behaviour like bundling or tying and discriminatory and predatory behaviour. Bundling or tying are practices by which firms may try to use their power in one market as leverage in another market. Discrimination between customers can be used to exploit market power. Predatory behaviour and discrimination are also examples of unfair means that companies use to monopolize markets.

A puzzling thing is that what is considered abusive behaviour can be both commercially rational for a dominant firm and fully legitimate for a company that is *not* dominant. One must, however, be aware that these commercial practices would not be sustainable for companies that are *not* dominant because they face sufficient competition. Customers just would not accept tying arrangements or the negative impact of discrimination when they have alternative supply available. It is for this reason that competition law normally only applies to unilateral behaviour in situations of market dominance. When the market does not work properly, regulation steps in.

The actual question of what constitutes dominance is of course a crucial one. From the perspective of economic theory one would argue that it is a position that enables one or more companies to restrict market supply and cause price to rise above the competitive level. The legal definition of economic dominance in the context of EC competition law is a bit similar. The European Court of Justice (ECJ) considers an undertaking dominant when it has a position that enables it to prevent effective competition on the market and behave to an appreciable extent independently of its competitors and customers.[9] This definition of the ECJ shows that in the context of competition law the question of dominance cannot be addressed without taking the dynamic aspect of competition into account. This implies that when a market is contestable because entry is easy, it cannot be considered a relevant anti-trust market. For this reason, such a market is not the proper basis for the assessment of market power.

Dominant firms must be cautious not to try to enlarge their economic power by unfair means or exploit their position in an excessive way. Competition authorities have the task to prohibit this, but this is not an easy task. The definition of the relevant market, the identification of dominance and the assessment of the behaviour that is presumed to be abusive can give rise to difficult legal and economic questions. The abundant literature on the Microsoft case proves the point adequately. It is especially in connection with the doctrine of abuse of economic dominance that complicated questions may arise with respect to high-tech and network sectors, as will be shown below.

3   COMPETITION LAW AND INTELLECTUAL PROPERTY

Having sketched the main features of competition law, we now address the interface between competition law and intellectual property (IP) rights. It is important to be aware of the fact that, in terms of incentives, both competition law and legislation in the field of IP rights must be considered as crucial for the promotion of economic progress. The freedom to compete can be considered as the stick that makes companies aware of the fact that a head start in the market place can be lost when competitors become more innovative. But competition also leads to the finding of new applications and through that, to the diffusion of innovation. On the other hand, IP rights can be seen as the carrot for innovation, because only well protected property rights guarantee that successful innovators can pick the fruits of their inventions. The existence of these rights will promote investments in innovative directions.

3.1 Competition Policy Addresses the Exercise of IP Rights

It is of great importance that the freedom to compete and the possibility to establish IP rights are well balanced (Barton 1997). It is primarily the legislator than must strike this balance by defining the scope of IP rights. This scope will in principle be taken for granted by competition law. But there is an important proviso to make. The ECJ has ruled that although the grant or existence of IP rights is not subjected to competition law, the exercise of these rights is (Faull and Nikpay 1999). What does this mean? With respect to the behaviour of undertakings, the court draws a distinction between the *use* and the *exercise* of IP rights. The court defined as 'the specific subject matter' of an IP-right (a) the exclusive right to use an invention with a view to manufacturing industrial products and putting them into circulation for the first time, either directly or by the grant of licenses, and (b) the right to oppose infringements.[10] This means that once a good has been sold in the EU by the holder of the IP-right or by its consent, this right is considered to be exhausted. From this it follows that contractual clauses, such as territorial restrictions in licence agreements, that hinder the free flow of goods in the EU, fall within the scope of EC competition law.

Furthermore, the exercise of an IP-right can give rise to an abuse of dominance. It must however be noted that the distinction between use and exercise is problematic, because we can consider a right as the sum of the ways it can be exercised (Korah 2002). Therefore, the scope of IP rights, and certainly also the economic value of such rights, to a certain extent depend on competition law and policy. Consequently, competition law is probably a more decisive factor for the value of innovations that are protected by IP rights than one might expect.

3.2 IP rights as 'Essential Facility'

The so-called essential facilities doctrine gives a specific illustration of the above. This doctrine is a very sensitive topic amongst antitrust practitioners, because more than any other doctrine in competition law it interferes with the private power to pick the fruits of one's property rights. An essential facility can be defined as an asset to which access is indispensable in order to compete on a certain market.[11] This means that the owner of an essential facility can effectively decide who can enter a certain market and who cannot. Such a facility can be a piece of infrastructure or any other type of asset. The essence of the essential facility doctrine is that under certain circumstances the denial of access to the facility constitutes an abuse of a dominant position. In the case *Volvo Veng* the ECJ ruled that a refusal to grant a licence (for designs of body panels for cars) cannot in itself constitute an abuse of a dominant position. Such a refusal can, however, be abusive when, *inter alia*, the firm that refuses to grant a licence overcharges for the spare parts in question. Another possibility is that it stops producing the products when market demand is still considerable.[12]

The consideration about the existence of unfulfilled market demand also plays a prominent role in the controversial *Magill* case.[13] The subject of the case was the refusal to grant a copyright licence for information on TV programmes. The three broadcasting companies involved produced weekly surveys of their own programmes and Magill wanted to produce a comprehensive guide covering the programmes of all three stations. The European Commission forced the broadcasters to supply the necessary information, which was upheld by the ECJ. The Court considered that the refusal to supply the information prevented the appearance of a new product which the stations themselves did not offer and for which there was a constant consumer demand. The implications of this ruling could be far-reaching (Korah 2002). It could mean an obligation to licence to anyone who is willing to offer the consumer a new product on the basis of the licence, especially when this product can be considered a relevant anti-trust market.

Now that it is established case law that competition law effectively limits the scope of IP rights, authorities may want to look behind the surface of IP-legislation by asking themselves whether and to which extent it is reasonable that IP rights protect a certain asset. Advocate General Jacobs, in his advice in the *Bronner* case, sees as one of the decisive special features of the *Magill* case that the copyright protection of TV listings is hard to justify with the motive to stimulate or reward creative efforts.[14] Such reasoning risks requiring an economic justification for any IP-right that might raise questions in connection with competition law. This would, it is submitted, mean a too strong subordination of IP legislation to competition law. The assessment of the conformity of an exercise of IP rights with competition law could better be made irrespective of the economic merits of that specific right. The alternative would lead to loss of legal security and raise complex economic questions in the assessment of cases.

4   COMPETITION IN THE NEW ECONOMY

Essentially the characteristic process of creative destruction can be described by the observation that monopolies in the initial market phase of knowledge industries are the *raison d'être* for innovation. High risks will only be taken when the rewards compensate for the risk of failure. Large investments can only be financed if profits are sufficiently large. Indeed, as these industries are characterized by both high fixed up front investments and low marginal costs many of these markets are initially characterized by a situation where pricing at marginal costs makes the recovery of full costs impossible. Therefore such markets tend to be natural monopolies. This is even more so when network effects come into play. In this section we want to explore the question how to make sense of competition policy when scale effects and network effects are major driving factors in the development of economic activities.

4.1 Network Effects and Scale Effects

The essential characteristic of a network industry is that the value of a product or service for a user depends on the number of other users of the same product or service. This is called the *'network effect'*. The users are 'connected' to the same network, sometimes in a physical, sometimes in a virtual sense. Examples are different sorts of telecommunication but also networks of bank accounts or credit card users and acceptants. A similar effect can be seen in industries where standardization is an important feature, such as consumer electronics or computer software. In such cases, the reactions of consumers and suppliers will often be interrelated. If more people choose a certain computer system, more suppliers will be interested to write new applications that in turn will make the system more interesting for consumers, and so on. In the same way, the more consumers choose a certain credit card, the more interested retailers will be to become a participant and so forth. From the perspective of competition policy a paradox may arise: while market power normally must be considered detrimental for the consumer, the existence of network effects may lead to the opposite conclusion. This is however not the case when a standard or network cannot be appropriated, so that the products of different suppliers can be part of one and the same network.

Apart from network effects, which can be labelled as 'demand side scale effects', also cost–based *scale effects* on the supply side can be important. High fixed costs (e.g. the creation of intellectual property) and low or no costs for the production of extra units (e.g. software copies) makes expansion easy and profitable. Furthermore, production circumstances can be such that capacity constraints are of little or no importance, in which case expansion of market positions can take place very rapidly. Both network effects and important scale effects can have a huge impact on the nature of competition. Competition will be tending to be *for* the market instead of *in* the market. This means that although many firms may invest in the development and commercialization of a new product, standard or system, only one, or at best a few, will succeed in acquiring a position on the market. In the most extreme case 'the winner takes all', that is to say, the whole market. In such cases, the winners of the competitive process will automatically achieve some kind of dominant position in the market in which they operate.

We will now address the question how to take account of the special features of the new economy in the practical application of competition law. In this analysis, three questions must be distinguished: firstly, how should markets be defined; secondly, when is economic dominance at hand; and thirdly, when must company behaviour be considered az abusive.

4.2 The Definition of Markets

The definition of the relevant market is at the heart of most competition law procedures. It is a necessary step in an accountable analysis of the impact of an agreement, a merger or a unilateral business practice on competition. A relevant market comprises the goods or services that meet a specific demand and for which no alternatives are reasonably available. With respect to networks the point can be made that a network does *not* always constitute a relevant market in itself. Networks are neither by definition a natural monopoly nor the only means by which a certain market demand can be satisfied. Sometimes alternative networks can co-exist, as is the case in telephony or in payment systems. Altogether the definition of the relevant market in network sectors does not seem to raise specific problems.

On the other hand, when markets are of a high-tech nature, market definition may be a difficult job, as several writers have observed. Competition in high–tech markets will often be of a non-price nature (Pleatsikas and Teece 2001) and can result in the temporary edge of a firm over its rivals. The central parameters of competition are quality and innovation instead of price and this must be taken into account in the definition of the relevant market. In the standard approach a product is considered to constitute a relevant market when a hypothetical monopolist is able to raise the price for that product 5 to 10 per cent profitably above the competitive level.[15] This approach is less appropriate in dynamic markets if the payback period for successful innovations is relatively short. Under such circumstances it would be more realistic to look at other competition parameters, such as the intensity of innovative activity and shifts in customer purchases (Ahlborn, Evans and Padilla 2001). Secondly, high–tech markets may be differentiated, with all kinds of specific user groups. By giving too much weight to specific product characteristics one could run the risk of defining markets too narrowly and overestimating market power. In such cases one must take a closer look at the degree and speed in which suppliers are able to adapt their products to the specific needs of different user groups. Thirdly, a wider time frame for assessing the scope of the relevant market may be appropriate. In high–tech markets competition takes place at the level of innovative activity. Therefore, firms that have competed or, more – importantly – will compete in a certain market within a period of, for example 4-5 years, should be considered as relevant players in that market (Pleatsikas and Teece 2001).

It is indeed a task of competition authorities to assess every case on its merits, taking into account all the relevant economic factors. Now fixed rules can apply on the great diversity of cases that may come under their scrutiny. Furthermore, it is generally accepted that an abuse case will rest more on an *ex post* analysis of the market as far as one must investigate what damage has already been done to competition. In contrast an analysis of the possible effects of an intended merger must necessarily be more forward looking. It is stressed that in both situations already at the level of market definition due attention must be given to the, possibly negative, influence that anti-competitive behaviour or mergers will have on the dynamics of competition.

4.3 Assessment of Market Power

Network effects and scale effects have always played a role in the natural monopoly sectors in the old economy. This was often the reason to label them as 'utilities' and bring them under either a special regulatory regime or direct government control. So what makes the new economy special? An important difference exists between networks that are based on tangible assets like physical infrastructure and the networks of the new economy that are based on non-tangible assets such as IP rights. It has been observed that in the last case a winning position will be much more vulnerable and that for this reason competition authorities need not worry very much about it (Evans and Schmalensee 2001). In other words, it is claimed that if in the new economy monopolies arise, they tend to be contestable as a result of a constant threat of innovation by rivals. If this were the case, competition law would indeed not have an important role to play. Contestable markets cannot be exploited on a long-term basis and therefore we need not worry too much about monopolization or abusive behaviour.

In essence, the above argument is not new as Schumpeter developed it more than half a century ago. First, he stressed the importance of innovation, which was in his view the cause of the already mentioned 'perennial gale of creative destruction'. But he also stated that monopoly power can seldom be exploited:

> Outside the field of public utilities, the position of a single seller can in general be conquered – and retained for decades – only on the condition that he does not behave like a monopolist.

This argument is more extreme as it states that most markets are, at least in the longer run, contestable. His *laissez faire* opinion on anti-trust intervention has never received broad acceptance, although the Cambridge school came near to it. But one can nevertheless say that Schumpeter's view has been influential as far as competition authorities usually do pay much less attention to exploitative abuses of dominance than to exclusionary practices that harm the competitive process itself. Although we may agree with him that market forces can prevent the exploitation of market power, we also must have an eye for the fact that powerful undertakings can develop strategies to influence the functioning of the market itself. Especially, they can try to deter entry of new competitors in a variety of ways. This is an issue that Schumpeter seems to have overlooked.

Must high-tech markets indeed be considered contestable? A contestable market is a market that is disciplined by competitors that are not in the market but have the means to enter (and exit) at short term and little cost. Under these conditions, even firms with little or no actual presence in the market can exercise a competitive threat. Suppose that an airline company has a monopoly on certain routes and airport slots and licenses pose no specific problems. From the perspective of the customer each route can be seen as a relevant market. But it would be realistic to consider such a market as contestable as far as airline companies can accommodate themselves quickly to new opportunities that the market offers. Monopoly profits would immediately attract entrants.

This example makes visible that neither network industries nor high-tech markets would deserve the qualification 'contestable'. Investments in knowledge, R&D and network infrastructures take time and are expensive. Furthermore, these costs are to a large extent 'sunk', so that entering the market is not without financial risk because a subsequent exit is costly. So the argument about the fragility of market positions in the new economy does not speak for itself. On the other hand, when a market is characterized by a rapid succession of innovations it can earlier be expected that existing market position may be lost in the near future. But this will to a large extent depend on the circumstances of a given case. Empirical evidence shows that dominant positions often are not long lived as long as technological development retains its pace, i.e. as long as the industry is not mature, for example, uncovered that the existing industry structure in terms of dominant firms was completely overhauled in about three-quarters of 46 historical case studies on the impact of radical innovations. In as far as these monopolies are transient because knowledge can be reproduced or because production techniques spread allowing for imitation, no eminent competition problem would seem to exist. Therefore, it does not make much sense to ask ourselves whether in general Schumpeter's weather forecast holds or not. The relevance of his argument must be determined on the basis of the circumstances of the case, and these circumstances can differ considerably. Innovation can have the force of a gale, not more than a breeze, or even be non-existent.

The above makes clear that competition authorities, when dealing with cases in high-tech industries, will address the question what the expectations with respect to the appearance of new products and new competitors will be. This factor this should have a substantial influence on the overall assessment of a case. If a sector is mature, market shares are often a central parameter in the assessment. If a sector is innovative, market shares say little because they do not reflect the ability to compete in the longer run. Therefore, the merging of two firms with large market shares but little innovative potential may cause little harm to the competitive structure of the market. But this argument also implies that an action (e.g. exclusionary behaviour or a take-over) may cause serious harm to competition even if the target of that behaviour is a company with little or no presence on the market, but with a high potential to be a future competitor. This view became apparent in the *Microsoft* case, in which the Court of Appeals for the District of Columbia considered that,

> It would be inimical to the purpose of the Sherman Act to allow monopolists free reign to squash nascent, albeit unproven, competitors at will – particularly in industries marked by rapid technological advance and frequent paradigm shifts. (Gifford 2001)

4.4 Monopolizing Behaviour in the New Economy

When a firm acquires market power as the result of a competitive process in which the winner takes all or most of the market, it may become dominant in the sense of competition law. However, the fact that the undertaking becomes dominant does not mean that it *infringes* competition law. It was shown above that this is only the case when the undertaking abuses its dominant position (under EC law) or monopolizes the market by anti-competitive or exclusionary means (under USA law). A first point to note is that in high-tech industries market power can be the efficient outcome of the competitive process itself, as a consequence of scale and network effects. Furthermore, the necessary investments in high–tech products may be both substantial and risky, in which case a high profit must be considered functional and *not* abusive (Ahlborn, Evans and Padilla 2001). This should be taken into account in order to preserve the necessary incentives for such investments. But, as was already noted above, competition authorities are usually not very keen on attacking this type of abuse anyway.

Must the specific features of high-tech or network markets be taken into account when exclusionary practices like predatory behaviour are to be considered? A low price will, according to the ECJ in the AKZO case, be predatory and therefore abusive if it is either below average variable costs or above that level but below average total cost when the intention was to eliminate a competitor.[16] US courts have also applied the 'recoupment test' by asking the question whether an accused firm has a reasonable expectation of recouping its losses from predation through future extra gains. Evans and Schmalensee (2001) and Ahlborn, Evans and Padilla

(2001) have argued that these tests are problematic in new-economy industries. Cost-based tests would be of no help to distinguish predatory from non-predatory behaviour, because it would be rational for every player in winner-takes-all competition to charge (very) low prices in order to win the race. It is however submitted that this argument only applies as far as firms have not yet reached the scale where the market will more or less automatically generate a dominant position. So when the market is starting to 'tip', predatory investments would commercially no longer be necessary or rational. Therefore, the above mentioned difficulty does not arise under EC law, as under this jurisdiction predatory behaviour is only forbidden for firms that are already dominant.

4.5 Refusal to Deal in Network Industries

Another example of company behaviour that can under some circumstances be an abuse of dominance is refusal to deal, which means refusal to supply a good, service or right, or refusal to give access to a network. Although in quite a few cases competition law has dealt with refusal to give access to certain infrastructures, the leading case in EC jurisprudence deals with something as unspectacular as the distribution of magazines. This shows that there is much truth in the following statement (Varian 2002):

> There was never a new economics to go along with the new economy. Sure, there was a lot of talk about increasing returns, network effects, switching costs and so on. But these are hardly new concepts; they've been part of the economic literature for decades. Furthermore, although these are important ideas, they aren't Big Ideas. They explain certain phenomena well, but they have a limited reach.

In the above mentioned cases *Volvo Veng* and *Magill* and also in another case, *Tiercé Ladbroke*[17] which dealt with the licensing of live film of French horse racing, there was no doubt that the products in question were unique. They could only be produced or disseminated with the consent of the IP rightholder. This is not necessarily the case with networks; in as far as it is possible to duplicate them. This was an essential element in the *Bronner* case. It dealt with a dispute between Mediaprint and Oscar Bronner. Mediaprint operates the only national home delivery service for daily newspapers in Austria. Bronner required Mediaprint to distribute his newspapers too. The question was, whether the refusal of Mediaprint to supply this service amounted to an abuse of economic dominance. In his opinion, Advocate General Jacobs took the opportunity to give an explanation of the US doctrine on essential facilities. Under this doctrine a company with monopoly power can be required to contract with a competitor when the following five conditions are met:

- The facility must be essential, that is to say indispensable to compete on the market;
- A competitor must reasonably be unable to duplicate the facility;
- The use of the facility on reasonable terms is denied;
- It is feasible for the facility to be provided;
- There is no legitimate business reason for refusing access to the facility.

The 'duplication' factor of this US doctrine became an essential element in the court's ruling. It said that Mediaprint would abuse its position by denying a competing publisher access to its network when it would be impossible for that publisher to set up its own network under reasonable economic conditions, alone or together with other publishers. In other words, when it is economically possible to duplicate a network the existing network should not be considered an essential facility.

The *Bronner* judgement shows that a network is an essential facility only when certain conditions are met. An assessment of the economic merits of the case under consideration is always necessary. The feasibility of setting up an alternative network, either by one party or in co-operation with others, is one of the essential questions that must be addressed in such an assessment. *Bronner* also shows that other means for providing a good or service must be taken into consideration. If good alternatives exist for the goods or services that are provided by the network, the network cannot be considered as the relevant market and the accessibility of the network is not essential for the competitive structure of that market. The network can under that circumstance not be considered an essential facility.

5 CONCLUDING REMARKS

Obviously, the relationship between regulation and innovation is a complex one. Clearly, regulation should not frustrate innovation. Innovation, however, sometimes frustrates regulators that have to exercise control in a changing environment. Rules can become meaningless overnight and the need for new regulation may emerge unexpectedly fast. Regulators should therefore keep some room for manoeuvre to be able to respond to a changing environment. They also must have an open eye for the consequences that these changes may have on their tasks.

Competition policy is by its very nature a much more flexible instrument than regulation. It is, however, also a much more modest instrument. Competition policy instruments must be applied with a clear economic understanding of the market. To some extent, future developments can be taken into account, but competition policy cannot 'engineer' the competitive process as precisely as the regulator does. So under general competition law, the market itself has a much larger task.

In the end, we are convinced that the tasks of general competition law and of regulatory intervention are essentially the same: to get markets working, to keep markets working and to stimulate the principal source of prosperity in our society–innovation

NOTES

1. The views expressed in this chaptere are not necessarily those of the NMa or the Dutch government.
2. An overview of the actual implementation of regulatory reform in telecommunications and electricity can be found in Boylaud and Nicoletti (2001) and Steiner (2001).
3. Note that these efficiency losses go beyond the static loss that measures the gains of regulatory reform in terms of the allocation of the factors of production ,as the impact of technology on both prices and quantities is explicitly taken into account in the OECD study.
4. Commission Regulation (EC) 2659/2000 of 29 November 2000 on the application of Article 85 (3) of the Treaty to categories of Research and Development Agreements [2000] OJ L 304.

5. Commission Regulation (EC) 240/96 of 31 January 1996 on the application of Article 85(3) of the Treaty to certain categories of technology transfer agreements [1996] OJ L 31.
6. See Case IV/M.269 *Shell/Montecatini* [1994] OJ L332/48. In this case the companies had to undertake to preserve a second source of polypropylene technology for licensing purposes before the concentration was accepted by the European Commission.
7. Case IV/M.469 *MSG/Media Service* [1994] OJ L364/1.
8. Case IV/M.553 *RTL/Veronica/Endemol* [1996] OJ L134/32.
9. Case 27/76 *United Brands v Commission* 1978, E.C.R. 207.
10. Case 15/74, *Centrafarm vs. Sterling*, 1974, E.C.R. 1147.
11. Case C-7/97 *Oscar Bronner GmbH v. Mediaprint*, E.C.R. I-7791, opinion of Advocate General Jacobs in para. 47.
12. Case 238/87 *Volvo AB v. Erik Veng Ltd.*, 1988, E.C.R. 6211.
13. Cases 241-242/91 *Radio Telefis Eireann v. Commission*, 1995 E.C.R.I-743. Cf note 13, para 63.
14. This is the so-called SSNIP test which is applied by competition authorities in the USA and the EU. 'SSNIP' stands for Small but Significant Non-transitory Increase in Price.
15. Case C-62/86 AKZO *Chemie v. European Commission* [1991] E.C.R. I-3359
16. Case T-504/93 *Tiercé Ladbroke* E.C.R. II-923 1997
17. This conclusion also follows from another judgement, *European Night Services v. Commission*, T-374, 375, 384 & 388/94 [1998] E.C.R. II-3141

REFERENCES

Ahlborn, C. D.S. Evans and A.J. Padilla (2001), 'Competition Policy in the New Economy: Is European Competition Law Up to the Challenge?', *European Competition Law Review*, 156–67.

Barton, J.H. (1997), 'The Balance between Intellectual Property Rights and Competition: Paradigms in the Information Sector', *European Competition Law Review*, 440–45.

Bergeijk, P.A.G. van, J. van Sinderen and B.A. Vollaard (1999), *Structural Reform in Open Economies: A Road to Success?*, Cheltenham, UK and Northampton, MA, US: Edward Elgar.

Boyland, O. and G. Nicoletti (2001), 'Regulation, Market Structure and Performance in Telecommunications', *OECD Economic Studies*, 32, 99-144.

Evans, D.S. and R. Schmalensee (2001), 'Some Economic Aspects of Antitrust Analysis in Dynamically Competitive Industries', National Bureau of

Economic Research, Working Paper 8268, http://www.nber.org/papers/w8268, 14 December 2004.

Faull, J. and A. Nikpay (1999), *The EC Law of Competition*, Oxford, UK: Oxford University Press.

Gifford, D.J. (2001), 'What is Monopolisation Anyway? The D.C. Circuit grapples with some Perplexing Issues', *The Antitrust Bulletin* (Winter), 797–833.

Korah, V. (2002), 'The Interface between Intellectual Property and Antitrust: The European Experience', *Antitrust Law Journal*, 69, 801–39.

Määttä, K. and M. Virtanen (2001), 'Regulatory Principles in Modifying the Act on Competition Restrictions in a World Characterized by Network Externalities', Paper, Helsinki Conference on Anti Trust Issues in Network Industries, Helsinki, August 3.

OECD (1997), *The OECD Report on Regulatory Reform – Volume II: Thematic Studies*, Paris: OECD.

Pelkmans, J. (2001), 'Making EU Network Markets Competitive', *Oxford Review of Economic Policy*, 17 (3), 432–56.

Pleatsikas, C. and D. Teece (2001), 'The Analysis of Market Definition and Market Power in the Context of Rapid Innovation', *International Journal of Industrial Organization*, 19, 665–703.

Posner, R.A. (2001), 'Antitrust in the New Economy', *Antitrust Law Journal*, 925–43.

Schumpeter, J.A. (1976), *Capitalism, Socialism and Democracy*, 5th ed, London UK: Allen and Unwin.

Summers, L.H. (2001), 'Competition Policy in the New Economy', *Antitrust Law Journal*, 69 (1), 353–9.

Varian, H.R. (2002), 'A New Economy With No New Economics', *The New York Times*, 17 (1).

White, L.J. (1998), 'Microsoft and Browsers: Are the Antitrust Problems Really New', in J.A. Eisenach and T.M. Lenard (eds), *Competition, Innovation and the Microsoft Monopoly: Antitrust in the digital market place*, Boston, US and Dordrecht, NL: Kluwer Academic Publishers.

4. The California Electricity Crisis: A Unique Combination of Circumstances or Symptom of a Structural Flaw?

Laurens J. de Vries

1   INTRODUCTION

The electricity crisis that plagued California between the summers of 2000 and 2001 shocked and fascinated people around the world. How could such a high-tech state lose control over the electricity system to the extent that service could no longer be guaranteed? The disastrous developments in California caused widespread doubt about the desirability of liberalizing electricity markets. This chapter will show that California's problems can only in part be blamed on restructuring, but that the security of supply is an often-overlooked vulnerability in restructured markets. The purpose of this chapter is to investigate only the causes of California's energy crisis, not the consequences for the state or the electricity sector, nor solutions to the crisis. We are interested in avoiding such a crisis and therefore we want to know how it developed.

This chapter starts by describing California's electricity system in the years preceding the crisis (section 2). Sections 3 and 4 describe the way California's electricity market was restructured. Section 5 provides a brief chronology of the crisis, while section 6 presents a number of trends that may point to the causes of the crisis. This serves as the basis for the analysis of the crisis in sections 7 and 8. Section 10 presents the conclusions. Readers with little time may jump directly to section 6 to start the analysis.

2   PRELUDE

Until 1996, electricity was provided in California by vertically integrated monopolies. The majority of the state was served by three investor-owned utilities, Pacific Gas & Electric, Southern California Edison and San Diego Gas & Electric. In addition, some cities provided electricity as a municipal service, the largest ones of which were Los Angeles and Sacramento. The privately owned utility companies were regulated by the State Public Utilities Commission, the municipal utilities were not. The utility companies, both private and municipal, produced much of their own electricity and owned the transmission and distribution networks. In 1978, the Federal Public Utilities Regulatory Policy Act partly opened the market for generation. In 1992, the Energy Policy Act further opened the market in wholesale generation, among others by facilitating access to the (mostly privately owned) transmission wires. The Energy Policy Act gave a strong impetus for the liberalization of the United States' electricity markets, even though it remained up to the individual states to take action. However, nationally only about 7 per cent of electricity was generated by non-utility companies by the year 2000 (Union of Concerned Scientists, 2000).

Prior to restructuring, the performance of California's electricity system was mediocre. Prices were high: by 1996, the average price in California was almost 40 per cent higher than the average price in the rest of the USA (EIA, 2002). This was caused in part by large cost overruns in the nuclear power program (Hirst, 2001). Large businesses pushed for liberalization, hoping that competition would lower the prices of electricity (Gladstone and Bailey, 2000). In the early 1990s, California was one of the first states to consider restructuring its electricity system. However, due to strong opposition, among others from Southern California Edison, the debate continued for a number of years before a compromise was reached in the form of Assembly Bill 1890 in 1996.

3   THE RULES[1]

The California State Legislature adopted bill AB 1890 with the purpose of creating a competitive market in electricity. This act, which took effect in April of 1998, only applied to investor-owned utilities, which were under the jurisdiction of the Public Utilities Commission of the State of California. Municipal electricity utilities, the largest of which were those of Los Angeles and Sacramento, were not required to restructure and most of them did not. The private utilities which were restructured served a little more than 80 per cent of the California market (CEC, 2000).

In order to encourage the development of competition, the electricity industry was partially unbundled. The incumbent investor-owned utilities were pressed to divest their generation assets, other than nuclear and hydro power.[2] They now needed to purchase a large part of the electricity which they delivered to their customers in the market. The electricity for small consumers they were required to purchase in a pool, the California Power Exchange (now defunct).[3] For most of its existence, the pool only allowed spot (day-ahead) contracts. Future and long-term contracts were not allowed in order to stimulate competition. However, an important side-effect of this rule was that it removed important risk management tools for market parties. The restriction of long-term contracts was changed in July 1999, when the power exchange started to offer a limited volume of long-term contracts. Apparently this much-needed adjustment came too late, or perhaps the utility companies underestimated the value of long-term contracts; in any case the utility companies engaged in too few long-term contracts to hedge their market risk (Woolfolk, 2001).

While the utility companies maintained ownership of the transmission system, they had to hand over control of the transmission network to the newly created Independent System Operator (ISO, also known as CAISO). Their role was reduced to distributing electricity, which they purchased in the pool or generated themselves, to their customers, and managing their distribution networks. Hence, after restructuring, the incumbent utility companies became known as utility distribution companies.

Rates for consumers were frozen at their 1996 levels and reduced by 10 per cent in 1998. This rate freeze was instigated by the large utilities in order to recover their stranded investments (Gladstone and Bailey, 2000).

The rate freeze was to remain in place for four years or until the utilities had recovered their stranded costs, whichever came earlier. The assumption was that competition would lead to decreasing wholesale prices, thereby increasing the utility distribution companies' profits. The customers' contribution to paying off the utilities' sunk investments was named the Competition Transition Charge. The level of this charge was determined by the difference between the fixed retail price and the wholesale price.[4]

When AB 1890 entered into force in April 1998, most customers of the former investor-owned utilities were allowed to choose their provider of electricity. However, the utility distribution companies had a service obligation only towards those customers who had not switched provider. Moreover, in exchange for the opportunity to find cheaper providers, customers who had switched no longer enjoyed the protection of fixed retail prices. As a result, few consumers switched provider, so that the incumbent utilities retained most of their customers and retail prices remained fixed for the great majority (Marshall and McAllister, 2000).

In summary, the main characteristics of the California restructuring process were:

- The incumbent utilities divested much of their generation assets
- Transmission was managed by an independent system Operator
- All purchases by the utility distribution companies were made in a mandatory power pool in which only spot contracts were allowed
- During the transition period (which lasted through the power crisis), retail prices were fixed for small consumers
- Not all of California participated in the restructuring process: a number of municipal electricity departments stayed out.

4   THE PLAYERS

The restructured part of the California electricity market was served by three large incumbent utilities. Restructuring turned these formerly vertically integrated utilities into utility distribution companies:

Pacific Gas and Electric served about 12 million people in the north and middle of California with gas and electricity. After restructuring, it owned about 7500 MW in generating capacity in the form of hydropower and a nuclear plant. It had to purchase about 60 per cent of its 82 000 GWh of annual electricity sales in the wholesale market (Pacific Gas and Electric, 2001).

Southern California Edison was nearly as big as Pacific Gas and Electric. However, it owned less than 3000 MW in generation facilities, consisting mostly of a majority stake in a nuclear power plant.

San Diego Gas and Electric sold only a little less electricity than its two counterparts, but owned almost no generating facilities (CEC, 2001a).

The generation assets which the incumbent utility companies had sold were purchased by private companies. After restructuring, about 40 per cent of the electricity sold in the state was generated by private firms, the largest ones of which were AES, Reliant, Southern (Mirant) and Duke. Public agencies such as municipal utility companies still produced nearly a quarter of all electricity. A slightly smaller percentage was provided by 'qualified facilities', which were Federally approved environment-friendlier facilities such as combined heat-and-power units and renewable energy plants. The utilities were required to buy from these qualified facilities, which typically were small and independently owned. Finally, the utilities themselves provided about 15 per cent of total production (Kahn and Lynch, 2000).

The California Public Utilities Commission controlled the tariffs which were charged to regulated customers, not only for electricity, but also for other privately owned utilities such as gas, water, and rail transport. After restructuring, its role in the electricity market was limited to setting the rates for the small consumers as long as they remained fixed.

The California Energy Commission (CEC) was an energy planning agency which survived the restructuring process. Its main activities were data collection and analysis and power plant licensing. It provided many of the data for this case study.

The restructuring law created two non-profit agencies to facilitate the operation of the market. The Independent System Operator took over control of the transmission network from the incumbent utilities. The California Power Exchange became the trading platform for most wholesale trade. The distribution companies were required to purchase their electricity there, so that it actually was a mandatory power pool for most transactions.

These two organizations were overseen by the Electricity Oversight Board, as part of its more general monitoring function.

Restructuring not only involved a shift of control from the State to the market, but also to the Federal government. The State had surrendered its authority to intervene directly in the market to the Federal Energy Regulatory Commission (FERC). The State's only power to intervene in market operations lay in the Electricity Oversight Board's ability to litigate with the FERC. However, during the crisis the FERC adopted a laissez-faire approach until the political pressure forced it to change its course.

5   CHRONOLOGY

The electricity system functioned smoothly during the first two years after restructuring took effect in April of 1998. Wholesale prices dropped and remained fairly steady, so that the restructured utility companies made a profit. In addition, they received substantial revenues from the sale of their fossil fuel generation assets. During the crisis, when the utilities asked the state for debt relief, these revenues became a point of contention, as they had been transferred to the utilities' parent companies and were not used to offset the utilities' mounting losses.

In May of 2000, two years after the restructuring act had taken effect, wholesale prices started to rise sharply, as Figure 4.1 shows. Due to the demand for air conditioning, in most of California electricity demand peaks in summer. A certain price increase was therefore to be expected, but in 2000 the prices were much higher than in the previous years. During July and August, the average electricity price at the power exchange was more than three times higher than at the same time in previous years.

San Diego Gas & Electric was the first of the three investor-owned utilities to recoup its sunk investments and therefore it was the first utility whose retail rates were freed. In the summer of 2000, shortly after their retail prices were deregulated, SDG&E consumers saw their power bills multiply in size. This caused a political uproar which led the State Public Utilities Commission to freeze the rates of San Diego Gas & Electric again. The combination of fixed retail rates and high wholesale prices caused all three utility distribution companies to lose money, but the expectation was that prices would decrease after the summer and things would return to normal again.

Many causes were suggested for the price increases, but it was clear that there was an acute shortage of power in the market. This shortage reached its first climax with rolling black-outs in the San Francisco Bay area in June of 2000. This outage was not actually caused by a general shortage of generation capacity, but by a local shortage combined with a lack of sufficient transmission capacity (Johnson and Woolfolk, 2000).

Figure 4.1   Daily average wholesale prices

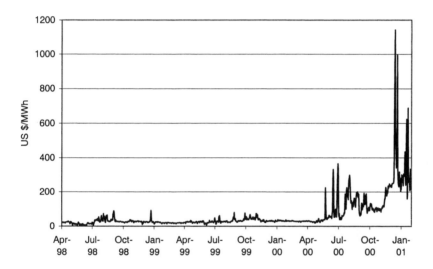

Source: Based upon data from the University of California Energy Institute

To much surprise and dismay, prices did not return to normal after the summer peak, but remained much higher than usual during the fall of 2000. The shortage continued even though demand declined. The continuing high prices caused the utilities' financial losses to grow quickly, as their obligation to serve their customers at fixed tariffs remained. The utilities agitated for a lifting of the fixed retail tariff, or at least for a rate increase, but as elected bodies, the legislature and the State Public Utilities Commission were extremely reluctant to do that. They continued to expect prices to drop again, so that the utilities could recover their losses. To reduce the gap between the utilities' purchase prices and retail prices, California appealed to the FERC to impose regional wholesale price caps, but the FERC refused (Allen and Booth, 2001). State-imposed price caps were ineffective due to generators' ability to 'launder' electricity by selling it to affiliates in neighbouring states and buying it back at much higher prices. As wholesale prices remained high, the combined losses of the two largest utilities exceeded USD 12 billion by February 2001, pushing them to the brink of bankruptcy.

The utilities' insolvency compounded the problems to the point that at the end of 2000 the situation became untenable. The large private generators were threatening not to deliver electricity to the utilities because the latter's creditworthiness had sunk to the lowest level. In addition, the utility distribution companies had not been able to pay the small, independent producers for so long that some of them could not afford to purchase fuel any longer or even risked bankruptcy themselves. The utilities' lack of creditworthiness also threatened their ability to purchase natural gas and deliver it to generation companies. These effects further jeopardized the supply of electricity. In December, the outgoing Clinton administration intervened by ordering generators to keep supplying electricity, whether they were paid or not. After Bush took office in January, he continued this order for a few weeks, but gave California notice that it must devise its own solution.

In January 2001 the crisis reached a new climax, when the independent system operator was forced to impose rolling blackouts throughout significant portions of the state for two consecutive days. At the same time, prices at the power exchange rose several times higher than the previous record highs, causing the collapse of the utility distribution companies. Towards the end of January the State of California finally took decisive action. Effectively abolishing the market altogether, the state took upon itself to purchase electricity for the teetering utilities. As the state became the single buyer of electricity, the power exchange, the credibility of which already had been undermined by manipulation by both generators and distribution companies, closed its doors.

The state had hoped to be able to use its purchasing power to drive prices down, but it paid two to three times the historical average electricity price for long-term contracts. In this way it did not only guarantee the flow of electricity, but also that Californians would be paying for this crisis for years to come (Nissenbaum et al., 2001). The cost of buying power was high; it was projected to cost the state USD 18 billion in the first year alone, which caused Wall Street to reduce the state's credit rating (Nissenbaum, 2001). The state intervention stabilized the supply of electricity, but at a high cost.

While there were more black-outs in May, the crisis ended by the summer of 2001. For a large part, this was probably due to Californians' energy conservation efforts, which reduced demand by up to 12 per cent. In addition, mild weather played a role and all possible means were developed to increase production. By the summer of 2001, more than 6000 MW in new generating plants had already been approved for construction, while the same amount was under review (CEC, 2001b).

As the crisis unfolded, a heated debate developed with respect to its causes and potential remedies. Opponents of deregulation were quick to claim the crisis as proof that a market in electricity was impossible. Proponents of deregulation countered that the way California had restructured was highly flawed so that it could not be considered proper deregulation. To begin with, they considered the fixed retail prices and the prohibition of long-term contracts at odds with a market. Opponents of environmental measures claimed that California's relatively strict environmental regulations had made all investment in power plants impossible. The state accused generators of price gouging. The generators washed their hands in innocence while making record profits, attributing the high prices to market conditions (Hebert, 2001; Holson and Oppel, 2001). Other suggested causes were high gas prices, high prices of NO_x emissions permits, low reservoir levels due to drought, falling imports from other states and an unprecedented growth in demand due to the fast development of the computer and internet industry.

6 TRENDS

To evaluate the different possible causes of the energy crisis, it is useful to separate physical reality from the many theories and accusations that were presented following the crisis. This section analyses several basic trends which help explain the development of the crisis: demand, installed generator capacity, generator outages and imports.

Firstly, the claim that the state was confronted with an extremely high and unforeseeable growth in demand appears to be a myth. As can be seen in Figure 4.2, electricity demand grew at a modest annual 1.4 per cent on average during the decade preceding the crisis, trailing population growth slightly. This means that per-capita electricity consumption decreased marginally despite the economic upturn. The growth in annual peak demand was also not substantial, according to the CEC (2000). In the late 1990s, peak demand in the ISO control area grew to about 46 000 MW. While there are regional variations within the state, the overall modest growth rate indicates that demand-side developments are not the cause of the general power shortage.

Figure 4.2   Electricity demand and population growth

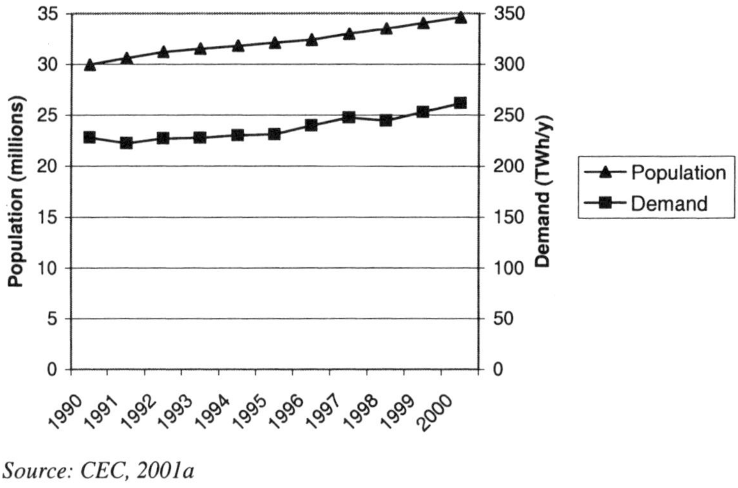

Source: CEC, 2001a

On the supply side, a remarkable trend was that very little generation capacity was added during the 1990s. As a result of decommissioning, the net available capacity actually decreased slightly during the decade prior to the crisis. In the summer of 2000, the installed generating capacity was close to 53 000 MW (CEC, 2001a). The actual available capacity in California was substantially less due to scheduled and unscheduled outages.

When comparing generating capacity to demand, it should be kept in mind that an electricity system needs reserve capacity to function. In California, operating reserves of 7 per cent are the norm for thermal capacity and 5 per cent for hydro capacity (California ISO, 2001).

The growth rate of generation capacity lagged substantially behind the growth in electricity consumption not only in California, but also in the rest of the Western System. Throughout the 1990s, the demand for electricity in the West grew on average by about 3 per cent per year, while the generation capacity increased by less than 1 per cent per year (FERC, 2000). As a result, the margins between available generation capacity and demand shrank throughout the Western System.

Figure 4.3   Generator construction year

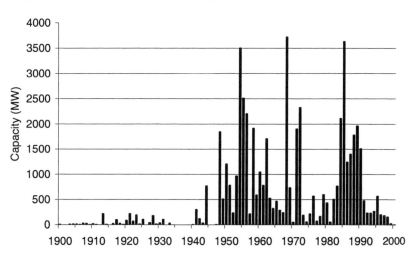

Source: CEC, 2001a

The scarcity may have been made worse by the high average age of the available generating stock, which probably reduced plant reliability. Figure 4.3 shows that nearly all existing plants were built before 1990 and that about a third was from before 1970. Historically, the ISO could assume that about 2500 MW was out of service at any time. During the crisis, the volume of off-line capacity grew to unprecedented rates, as is shown in Figure 4.4. While the outage rate was somewhat low during the summer of 2000, during much of the winter more than 10 000 MW was off-line and at point the outage rate exceeded 30 per cent of total installed generating capacity.

Figure 4.4   Monthly average off-line capacity

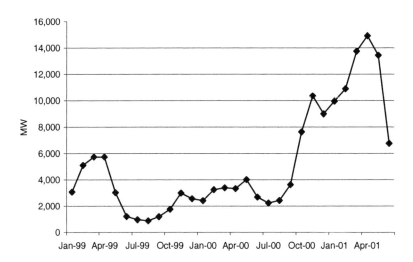

Source: Based upon data from the California Energy Commission (www.energy.ca.gov/electricity/1999-2001_monthly_off_line.html), 16 December 2004.

The last factor to be considered here is California's reliance upon electricity imports. Figure 4.5 shows that California has relied substantially upon imports to meet its electricity demand during the last two decades. While California's relative dependence upon imports has been declining (as the absolute amount remained stable), the state still was highly dependent upon imports at the time of the crisis. In 1999, the share of imports in total consumption was 18 per cent. Imports typically are higher during the summer, when the Pacific Northwest has its off-peak season and can export more of its large supply of hydropower.

In 2000, total imports were 28 per cent less than the year before (California ISO, 2001). There were two main causes of these import reductions. In 2000 a drought hit the northwest, as a result of which hydropower production was down significantly and the area could export much less than usual. In the winter of 2000-2001, the Bonneville Power Administration had about 4000 MW less capacity than usual due to the drought, which was one of the worst in 70 years of record keeping (Bonneville Power Administration, 2001). In addition, strong economic growth and population growth in surrounding states, coupled with lagging investment, caused these states' power surpluses to shrink.

Figure 4.5   Imports and in-state generation

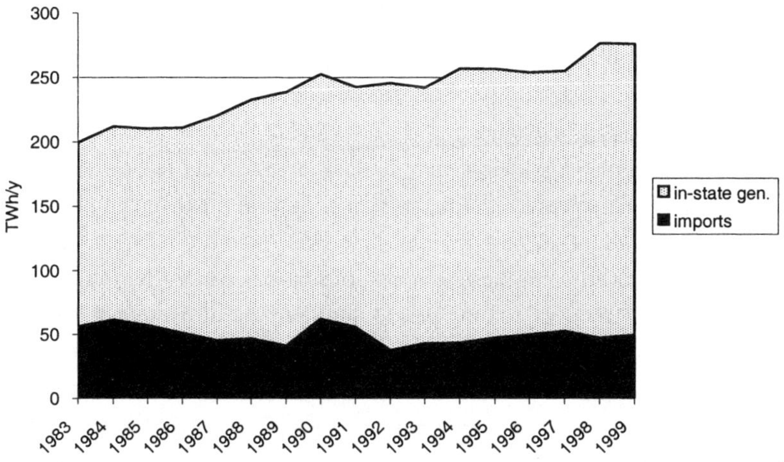

Source: Based upon data from the CEC.

In summary, the image that emerges from these trends is that the reserve margins (the difference between generation capacity and imports on the one hand and demand for electricity on the other hand) steadily shrank throughout the 1990s. Demand did not grow exceptionally fast (neither peak nor average demand), but it did grow. This growth was not matched on the supply side, where both generation capacity and imports remained stable. During the crisis imports dropped significantly and generator outages increased dramatically.

7   PHYSICAL CRISIS

The question that the California crisis provoked in every other restructured electricity market was 'Can it happen here?' To know the answer, it is essential to understand what went wrong in California. In particular, the question should be addressed which aspects of the crisis were unique to California, or simply the result of bad luck, and which factors might occur in other systems as well.

A basic flaw in the California market was the fact that prices were fixed for a majority of consumers. Not only did this cause the financial downfall of the utility distribution companies, it also meant that consumers did not react to the high electricity prices.[5] Had consumers been able to react to the electricity price, the blackouts probably would not have occurred, nor would prices have risen so high. However, the lack of consumer responsiveness is not unique to California. In other systems, in which consumer prices are free, consumers rarely know the real-time price of electricity, so that they still cannot react to it. In these systems, the flaw is caused by the fact that the electricity bill covers a long period and the time of use is not metered. Had the consumers in California been exposed to the real market prices, they would still have received an incentive only to reduce their total electricity consumption as average prices rose. There would have been no incentive to reduce consumption when it was needed most, during peak hours. In fact, the crisis would have been alleviated substantially if consumers had only shifted consumption from peak hours to off-peak hours, but in the absence of time-of-use billing there is no reward for doing so.

The problem of the low demand price-elasticity needs to be addressed in all electricity markets, but we cannot assume that this was the only cause of the crisis in California. Even with full demand-side participation, generation capacity will still need to be adequate to meet demand peaks. We need to turn to the supply side of the market to investigate why it failed to produce enough generation capacity to meet demand. California started from a situation of plenty reserve capacity in the late 1980s, but during a decade with no net increase in generation capacity, this reserve capacity was absorbed by the growth in demand. Even when demand grows as moderately as it did in California, a stagnation of investment in supply capacity is bound to cause a shortage sooner or later. This aspect of the crisis we will call the physical crisis, as opposed to the financial aspect of the crisis, a distinction which The Brattle Group also makes (Carere et al., 2001). It is often suggested that environmental restrictions and NIMBY-type opposition made it difficult to obtain building permits for power plants in California (cf. Yardley, 2001; Berry, 2001). However, the fact that some projects for which the necessary permits had been acquired were not built, suggests that other reasons were dominant (Carere et al., 2001). Why, then, was there no new construction until it was too late?

One apparent reason for the lack of power plant construction was regulatory uncertainty (Carere et al., 2001; Hirst, 2001). The debate about restructuring started in the early 1990s while the law took force in 1998, so that during most of the decade the future of California's electricity system was unclear. Since restructuring, investors may have been reluctant to invest until they had developed some experience with the new system. The forced absence of long-term and future contracts eliminated possibilities to hedge the investment risk in generation capacity, which further discouraged new construction.

The low prices before the crisis discouraged the development of new generation capacity. Due to the lack of experience with the market in California, investors did not know when to expect price rises, nor did they probably realize how high the prices could rise during a shortage. Once the prices rose, there was not enough time to construct new capacity. Planning and building a new generation plant may take several years; the permit process may extend the lead time with again as much time. Investment in generation capacity in reaction to price peaks inevitably is slow, as a result of which there is a risk of cyclical investment behaviour. The possibility of the development of a business cycle was anticipated by Ford, who made a computer simulation of the California electricity market (Ford, 1999, 2001). The theory that electricity markets are subject to a business cycle was further developed by Stoft (2002).

The fact that there was little investment in generation capacity throughout the western states means that the cause of the crisis was not limited to California alone. A system-wide lack of investment, coupled with often higher growth rates of electricity consumption in surrounding states, actually caused a regional crisis (Hirst, 2001). The reason that the crisis manifested itself primarily in California is that California relied heavily upon imports. When surrounding states saw their electricity surplus disappear, they reduced their exports. Why the surrounding states did not invest was not investigated in this project. Perhaps regulatory uncertainty also played a role there, as some states were also (considering) restructuring. Otherwise they simply may not have been interested in constructing generation capacity as long as they had more than enough capacity to meet their own demand. The NIMBY phenomenon may have played a role, as it is even more difficult to make the case for power plant construction in a state with a power surplus.

There were many factors which exacerbated the physical crisis, such as the drought which reduced the supply of hydropower (much of which was imported), the hot summer of 2000 which increased consumption, and technical problems with California's many old generators. However, these same circumstances would not have caused shortages a number of years earlier, when the system still had enough reserve capacity. The lack of investment in generation capacity had brought the system to a point where it could no longer cope with irregular circumstances. The reason the crisis occurred in the summer of 2000 is that a number of unusual circumstances occurred simultaneously. Had the summer of 2000 been wet and cold, the crisis might not have occurred until a year later. However, a shortage of electricity was bound to occur sooner or later, as long as no new generation capacity was being built.

An aggravating circumstance which stands out is the shortage of transmission capacity. The San Francisco Bay area blackouts in June of 2000 could have been avoided if the transmission capacity into the area had been larger. At the time of these first blackouts, the state actually had a power surplus, but the necessary power could not be transmitted to the Bay area. The problem with transmission is not just one of capacity: due to the deteriorating quality of the networks, the net available capacity has been falling gradually since the late 1980s (Hirst, 2001).

Given the lack of generation capacity, the physical shortage would probably also have occurred if the electricity industry had not been restructured. Generation companies might still have underestimated the need for new capacity until it was too late, with power interruptions as a result. The financial chaos that ensued, however, was a product of the new organization of the sector.

8 FINANCIAL CRISIS

In any market, scarcity can be expected to increase prices. The situation in California was exceptional, however, in two respects: wholesale prices rose to extreme heights for a long period of time, and retail prices remained fixed. This particular combination caused a financial crisis, the damage of which may rival the costs of the actual power outages. Since the beginning of the summer of 2000, wholesale prices exceeded retail tariffs by a large margin. At times, wholesale prices rose to more than ten times the retail price. The utility distribution companies, who had few long-term contracts and an obligation to serve their small customers, were forced to purchase their electricity at these high prices and sell it at the fixed, low retail price. As a result, the utilities' losses quickly mounted to billions of dollars. By early 2001 they became insolvent, causing a collapse of the system.

The utility distribution companies' deteriorating financial situation complicated and aggravated the crisis. The utilities' suppliers became reluctant to deliver electricity and gas to them, which further threatened the delivery of energy to their customers in California. In addition, the utilities' months-long failure to pay small, independent producers for the electricity they delivered drove independent electricity producers also to the brink of bankruptcy, which posed another threat to the supply of electricity. Thus the financial crisis contributed to the physical shortage of electricity, creating a feed-back loop that worsened the crisis.

The financial crisis contributed substantially to the social costs of the crisis, because it left California without a functioning electricity market. This forced the State of California to intervene by purchasing electricity on behalf of the utility distribution companies. Not having any experience in the market and entering it when prices were high, the state engaged in many long-term contracts at prices far above the average market price.

The financial crisis gives rise to two questions: why were the retail rates fixed and why were wholesale prices so high? The first question is the easiest to answer. The utilities themselves had lobbied for fixed retail prices, ironically because they thought this would protect their profit margin. Assuming that the market would bring wholesale prices down, they hoped to avoid a price war and protect their profits by fixing retail rates during a transitional period. The legislature's justification for permitting this was to allow the utilities to recover their stranded investments.

The second question is more complex. When a shortage of supply exists in a market, one can expect prices to increase, especially in an electricity market where demand has a low price-elasticity. However, it is questionable whether this effect alone can explain prices of ten times the historical price. A first explanation is that a number of input costs had increased. The price of natural gas in California soared in the fall of 2000 (CBO, 2001). At first, this appeared to be caused by scarcity due to the high demand from electricity generators and a break in a pipe line. Later, however, evidence emerged that market manipulation by gas supply companies caused at least part of the increase in gas prices (FERC, 2002; Oppel and Bergman, 2002; Sheffrin, 2002). Other input costs rose as well. The reduced availability of hydropower due to the drought meant that more electricity had to be generated from fossil fuel plants, as a result of which the price of NO_x emissions increased substantially (Joskow and Kahn, 2002).

However, an extensive analysis of input costs and generator availability to determine the causes of the high electricity prices in the summer of 2000 shows that the high electricity prices cannot fully be explained by the cost of production and the inelasticity of the demand curve (Joskow and Kahn, 2002). The unusually high volumes of unavailable capacity during the crisis (see Figure 4.4) gave rise to the suspicion that generation companies were withholding capacity in order to increase the prices.

9   MANIPULATION

The suspicion of capacity withholding already arose during the crisis. It was counter-intuitive that the first state-wide electricity shortage would develop in January, during the low season. Generation companies argued that the high outage rates at that time were a caused by deferred maintenance during the previous half year, when the continuing shortages had required the utmost from the aging generation facilities (Kaplan and Guido, 2001). The evidence of capacity withholding mounted, however. Joskow and Kahn observe that, in a situation of scarcity and with low price-elasticity of demand, generators have market power, that they are in a position to abuse this market power even without needing to collude formally, and that they have strong incentives to do so. Using publicly available data, they show that capacity withholding is the only plausible explanation for a significant part of the high prices. Therefore they conclude that the abuse of market power contributed significantly to the crisis. Stoft corroborates this analysis in a more theoretical way. He shows how a generator with even a small market share is able to increase its profit by withholding part of its generating capacity during a period of tight supply (Stoft, 2002). More evidence of the abuse of market power emerged from the Enron bankruptcy proceedings, where memos were found which explained the different methods (Behr, 2002; FERC, 2002). The California Public Utilities Commission concluded eventually that a majority of the outages was caused by strategic withholding.

The withholding of generation capacity by the electricity generating firms severely aggravated both the physical and the financial aspects of the crisis. It greatly increased the social cost of the crisis and contributed to the bankruptcy of the utility distribution companies. It would be a mistake, however, to consider the manipulation the main cause of the crisis. In the absence of investment in generation capacity, a shortage of electricity would have occurred sooner or later, also if the market had not been restructured. And given a scarcity of electricity, the wholesale prices would have risen and the fixed retail prices would have caused heavy losses for the utility distribution companies. Had the retail prices not been fixed, the utility distribution companies would have been able to pass the high wholesale prices along to consumers and avoid losses. However, the evidence from San Diego suggests that unregulated retail prices might have caused a political crisis instead, of at least the same proportions.

The risk of generating capacity withholding is an important lesson for other electricity systems. This phenomenon is by no means constrained to California, but can occur in every electricity system with a low price-elasticity of demand when generation capacity is scarce.

10 CONCLUSIONS

The fundamental problem of California's electricity market was a lack of investment in generating capacity. For too long, too little was invested in generation capacity, not just in California, but also in the other states of the Western interconnected system. The shortage of generation capacity was aggravated by a number of circumstances such as drought (which reduced the available hydropower), heat (which temporarily increased demand), generator failures and transmission capacity constraints. This inevitably led to a crisis in which the supply of electricity was not sufficient to meet demand. As the largest net importer of electricity in the region, California bore the brunt of this crisis when the drought reduced electricity generation in neighbouring states.

The pattern of underinvestment predated the restructuring law, which means that the crisis cannot be blamed entirely upon the market reforms. However, the new market structure did fail to signal the need for new generation capacity in time. The most likely cause of the lack of investment within California is regulatory uncertainty during the time leading up to the restructuring of the market, exacerbated by a flawed market design. A more fundamental tendency towards a boom and bust cycle probably also played a role.

A fundamental flaw in the restructuring law was that retail prices were fixed while wholesale prices were determined by the market. This caused the physical shortage to develop into a financial crisis. California's electricity distribution companies were forced to purchase electricity in a wholesale market in which, during the crisis, prices rose much higher than the regulated retail tariffs for which they had to sell much of their electricity. The fact that utilities had not been able to hedge their price risk by engaging in long-term power contracts aggravated the situation. The combination of high wholesale prices and fixed, low retail prices resulted in high financial losses for the utility distribution companies which eventually brought them into severe financial difficulties, bankrupting one of them and forcing another to sell off a substantial part of its assets.

Prices rose to extreme heights during the crisis for a number of reasons. Firstly, electricity demand in California was nearly price-inelastic, as a large portion of consumers purchased electricity for fixed tariffs. Thus high prices did not lead to a reduction in demand, which could have dampened the price increases. Secondly, the costs of certain inputs, most notably natural gas and NO_x emissions credits rose substantially during the crisis. Finally, the abuse of market power severely aggravated the crisis. By withholding generation capacity, generating companies increased prices far above their competitive levels and contributed to the power outages.

11 LESSONS FOR OTHER ELECTRICITY SYSTEMS

Several lessons can be learned from the experience in California. First, it is essential for the long-term stability of the system that there are adequate incentives for investment. In California, these incentives existed – witness the high prices – but did not manifest themselves in time: only when there already was a shortage did the market develop strong signals that more capacity was needed. The consequence was a period of tight supplies before new capacity became available. This raises the possibility of a business cycle.

A second lesson is that in electricity markets with a low demand price-elasticity, even generating companies with a small market share have market power during periods of scarce supply. The reason is that in such a situation it is possible to increase prices substantially by withholding only a small amount of capacity, so that even small generators have an incentive to withhold capacity. This means that the abuse of market power which was observed in California was not just an artefact of the market rules in California, but is a phenomenon that may occur in any electricity market with low demand price-elasticity during periods of scarce supply.

Finally, the crisis demonstrated the high social cost of consumers being completely isolated from the market. The fact that consumers did not respond to high wholesale prices (because consumer prices were fixed) contributed substantially to the crisis, as demand was not reduced when supplies were tight. The high response to the call for voluntary conservation and load-shifting to off-peak hours during the crisis demonstrated that demand price-elasticity can be significant.

NOTES

1. Except where indicated otherwise, the following description of the main provisions of the restructuring law is adopted from the California Energy Commission (1998).
2. Note that in Europe unbundling is directed at separating networks, being considered a natural monopoly, from competitive functions, while in California unbundling involved the divestment of generation assets by the incumbent utility companies. The utility distribution companies were allowed to retain control over their networks as well as deliver electricity to the customers on those networks.
3. The name California Power Exchange is confusing, as the word exchange usually indicates that participation is voluntary, while the term pool typically is used for mandatory trade platforms.
4. As wholesale prices started to exceed the fixed retail prices during the crisis, the CTC for the protected customers became negative. More simply said, the utility distribution companies lost money on their power sales, rather than recovering stranded costs.
5. Only after the rolling blackouts occurred and a public outreach campaign was started, supported by some financial incentives for conservation, did consumers start to reduce their demand. This was, however, not a reaction to the actual prices in the market.

REFERENCES

Allen, M. and Booth, W. (2001) 'Spread of California Crisis Concerns Bush, Western Governors Get Assurances of Action', *Washington Post*, January 30.

Behr, P. (2002), 'Papers Show That Enron Manipulated Calif. Crisis', *Washington Post*, May 7.

Berry, J.M. (2001), 'U.S. Officials: Impact of Calif's Crisis Muted for Now', *Washington Post*, January 20.

Besant-Jones, J. and B. Tenenbaum (2001), *The California Power Crisis: Lessons for Developing Countries*, World Bank, Energy and Mining Sector Board, http://www.worldbank.org/html/fpd/energy/pdfs/e_calexp1002.pdf, 14 December 2004.

Bonneville Power Administration (2001), 'Cold Weather Spurs Energy Consumption; More Power Needed from Columbia River Dams', News release, February 13.

California ISO (2001), *CAISO Summer (2001) Assessment*, www.caiso.com/docs/09003a6080/0c/af/09003a60800cafcd.pdf, 22 March

Carere, E., P. Fox-Penner, C. Lapuerta and B. Moselle (2001), *The California Crisis and its Lessons for the EU*, Cambridge/Washington, US and London, UK: The Brattle Group.

CBO (Congress of the United States, Congressional Budget Office) (2001), 'Causes and Lessons of the California Electricity Crisis', http://www.cbo.gov/showdoc.cfm?index=3062&sequence=0, 14 December 2004.

CEC (California Energy Commission) (1998), *New Options for Agricultural Customers: California's Electric Industry Restructuring*, State of California Energy Commission P400-97-005.

CEC (California Energy Commission) (2000), *California Energy Demand 2000–2010, Technical Report to California Energy Outlook,* Docket #99-CEO-1, http://www.energy.ca.gov/reports/2000-07-14_200-00-002.PD, 14 December 2004.

CEC (California Energy Commission) (2001a), www.energy.ca.gov, 16 December 2004

CEC (California Energy Commission) (2001b), Energy Facilities Siting/Licensing Process, www.energy.ca.gov/sitingcases/index.html, 14 December 2004.

EIA (Energy Information Administration) (2002), *Status of the California Electricity Situation*, www.eia.doe.gov/cneaf/electricity/california/california.html, 14 December 2004.

FERC (Federal Energy Regulatory Commission) (2000), *Staff Report to the Federal energy Regulatory Commission on Western Markets and the Causes of the Summer (2000) Price Abnormalities,* www.stoft.com/x/cal/(2000)1101-FERC-staff-all.pdf, November 1.

FERC (Federal Energy Regulatory Commission) (2002), Initial Report on Company-Specific Separate Proceedings and Generic Re-evaluations; Published Natural Gas Price Data; and Enron Trading Strategies; Fact-Finding Investigation of Potential Manipulation of Electric and Natural Gas Prices, FERC, DOCKET NO. PA02-2-000.

Ford, A. (1999), 'Cycles in Competitive Electricity Markets: a Simulation Study of the Western United States', *Energy Policy*, 27, 637–658.

Ford, A. (2001), 'Waiting for the Boom: a Simulation Study of Power Plant Construction in California', *Energy Policy,* 29, 847–69.

Gladstone, M. and B. Bailey (2000), 'State's Long Road to Current Problems', *San Jose Mercury News*, www.bayarea.com/mld/bayarea/archives//, November 30.

Hebert, H.J. (2001), 'Solution Eludes Power Players, State and Federal Officials, Utilities Representatives and Power Producers and Brokers hold a Meeting to try to ease Californias Electricity Crisis', *The Associated Press*, January 10.

Hirst, E. (2001), *The California Electricity Crisis: Lessons for Other States*, Washington, US: Electric Industry Restructuring.

Holson, L.M. and R.A. Oppel Jr. (2001), 'Trying to Follow the Money in Californias Energy Mess', *The New York Times*, January 12.

Johnson, S. and J. Woolfolk (2000), 'Power Shortage Worsens, State Pushed to Brink of Black-outs as Supply Falls', *San Jose Mercury News*, December 8, www.bayarea.com/mld/bayarea/archives//, 14 December 2004.

Joskow, P.L. and E. Kahn (2002), *A Quantitative Analysis of Pricing Behaviour In California's Wholesale Electricity Market During Summer 2000: The Final Word*, http://econ-www.mit.edu/faculty/pjoskow/files/Joskow-K.pdf, 14 December 2004.

Kahn, M. and L. Lynch (2000), *California's Electricity Options and Challenges, Report to Governor Gray Davis*, Electricity Oversight Board and California www.cpuc.ca.gov/published/report/GOV_REPORT.htm, August, Public Utilities Commission.

Kaplan, T. and M. Guido (2001), 'Blackouts Roll Across the Bay Area', *San Jose Mercury News*, January 17, www.bayarea.com/mld/bayarea/archives//.

Marshall, M. and S. McAllister (2000), 'Potential Outages Could Produce Shocking Costs, Tech Firms Alarmed by Power Crunch', *San Jose Mercury News*, December 9, www.bayarea.com/mld/bayarea/archives//.

Nissenbaum, D., C. Devall. and J. Woolfolk (2001), 'Gov. Davis Announces 40 Long-term Contracts, Conservation Still Needed to Prevent Summer Blackouts', *San Jose Mercury News*, March 5, www.bayarea.com/mld/bayarea/archives//.

Nissenbaum, D. (2001), 'Power Bills Drain Budget Surplus', *San Jose Mercury News*, 8 May, www.bayarea.com/mld/bayarea/archives//.

Oppel, R.A. and L. Bergman (2002), 'Judge Concludes Energy Company Drove Up Prices', *The New York Times*, 23 September.

Pacific Gas and Electric (2000), *Annual Report*, www.pgecorp.com/financial/reports/pdf/FS_(2000)final.pdf.

Sheffrin, A. (2002), 'California Power Crisis: Failure of Market Design or Regulation?', *IEEE Power Engineering Review*, 22 (8), 8–11.

Stoft, S. (2002), *'Power System Economics, Designing Markets for Electricity'*, Piscataway, US: IEEE Press.

Union of Concerned Scientists (2000), *Public Utility Policy Act Briefing*, www.ucsusa.org/energy/brief.purpa.html.

Woolfolk, J. (2001), 'Deregulation Overlooked Long-term Power Buying', *San Jose Mercury News*, January. 11, www.bayarea.com/mld/bayarea/archives//.

Yardley, J. (2001), 'Texas Learns in California How Not to Deregulate', *The New York Times,* January 10.

5. Dilemmas in Network Regulation: The Dutch Gas Industry

Aad F. Correljé

1 INTRODUCTION

Currently, all over the world, infrastructure-bound industries, like telecom, public transport, water and energy supply, are in a process of structural change and liberalization. Among the main stated objectives are the provision of choice to customers and the stimulation of efficiency and innovativeness in the industries, through their exposure to the 'dynamism of the market'. The Dutch energy regulator DTe, for example, states that gas supply has to be turned into a demand-driven sector with an emphasis on freedom of choice for suppliers to the consumer, to realize the objective of stimulating economic efficiency and an improved international competitive position for the Dutch energy industry, leading to lower prices, improved services, a differentiated offer of services to consumers and the stimulation of innovation (DTe 2004a). To this end, the prevailing structure and management of utilities has been broken up and new systems of governance are created. Incumbent utilities' supply monopolies are dismantled and forced to compete with alternative providers, either directly *in* the market, or through tendering procedures *for* the market. Generally, those segments of the utilities that potentially allow for rivalry between suppliers are opened up for entry to newcomers. Sometimes, the incumbent is split up into a number of firms. Other segments, which are considered a natural monopoly, are singled out and placed under some form of regulatory oversight, to secure their continuous, economically efficient operation in such a way that users are given non-discriminatory access to essential facilities, at an acceptable price. Moreover, there are shifts in the ownership of the firms; ranging from full-fledged privatization in some sectors and countries, to all kinds of hybrid public/private partnerships, at varying degrees of distance from their share-holders (see for example Juris 1998; Shuttleworth 2000; Newbery 2001; Vogelsang 2003; Correljé 2004).

Processes of structural change have a radical impact upon the economic and technical performance of the network industries. Shifts in governance and economic performance of firms and sectors go hand in hand with shifts in preferences regarding technologies, investments and marketing strategies of suppliers. In some areas, such as the worldwide web, mobile telephony and green power supply, for example these changes are well appreciated as signs of modernization and progress. In other fields, unwanted 'side-effects' like rising prices, price volatility, failing services, lagging investments and corporate mismanagement, are making consumers and public authorities increasingly hesitant towards the real-world consequences of liberalization. These may differ considerably from the economic textbook promises and the rallying slogans of liberal politicians. Other signs of discomfort are heard from the regulated industries, including incumbents as well as new entrants and financial institutions, complaining that new systems of governance and regulators' approaches actually threaten the viability, stability and performance of the industries (Correljé et a.l 2003a).

The debate on the potential role of markets and regulation has thus become increasingly complex. In the 1980s and 1990s, in the context of a largely theoretical debate, liberal 'believers' could argue that economic benefits could be reaped through structural change, while communitarians would maintain the opposite view. Since then, on the basis of real-world experiences in a range of countries and industries, the debate has taken a shift from a prescriptive stance to a more evaluative character (see Berg et al. 2002; Helm 2003; Thomas 2004). This evaluation is increasingly voiced in critical terms, referring to the well-known disasters such as the California blackouts, the Scandinavian electricity price hikes, the UK railroad accidents, etc. These examples often point to *wrong*, uninformed choices for market design and regulatory approaches made in the past, as the premier cause of these problems (See for Dutch examples: Köper 2003; Van Damme 2004; Nillesen and Pollitt 2004;).

In this chapter, however, we will maintain that the simple use of the qualification 'right' or 'wrong', in respect of a choice for a market and ownership structure and for a regulatory approach, may be flawed. It is based on the simplistic assumption that alternative – and better – choices by the government and the regulator could have produced the conduct aspired to and performance promised to voters and customers (see also EB, 2003, no. 11, p. 3). It thus presumes that there exist 'off-the-shelf' regulatory packages, providing a choice of instruments that, if the right parameters are employed, yield the preferred behaviour in terms of supply, demand and prices.[1]

We also assume that market behaviour evolves in close association with shifts in the market structure and in the regulation of a market, etc. But, in contrast to this 'off-the-shelf' approach, we will also argue that the design, the implementation and the 'maintenance' of regulatory systems are a dynamic learning process, evolving over time. In part, this process is driven by exogenous pressures, as regulation has to cope with dilemmas in respect of, for example, stranded assets, the position of the incumbent *versus* newcomers, technological development, the growth of markets, specific public values and other policy objectives. Solving these dilemmas requires adjustments to the scope, the scale and the approach of regulation and takes place under influence of actions taken by stakeholders in the industry, governments, European, national and local political representative bodies, labour unions, consumers organizations, NGOs, research institutes and consultancies, etc. (see Baldwin and Cave 1999).

Parallel to these interest-related exogenous pressures, however, a process of endogenous, collective learning drives the development of a regulatory system. We will argue that the main actors, i.e. the firms in the industry, the regulator and the political realm gain new insights time and again. These actors use such new insights to optimize their behaviour in respect of their newly perceived context by revising their strategies *vis-à-vis* each other and the changing market (see also Janssen 2004). We distinguish such *quasi optimizing* behaviour from *strategic* behaviour, as the latter seems to suggest that – within a context of asymmetric insights – firms make use of the regulatory lacunae of which they know the consequences, on the basis of their predefined interest.

This evolutionary perspective implies that both the regulator's actions, as well as firms' responses to these actions and the articulation of public values, are to a certain degree the products of a process of discovery. As will be explained below, these discoveries do arise as a consequence of the way regulatory frameworks are founded upon neo-classical and Austrian economic theories, their narrow focus on specific sets of issues, their inherent incompleteness in the real world and the continuous detection of new, previously undefined, facets that have to be incorporated in the regulatory system. This perspective enables us to understand why regulation will never be 'finished'; why the policy-maker and the regulator will always be 'too late' or 'incomplete' in capturing and modifying the industry's behaviour, why some firms thus benefit more than others and why new *public values* keep on showing up. It thus explains the possible reticence of the industry to invest in assets and to participate fully in the 'regulatory game'. It also suggests, however, that the simple, momentarily, qualification 'right' or 'wrong' for a regulatory *approach* may imply a flawed perspective. Indeed, the question arises how an effective and efficient *process* of regulatory development can be established and managed. This process perspective is generally neglected in the policy-making process and in the applied academic research informing this process.

An analysis of the post-1990 development of the Dutch regulatory framework for the natural gas market yields an illustrative application of this evolutionary perspective on the development of regulation. We will interpret the emergence of this framework as a sequence of 'discoveries', unravelling step by step the set of technical and economic functionalities of the gas supply system. Until the mid-1990s these functionalities had been embedded, or internalized, within the overall gas supply structure of the NAM/Gasunie public–private partnership. Yet, once the Dutch government began to dismantle this structure, it began to 'escape' from the framework. Of course, the plight of the regulator, DTe, became to re-internalize these functionalities in a newly established framework, based on the paradigm of free market coordination. A further elaboration of this evolutionary perspective will be undertaken in Section 2 below. Section 3 will briefly sketch the sequence of key governance paradigms in network sectors. Section 4 will evaluate the post-1996 process of regulation of the Dutch natural gas industry. Section 5 will interpret this evolution and is followed by some concluding remarks.

2 REGULATION, MARKETS AND INSTITUTIONS

A dynamic perspective on the nature of regulation of industries and markets may be built upon the work of Douglass North (1990, 1994), analysing the development of institutions that facilitate the functioning of today's highly complex economic and social systems, and that of Michel Callon (1998a,b), paying attention to the particular design and content of those institutions. North's view draws on the well-known idea that, in order to engage in economic transactions in an economy, actors have to incur *transaction costs* for acquiring information on the transaction, the reputation of their partners, the enforcement of the transaction, etc. He argues that institutions (must) exist because of their contribution to the reduction of those *transaction costs*, by canalizing and ordering the behaviour of economic actors:

> Institutions provide the structure for exchange that (together with the technology employed) determines the cost of transacting and the cost of transformation. The greater the specialization and the number and variability of valuable attributes, the more weight must be put on reliable institutions that allow individuals to engage in complex contracting with a minimum of uncertainty about whether the terms of the contract can be realized. (North 1990: 34)

North distinguishes i*nformal constraints and formal constraints* in a hierarchical order as the constitution, laws, rules, obligations, rights, contracts, and the *enforcement of the constraints*. It is obvious that these behavioural constraints also include the regulation and systems of governance for network infrastructures. Often the state is a coercive force. But whereas neo-classical economics only invokes the state as a means of final resort, to enforce rights and to repair cases of unequivocal *market failure* or *imperfect markets*, North and Callon emphasize the omnipresence of the state in society. The state generally supports institutions that facilitate the functioning of markets and of the economy and of society as a whole and contributes to the *framing* of actors in their mutual relations.

Generally, the basic structure of institutional frameworks will be rather stable. This is a path-dependent consequence of the large number of interrelated institutional parameters, the high cost of adjustment and the fact that changes require complex and expensive negotiations with other parties involved (North 1990: 68). Yet, even these relatively stable systems are subject to gradual change, or to radical alterations as a result of exogenous shocks. Driving forces behind those adjustments are changes in relative prices – or the sheer availability – of labour, capital, raw material, information, and the manner in which they are perceived within the mental models of the relevant actors, in combination with the shifts in 'taste' and ideology that may alter those mental models (North 1990: 83, 104; 1994: 362).

In respect of these shifts, North (1994: 361-3) attributes a fundamental role to learning by individuals and entrepreneurs of political, administrative and business organizations. Learning, he argues, entails developing a structure by which to interpret the varied signals received by the senses. Experiences of a physical and socio-cultural nature underscore the development of a mental model to explain the environment, relevant to some goal, and to frame relationships with other parties involved. Such models will evolve reflecting the feedback derived from new experiences, sometimes strengthening the initial model, sometimes inducing modifications. As belief structures, these individual models form the basis of societal and economic structures, when widespread acceptation turns them into mechanisms, or institutions, to structure and order the environment, including systems of regulation and governance.

Taking a slightly broader perspective than North, Callon (1998a,b) argues that actors in society are part of an *actor–network* system, connected through their mutual relations. Such relations with other actors and organizations are based on relative interests and objectives and involve strategies, habits, rules, contracts, regulation, public/private arrangements, norms, and standards. The formal and informal institutions embedding these relations are, according to Callon, established through a process of *framing*, that organizes the real, chaotic, world for the several actors and organizations: 'Framing demarcates in regards to the network of relationships, those which are taken into account and those which are ignored' (1998b: 250-5). Crucial to the process of framing is that actors become able to form – in a *calculated* way – opinions and perceptions on their position *vis-à-vis* other actors and of the consequences of their choices in transactions and, thus, may reduce costs and risk.

As regards the market, framing involves the demarcation of a specific stage, within the overall network of interdependencies, within which negotiations ands transactions take place between actors. Actors that are better equipped to calculate their own position relative to others, have a relative comparative advantage in a market. Confirming North's attention for the evaluation and validation as the main role of institutions in economic exchange and calculation, Callon underlines the development of measures, conventions and procedures for validation and comparison. He stresses the role of sciences like accountancy, marketing and economics in the development of instruments of measurement, performance, comparison and interpretation – in response to a social and political demand for practical insights to solve problems in the organization of (economic) transactions (Callon 1998: 23–8). Actors may invest in developing the knowledge and insights that allow them to outperform others, including the regulator or the government.

North argues that this is a complex process (1994: 365) and that the search for knowledge, insights and the consequent mental model building is not by definition successful. Indeed, often regulating organizations and firms won't know where they are heading and what they will find there. Moreover, institutional development is to a certain extent dependent on the political process and the relative position of interest groups therein. Like the search for process and product innovation and efficiency improvements (see Nelson and Winter 1982; Weisman and Pfeifenberger 2003), we argue that the *discovery* and *implementation* of elements of regulatory frameworks and governance structures for markets are risky activities too, the outcome of which can not be predicted (see also Agrell and Bogetoft 2004). Such attempts may form the basis of societal and economic structures, but not until widespread acceptation turns them into 'real' institutions. Mirroring this process, also the evolving strategies of firms in the regulated sector are the temporarily results of a complex path of belief, discovery and reflexive learning.

The framing of groups of actors and their relations is neither exclusive, nor complete or stable. North argues that the 'coverage' of the system of institutions will have to remain limited to the apparently most pressing aspects. Bounded rationality and sheer cost reduce the degree to which aspects of behaviour and transactions can be 'covered' effectively, rendering uncovered actions, activities and their consequences *external effects* (1990: 61). Callon also refers to *external effects*, which he baptizes *overflow*. Overflow emerges when aspects or effects of actors' behaviour or transactions are not included in the *frame*: 'overflows escape from the co-ordination frame in place'. As with classical external effects, the consequent lack of co-ordination and compensation impedes efficient transactions and adjustments to behaviour to take place (Coase 1960).

The inherent incompleteness and non-exclusiveness of the framework of relations in combination with the actors' learning stimulates these actors to seek a reframing of relations to their own advantage. This suggests the existence of a continuous process of framing and reframing, as a consequence of the interaction between the institutional framework and the 'requirements' put forward by (economic) activities. Actors, discovering new solutions and approaches, may decide to 'invest' in changing the rules, through lobbying influencing the public opinion and political action and through the development of new knowledge and insights (North 1990: 78, 79, 87). It is crucial that some of the parties, or groups, involved will be better equipped and quicker to interpret and understand what it is all about. This will give them a lead in reaching the most advantageous position *vis-à-vis* others. Indeed, small groups of actors with determinate interests will generally be more effective than large numbers of actors with dispersed interest and vague perceptions (North 1994: 362). Moreover, particular groups may not present at all in the initial stages of the process. Taking note of the above, it is easy to understand how – *in abstracto* – processes of structural change and liberalization in the network sectors can be described and interpreted along the lines of institutional change.

Callon (1998b) suggests a number of stylized steps in the operationalization of the process of (re)framing. These are:

- Identification and explanation of external effects, or overflow;
- Identification of actors involved and their roles within or outside the frame;
- Measurement of perceived externalities and their valuation;

- Negotiations for a revised framework;
- Transactions within the new framework.

It is crucial to acknowledge that this process of framing is guided and informed by underlying technological, accountancy, marketing and economics *paradigms*. These paradigms, or mental models, are employed as a kind of lens to *identify* and *interpret* functional, technical, organizational, economical and regulatory facets of the externalities that are relevant for reframing, within the context of the infrastructure system's operation and performance. So, eventually, such paradigms define both the phenomena to be observed, as well as (elements) of a solution to their internalization. The paradigm employed will provide a hint towards the measures and indicators for functions, volume, quality, performance, effectiveness and efficiency through which external effects become tangible. It, thus, may yield the initial ideas about the principles and approaches on the basis of which the reframing exercise can be undertaken. So, it will be obvious that via additional investments in research and policy advice and through their use in the real world, these ideas can be further given the operational shape and status required, turning them into commonly accepted elements of the institutional framework.

3   PARADIGMS FOR STRUCTURAL CHANGE IN THE NETWORK SECTORS

In brief, the paradigmatic underpinnings of the structuring of the network sectors, since the end of the 1970s, underwent a shift from a traditional neo-classical view on the functioning of markets, towards paradigms that were based on monetarist and public choice theories. The standard neo-classical approach justified state intervention on the basis of the concepts of *market failure* and *public goods*, in which Pareto-optimal decision-making was not to be expected in the gas and power sector. Traditionally, the *natural monopoly* character of such services had justified regulation and public ownership. So, the state had to jump in and remedy imperfections and failures, including problems of excessive market power, externalities, lumpy investments, spillover, etc. (see for example Stiglitz 1986). In the

US, privately owned utilities were regulated by sector specific-federal and state agencies. In Europe, the utilities were owned by the state, municipalities or other regional bodies. The regulators in the US and public ownership in Europe also secured the *public interest* elements or *public values* associated with these services, involving issues of safety, security of supply, acceptable prices for specific types of users, objectives of local and sectoral development, the supply of jobs, and – more recently – sustainability and environmental protection (see Foreman-Peck and Milward 1994).

By the late 1970s, this perspective was replaced by the kind of 'liberalism' associated with the late Ronald Reagan and Margaret Thatcher. Efficiency, economic reform and political power were sought through a reduction of taxes, 'rolling back the state' and by bringing market-driven competition (Helm 2003; Parker 2000). Indeed, perfect competition – modelled after the revised economic textbooks – was to be imposed upon public sectors wherever possible (see Friedman 1962; Demsetz 1968). Gradually, and initially only in a number of Anglo Saxon countries and Chile, free access to consumers and markets, competition in production and retail sectors and privatization were introduced as the basic objectives of structural change in the energy sector. After the adoption of the Single European Market objective in 1985, these objectives became the points of departure for the European Commission, as the main instruments to tear down the prevailing barriers to trade (see CEC 1988; Haaland Matláry 1997).

More recently, particularly through the developments in the UK deregulation of utilities, the Austrian school has become involved as an important source of wisdom (see Laffont and Tirole 1993; Robinson 2000). This is because the Austrian ideas provide the basis for dynamic regulation, in which price cap regulation (RPI-X) entices operators to bring down their costs, while letting them keep the increased revenues for some time (see Littlechild 1983), for yardstick regulation of costs and tariffs and for efficient trading and auctioning facilities in the gas and electricity industry (see Newbery 2000). In contrast with the traditional static equilibrium approach in neo-classical economics, the Austrians focus on the dynamic process in competitive markets (Kirzner 1997). This, as is argued, contributes to the process of creative entrepreneurial discovery, quality and innovation, instead of to static cost cutting and an extrapolation of the monopoly situation. It is assumed that consumers will employ their free choice primarily to select quality and added value; price being only one factor among the many (Ferguson 1988; Robinson 2000). A further requirement for 'dynamic' competition and for harvesting its advantages is that new concepts and solutions can enter the market. So, the success of competition is often defined as the number of (new) competitors in the market. Consequently, the process of liberalization is fully geared towards safeguarding the entry of new entrepreneurs in the market. All new entry is seen as beneficial and, thus, incumbents must be obliged to sell their products and services as if they were a 'stand-alone business', incurring the full costs of each new entrant (see on this Shuttleworth 2000). As will be shown below, the Dutch policy in the energy sector moved away from the traditional utilities perspective in the mid-1990s and immediately adopted the Austrian approach. Yet, this did not mean that it took into consideration the more fundamental dynamics of market restructuring and the framing issues outlined above.

4   A NEW REGULATORY FRAMEWORK FOR THE NETHERLANDS' GAS INDUSTRIE

After a period of discussion and governmental internal deliberation on the organization of the energy sector, the actual liberalization of the Dutch gas market took off with the presentation of Minister Wijers' Third White Paper on Energy, by the end of 1995 (MEZ 1995). Until then, Dutch energy policy-making had ferociously rejected the EU Commission's objective of liberalization. Indeed, it had been considered a threat to the prevailing organization of the Dutch market and the associated policy and business objectives, like the policy to stimulate the production of gas from small off-shore fields, the revenues to the state, environmental policy objectives, the use of gas prices as an instrument of regional and sector development policy and the interests of the private shareholders in the Dutch gas production, Shell and Exxon and a range of smaller oil companies. The new White Paper, in contrast, highlighted the competitive advantages an early liberalization of the energy sector would bring to the energy-intensive

Dutch economy and pointed to *first mover* advantages to the energy industry itself. It proposed a phased introduction of a free choice for gas and power suppliers to, respectively, the large, medium-sized and small consumers of energy (see Correljé 1997 Correljé et al. 2003b).

The following sections will highlight a number of specific aspects in the process of restructuring. From the 1990s onwards, as is observed in section 5, there is a gradually expanding set of actors and parties actively involved in the discussion around the restructuring. Sections 6 to 8 trace the continuous growth in the elements of the gas supply system that were to be *regulated*, looking at the formal manifestation of the restructuring of the Dutch gas sector. This involved a sequence of rules, consisting of the two EU Gas directives and a number of regulations; the two Dutch Gas Laws and a number of revisions and decrees (AMVBs); the consecutive Guidelines for the execution of the Gas Law, plus Decisions and Licenses for specific firms, by the DTe, the Dutch regulatory agency; and a series of operative rules and procedures by Gasunie and the local distribution networks, owned by Nuon, Essent, Delta and Eneco. The more informal elements of this process of restructuring are much more difficult to identify, as these involve the strategies and interaction of the several actors involved. Nevertheless, to a certain extent these elements can be observed in their contributions to consultation procedures, in reactions in the press and in lobbying activities.

It will become clear that, on the one hand, there is an expansion in the number of elements of the system that are to be reframed, either in the formal meaning of being regulated, or in the way of being covered by the firms' business routines (see Nelson and Sampat 2001: 42–7). On the other hand, an increasing degree of detail seems to be required in the way the operation of the system is to be regulated. Many aspects that had been arranged more or less informally via self-regulation between the State, Gasunie and the distributors, now appeared to require formal, explicit, rules, procedures and standards.

5   THE ACTORS INVOLVED

Traditionally, four main types of actors were involved in the Dutch gas industry (see MEZ 1962). These involved, firstly, the Dutch *State* (represented via the Ministries of Economic Affairs and Finance and as a shareholder in Gasunie and Energie Beheer Nederland (EBN)). Secondly, there were the *oil companies*, including Exxon and Shell, via their joint venture the Nederlandse Aardolie Maatschappij (NAM) and as a shareholder in Gasunie, and a number of other gas-producing companies active in a range of concessions, jointly with EBN. Thirdly, there were 20 or so local *distribution companies* in the Netherlands, represented by Energiened, selling the gas to Dutch consumers. Fourthly, a few foreign transmission companies and utilities were involved in importing gas from the Netherlands, including Ruhrgas, Distrigaz, Gas de France, NAM, etc. After a turbulent period of the 1970s, contacts and negotiations between these several interests had been maintained within a relatively stabile, well-organized framework, shielded from all too direct political and societal involvement (Correljé et al. 2003b; Roggenkamp and Bos 2001).

The post-1995 restructuring and opening of the industry brought a range of other actors into the Dutch gas sector. Some of these actors were genuinely new, while others simply gained a different, more outspoken, international position. Directly involved with regulation, the main new actors were the EU Commission and the Dutch *regulator* DTe. Another new figure became the stand-alone *transport system operator* (TSO) – a function previously covered by Gasunie and the local gas distributors – Gasunie Transport Services (GTS). The local network operators were split off from the former distribution companies. Most of these actors joined their peers in EU-level organizations to discuss, develop and articulate their interests *vis-à-vis* other parties involved. As from 1999, the European gas regulators via the Council of European Energy Regulators (CEER) joined the European Gas Regulatory Forum, meeting regularly in Madrid, to exchange experiences and develop common regulatory approaches. The TSOs formed *Gas Transmission Europe* (GTE). The former European distribution companies, joined in the *Groupement Européen des Entreprises et Organismes de Distribution d'Energie* (GEODE).

The process of restructuring also brought new entrants to the Dutch market, including the newly established Gasunie trading branch, Gasunie Trade & Supply (GT&S), and foreign traders associated with gas producers and transmission companies, such as, for example, Gas de France (GdF), Total, Norsk Hydro, Dong, BP, Ruhrgas, Wingas, etc. At the international level these producers are associated in the International Gas Union (IGU) and the International Association of Oil & Gas Producers (OGP). Another group of new participants involved the trading branches of the former Dutch local utilities, like Essent, Nuon, Delta, and Eneco, and foreign colleagues, like RWE, Statkraft, EWE, etc. A number of independent, trading firms newly appeared in the market, like Hess, Entergy Koch, etc. Many of these firms joined the Dutch traders association, VOEG, to have their interests represented in contacts with the Ministry of Economic Affairs, DTe, and the network operators. At the EU level they joined the European Federation of Energy Traders (EFET).

Along with the phased opening of the three segments of consumers, these users began to appear as actors in the market. The large consumers organized in the VEMW and at the EU level in the IFIEC (the International Federation of Industrial Energy Consumers) and Eurelectric, for the power sector, began to take action to influence the process. The *Productschap Tuinbouw* and *LTO-Nederland* are interested organizations representing medium-sized users, particularly in horticulture. Small users are not represented by specific organizations, apart from the *Consumenten Bond*, the consumers association, and depend on the extent to which political parties are putting the interest of the small consumers, which of course are also voters, upon their political agenda (see Knops et al. 2004).

Through a variety of mechanisms, like interest group meetings and working groups, public hearings, parliamentary action, lobbying activities, applied academic and consultancy studies, etc., these organizations began to influence the process of restructuring. In due course, their input became increasingly focused and articulated. Therewith they gradually became aware of how they could be of influence in the regulatory process and what the consequences of the several regulatory options and choices in the process would be for their role in the developing market. Also their orientation in the international context, via the EU-level organizations, was an important factor. In this respect, it is interesting to observe that the initial positions pro and contra the process as such, gradually became more subtle and evaluated towards preferences for specific regulatory solutions.

6 THE EU GAS DIRECTIVES 1998 AND 2003

The EU Council accepted the Gas Directive in December 1997; it entered into force on 10 August 1998 (98/30/EC) and had to be implemented by the Member States two years later. The main elements of this Directive were broadly formulated as: (1) the provision of regulated *or* negotiated third party access (TPA) to the national transmission and regional distribution networks; (2) a step by step introduction of free choice of suppliers to eligible customers, defined as percentage shares of the respective markets; (3) separate accounts for generation, transmission, distribution and any other activities, but no explicit unbundling.

Progress in Member States implementing the Directive was varied. On 26 June 2003, the European Parliament and the Council adopted a new Gas Directive. This new Directive (2003/55/EC) was more explicit and more stringent in a number of aspects and, thus, reduced the leeway in national implementation: (1) it demanded TPA to transmission and distribution networks on the basis of published and regulated tariffs, instead on negotiated tariffs; (2) it established the right for all non-household gas customers to freely choose their supplier no later than 1 July 2004, while all of them should have this right by 1 July 2007; (3) instead of only separate accounts, it required legal unbundling of transmission and of large and medium-sized distribution companies. Genuinely new elements were: (4) that it required the establishment of a regulatory authority in each Member State with a universal minimum set of responsibilities; and (5) that access to storage facilities should be provided either on a negotiated or regulated basis. By January, in addition, the Commission published a series of clarifying notes that made the provisions more stringent (DG TREN 2004).

DG TREN monitored the national implementation of the Directive regularly and, in March 2004, it concluded that: 'For gas, it would seem that further progress is dependent on improved conditions for cross border exchanges and the development of a coherent tarification and capacity allocation regime at EU level. The implementation of the Madrid Guidelines and their development through the process set out in the *Commission's Proposal for a Regulation* will allow such improvements to be made' (CEC 2004).

The abundant documentation around the consultations of the European Gas Regulatory Forum in Madrid gives a clear insight in the way in which the regulatory instruments, concepts and *guidelines* (CEC 2003) are developed step by step.[2] It also vividly illustrates the contribution to this process of the several interested organizations referred to above.

7   A NEW FRAMEWORK FOR THE DUTCH GAS SECTOR

By the end of 1997, at about the same time as the acceptation of the first EU Gas Directive, the Dutch Ministry of Economic Affairs published a preliminary gas policy paper, *Gasstromen*, which contained the loosely drawn principles of a restructuring of the Dutch gas industry (MEZ 1997). In August 1998, DTe was established, as a 'lean and mean' organization under responsibility of the Minister of Economic Affairs, with explicitly stated tasks of market supervision and the execution of the Electricity and the Gas Law.[3] Clearly, in the ensuing process, DTe took the executive role to its limits of its marching orders and engaged in regulation, rather than just 'supervision'.

7.1 The Gas Act 2000 and 2004

In March 1999 a draft Gas Act was sent to Parliament, which it passed in June 2000. The *first round* of adjustments, as outlined below, emerged from basic provisions in the Gas Act. These involved, to start with, a timeschedule for freedom of choice of suppliers to the three main categories of consumers. Large consumers using more than ten million cubic metres annually, with a market share of around 45 per cent of total demand, would immediately enjoy the freedom to negotiate their gas supply contracts. From 1 January 2002, freedom of negotiation was given to medium-sized consumers with a gas consumption of between 10 and 0.17 million cubic metres. Parliament would have to decide when small users, consuming less than 0.17 million cubic metres (around 20 per cent of the market) would follow. Eventually, this happened in July 2004.

A second main issue was the opening up of the production and the trade in gas and the stimulation of new entrants and competition in the sector.[4] Traditional and new producers and traders in the Netherlands would be allowed to sell their gas, without the commercial involvement of Gasunie and/or the traditional utilities, to the several categories of consumers. To this end, these parties should achieve access to Gasunie's high-pressure transmission system and the lower pressure distribution networks of the local utilities. Initially, it was intended that Gasunie and the distribution companies would remain the owners of their transport systems to maintain the advantages of scale and scope and the coordination of gas supplies from the Groningen field and other fields and imports.

A third element was that, to secure a non-discriminatory provision of transport services and to facilitate regulatory oversight in these operations, Gasunie was required to administratively unbundle the operation of its high pressure national transport system from its trading activities; the 'Chinese wall'. The local distribution companies, in contrast, were to be split up legally into network operators and gas suppliers/traders. The Gas Act provided a hybrid *Third Party Access* (TPA) regime, through which the traders, producers and consumers could hire transport capacity and ancillary services from Gasunie and the local network operators. *Guidelines* by DTe had to draw the lines along which Gasunie and the local network operators had to publish their *Indicative Tariffs*, on the basis of which potential shippers would have to negotiate the actual prices and conditions for services.

By 2004, a number of provisions in the 2000 Act were overtaken by the so-called Intervention and Implementation (I&I) Act, that implemented the provisions of the 2nd EU Gas Directive. Thus, the Act required a move from partly negotiated, hybrid, access conditions, towards regulated access tariffs and access conditions to gas transmission and distribution networks and to gas quality conversion services. It required a legal – instead of administrative – unbundling of Gasunie's transmission network and the establishment of a TSO (GTS) for the national high pressure grid. In addition, the Act provided the Minister with the right to establish a gas exchange (Art. 66b) and to demand a release of contracted gas and capacity by the incumbent or by other parties (Art. 66a). Therewith, the Act followed the 2nd EU Directive, though it was more stringent in respect of legal unbundling of GTS, and the Minister's rights in respect of the exchange and the release programme. The I&I Act also put an end to the publication by DTe of the Guidelines on access tariffs and conditions. On the basis of a singular technical code, drawing on the Guidelines 2005, the industry would have to annually submit proposals for such access conditions for approval to the Director of DTe. This implied that the initiative was moved away from the regulator towards the industry.

7.2 The Split-up of Gasunie

Parallel to the development of a regulatory framework, it was announced that the Ministry of Economic Affairs was contemplating a new set—up for the Dutch gas industry, the structure of which was seen as increasingly awkward in the context of a liberalizing energy market. Hence, the Minister was re-negotiating the role of the State and the oil companies in the system (MEZ 2001). In April 2002, to the surprise of many, the minister of Economic Affairs, Joritsma, declared that Gasunie, as the wholesale trader and transporter of most of Dutch gas, would be dismantled (MEZ 2002; EB 2002, no. 5, 3). Gasunie was to be split into three parts. The trading branch, GT&S, would be split in two, and transferred to the trading departments of the two shareholding oil companies, Shell and Exxon/Mobil. The transmission branch, already administratively unbundled as GTS, would become the fully State-owned network operator, providing non-discriminatory access to all gas producers, traders and consumers.

Among the main issues the Dutch State and the oil companies had to resolve was the way in which the small fields policy and the long-term depletion policy could be maintained, given that Gasunie, the traditional 'keeper' of this policy, would disappear. A second fundamental factor in the negotiations between the State and the oil companies was the valuation of both GT&S's activities and the GTS network, and the way in which the shareholders will be compensated when the company is split up. A main difficulty in this regard is the fact that the value of the assets involved would be a composite function of state-influenced factors, like the regulation of the system and issues of taxation, and of factors fully external to the system, such as the price of oil and the future European gas market (see Correljé et al. 2003b; EB, 2003, no. 4, 1).

In the midst of these complicated and politically sensitive negotiations, firstly, the responsible Minister withdrew and, subsequently, the whole Balkenende government resigned, after only 87 days in office, in October 2002. In December 2002, the Ministry of Economic Affairs wrote a letter to Parliament in which it explained the lack of progress. Yet, to an increasing extent, the parties had become aware of the sheer lack of clarity in respect of the consequences of whatever new structure would be chosen. Not much has happened until June 2003, when the new Minister of Economic Affairs, Brinkhorst, announced the legal separation of Gasunie Transport Services. In October 2003, Brinkhorst announced that the process of deeper dismantlement of GT&S would be put on a temporarily hold, possibly to be resumed at a later stage. A year later, in October 2004, a full legal and economic separation of the networks of all former gas and power distribution companies was announced. Shortly thereafter the Minister declared that also Gasunie would be split up into a fully publicly-owned transport system and a trade and supply firm; the latter would continue under the ownership of the state and the two oil companies. With this solution the Dutch Government fully obeyed the rules of the EU Gas Directive – and went even beyond – in respect of the transport system. Further decision-making on the trade branch may be expected.

8   REGULATION: AN EVOLUTION IN FIVE ROUNDS

On the basis of the framework outlined above, a series of landmark actions took place in the gas sector that clearly illustrates the reflexive and evolutionary character of the process of regulation – within the context of a genuine conflict of interest between incumbent parties and new entrants, of course. In the following sections we will highlight the main rounds, focusing on the interaction between the way in which DTe contemplated and formulated its *Guidelines* as from 2000 onward, and the manner in which the sector, particularly Gasunie, adjusted its regime for trading and network access[5] and revised its business practices and routines.

8.1 The First Round: Unbundling the Past

According to the 1st EU Gas Directive and the Gas Act, Gasunie would have to provide negotiated access to its system. In 1998, it made a first move by introducing its *Commodity Services System* (CCS). This system established separate tariff components for the different elements of a gas transaction, like the volume of gas supplied (commodity charge), the contracted transport (transport charge) and handling capacity (capacity charge) and the location of entry into the Gasunie system (distance charge). It did *not* provide for the separate purchase of these components, however (Gasunie 1989). This structure replaced the former system, in which all these elements had been made available via an *all-in* tariff, at a price determined only by the annual volume of gas purchased and the type of user. The division into these tariff components represents a clear example of an attempt to 'reframe' the several separate elements of the commercial relationship around the supply of gas, between the gas supplier (i.e. the NAM and the other companies), the transporter and wholesale trader (Gasunie) and the several types of large consumers. Following the steps of the Callon scheme for internalization (1998b), outlined above, there is: (a) the identification and explanation of previously external effects, i.e. the volume of gas contracted *during a specific period* and the transport *capacity* for a *specific route*; (b) the identification of actors involved and their roles either within or outside the frame, highlighting the now separate roles of the gas producer, the wholesale supplier (but not yet the trader), the network operator and the customer; (c) the measurement of perceived externalities and their valuation, involving the volumes, capacity requirements, gas quality, time, and contract duration and distance.

This proposal for a new framework for transacting was, of course, followed by tough discussions between Gasunie and its customers on the identification of these elements, and their measurement and valuation. The main questions that arose were, for example, whether a *cost-plus* or a *market price*-based pricing principle should prevail; about the duration of the contracts for the separate elements, and the question as to whether these elements could be provided on a separate basis. As will be shown in this section, in each round of regulation these types of discussions arose around new – and sometimes old – issues, at an increasing level of detail.

8.2 The Second Round: Setting the Scene

In August 2000, DTe published its *Temporarily Guidelines 2001* for gas transport and gas storage, outlining principles, conditions and tariffs structures for access to these facilities in a rather schematic manner (DTe 2000). DTe made clear that these guidelines would only be provisional; to be substituted the next year by a *definitive* version, as main elements still had to be developed. Also a consultation procedure with the firms in the sector and their organizations was announced. The *Guidelines 2001* contained a limited number of issues. Gasunie was required to separate its services into *basic* and *special* services, while establishing an indicative cost-based tariff structure for basic services, like transmission and balancing, quality conversion and gas storage. Negotiations had to be concluded within a *reasonable* period, while the *most favoured tariff* clause would apply.

A wide array of comments was received from the several parties involved in the sector and made public via the DTe website (see also EB, 2000: 8, 4). Generally, traders and customers argued that the Guidelines were not specific enough, while identifying additional elements through which access to the market should be impeded. Gasunie and the gas producers, in response, referred to the investment problems emerging from access on a cost-based basis. It was also argued that, in fact, DTe was requiring regulated TPA, instead of the hybrid TPA provided for in the law. These measures were said to jeopardize the *small fields* policy and the security of supply to captive consumers, through their incentives for traders to speculate in capacity hoarding, while reducing incentives to adequately invest in capacity. Generally, it was stated that the competitive power of the Dutch gas industry would be eroded.

Nevertheless, reacting to these Guidelines, by January 2001, Gasunie announced a set of measures which, beside a 6.5 per cent lowering of tariffs for transport services, included firstly, the voluntary dismantlement of the prevailing CSS system of tariffs and, secondly, the partition of its activities into two entities, the one taking care of transport services and the other undertaking trade and supply. The CSS was generally considered unworkably complicated, while the latter measure obviously was taken to avoid too much discussion on Gasunie's role as the incumbent supplier.

8.3 The Third Round: Conflict and Struggle

In June 2001, the presentation of the DTe consultation document for the Guidelines 2002 announced the third round of restructuring, developing more advanced regulatory notions (DTe 2001a; BET 2001). A number of requirements were formulated. Gasunie would have to provide a basic transport service, including guaranteed transport and a matching of the contract periods for transport and balancing services, a backhaul transport service and secondary trading of basic services. It would have to set up an entry–exit-based transport tariff, instead of the prevailing point-to-point regime. All transport and other services should be based on the efficient cost-plus based principle. Imbalance should be made tradable among shippers, with a cost-based orientation of the balancing services (tariffs and penalties). Information should be provided on available capacities, costs for basic services and the results of negotiations on deviating tariffs and conditions and other information necessary for successful negotiations on efficient cost levels (DTe 2001a: 67; EB 2001, no. 5, 4).

In August 2001, the *Guidelines for Transport and Storage 2002* (DTe 2001b,c) were published and included most of the elements announced in the consultation document, earlier that year. Only the entry–exit approach for network access was postponed until 2003. Gasunie, however, blamed DTe for being incompetent in gas issues and argued that it went way beyond its legal remit. Gasunie also had serious objections against the proposed form of the entry–exit tariff structure and wanted a more extended version. It also refused to accept a balancing period longer than an hour and refused to offer a basic backhaul service (EB 2001, no. 7, 2). The confrontation became increasingly sharp, when Gasunie Transport Services (GTS 2001) published its tariff regime for 2002, which implied the outright rejection of some elements of the DTe Guidelines, like the entry–exit regime (EB 2001, no. 8, 3).

Eventually, in December 2001, Gasunie and the other network operators were given a *binding instruction* (DTe 2002a). Therewith DTe forced GTS: (a) to reduce its tariffs by 5 per cent annually over the period up to 2005; (b) to provide information on the available entry and exit capacities; (c) to set-up a balancing regime and an entry–exit based tariff system; (d) to provide indicative tariffs for short term transport contracts based on *efficient economic costs;* and (e) to implement a back-haul regime (EB 2002, no. 1, 6). A month later, GTS gave in under protest and adjusted its tariffs, while it made daily supply contracts available (EB 2002, no. 2, 7). In the meantime, though, persistent complaints were heard from consumers and the traders' interest organizations, that GTS did not provide any unbundled flexibility to the shippers, but only simple transport services. This was a serious problem to independent shippers and suppliers, as these were generally unable to adjust their supply in such a way that it precisely matched the load patterns of their contracted consumers. The incumbent GT&S, in contrast, could supply this flexibility from its own contracted suppliers, including the Groningen field (EB 2002 no. 3, 4; Jacobs Consultancy 2001).

8.4 The Fourth Round: New Contours

By July 2002, DTe published draft Guidelines for transport and for storage 2003 (DTe 2002b,c). Following upon a study on storage issues (Brattle 2002), this draft contained a more developed – as compared to earlier concepts – proposal for a National Balancing Point (BNP), a virtual point in the grid, at which all gas within the system could be traded between the shippers. Another important aspect was the request for short-duration transport contract (1 hour), in line with GTS's hourly balancing requirements. The discussion on cost-plus *versus* market as the basis for transport tariffs was continued, but not solved. Yet, in its *binding decision*, DTe (2002a, 25) admitted that GTS might be in position in which the cost-plus approach would induce perverse gas flows through the Dutch system, as was maintained in a study carried out for Gasunie (Jepma et al. 2001). In addition, GTS was allowed to make use of a more complex tariff basis for its entry–exit system, reflecting a capacity and a distance component. For the first time, DTe really stressed the need to introduce the mutual, secondary, tradability of transport, capacity and other elements contracted from GTS, to balance the shippers' positions in the system *ex post*.

Gasunie, in reply, maintained in respect of these issues that it was not able as yet to oversee the consequences of an NBP. It also argued that short-term contracts were not necessary. It, however, announced the analysis of the consequences of a set of facilities and approaches, in respect of the transport system (entry–exit, contract duration, tariff principles, backhaul), gas quality conversion (contract duration, tariff principles, availability), and balancing (allocation of tolerance, penalties, tradability of tolerance, provision of flexibility) (GTS 2002a).

It can be concluded that in this round the positions DTe and GTS came closer in a number of ways. The willingness of the parties to consider the meaning of the proposed approaches and the consequences thereof paved the way for a more constructive relationship. In July 2002, GTS published its Tariff Statement for 2003 (GTS 2002b) and shortly thereafter, in August, DTe published the Guidelines 2003 (DTe 2002d,e) for transport and storage. It was the aim to extend the sell-by date of these Guidelines, at least until any new radical changes would be required. And, in general, it can be observed that the perspectives came closer again.

The Guidelines 2003 maintained the distinction between GTS and the local distribution networks. The former was allowed to base its tariffs on *market value*, whereas the distributors' tariffs should be based on incurred cost. In respect of the balancing regime, it was announced that GTS would have to acquire gas supply flexibility from GT&S, to be made available in addition to its own line-pack capacity to shippers, separate from gas supplies by GT&S. Moreover, DTe required an adjustment of the tolerance regime, with a declining tolerance at lower temperatures, to allow for the associated throughput requirements of the system. Therewith, in principle, the short-term balancing problem to shippers could be solved, at a cost. GTS also announced the introduction of an entry–exit tariff system with only a moderate impact of distances, in combination with the provision of a short-term and a short-haul transport service, essentially along the lines of DTe's wishes. In addition to this, GTS introduced the *Title Transfer Facility* (TTF), through which shippers would be allowed to trade volumes of gas plus required transport service when these volumes were already in the transmission network. Other important features that came into development were a secondary market for transport contracts, interruptible transport services and access to quality conversion facilities. There was, however, no reference to the establishment of a *National Balancing Point*. The main comments of the users organizations were, firstly, that the choice for an entry–exit system with fixed nominations for entry and exit points would impede the development of trade within the system and, secondly, the rejection of the cost-plus basis for the GTS tariffs, in favour of the market value principle (EB 2002, no. 8, 3; no. 9, 3).

8.5 The Fifth Round: The Devil is in the Detail

Nevertheless, a number of fundamental impediments remained in place, as was concluded in a report by the Brattle consultancy, hired by DTe. Brattle had identified four main problems to shippers who wished to serve the small customers in 2004. Firstly, there was no access to quality conversion facilities to convert H-gas to L-gas, as most of the capacity was dedicated to Gasunie. Indeed, until 2009 all capacity was contracted (EB, 2004, no. 5, 7). Secondly, there was difficult access to flexibility services, like storage capacity, line-pack, or flexible production. Thirdly, there was lack of firm import capacity to import H-Gas from neighbouring countries. Fourthly, even if competing H-Gas suppliers would be able to obtain the required import capacity, quality conversion capacity, and tolerance services, these suppliers would not be able to offer a reliability comparable to that of the Groningen field.

By early 2004, DTe took over most of these conclusions, and added its own evaluation and proposals to adjust the Guidelines for 2005. It also explicitly asked interested parties to react on the information and questions presented. Interestingly, for quite a few of the observed problems, no solutions could be formulated, as yet (DTe, 2004a; EB 2004, no. 2, 2).On the basis of this information, DTe formulated its draft Guidelines 2005 (2004b,c). These Guidelines contained a number of novelty features in response to the issues referred to above. The many reactions of involved actors and interest groups to this draft were taken on board (see EB 2004, no. 6, 8) and, with a slight delay DTe eventually published the definitive Guidelines 2005 (DTe 2004d,e). A *basic backhaul* service (Art. 3) was expected to enhance the import capacity, as the inflow of gas into the Netherlands without capacity expansion could be achieved by reducing the outflow of exported gas. In respect of Balancing (Art. 6), DTe strove to stimulate an efficient use of transmission system without jeopardizing the integrity of the system, to this end it aimed to achieve an efficient maintenance of system balance through penalties that reflect the costs incurred and the establishment of a gas spot market. It also sought to establish a secondary market for interruptible services (Art. 10). Other crucial elements were the stimulation of transparency and information management (Art. 11 and 12), the socialization of the cost–based fixed element in the conversion tariffs, plus a variable element (Art. 22) and the differentiation between the fees for firm, basic and interruptible services (Art. 23).

In response to the new Guidelines, GTS published its Tariff Statement for 2005. The position of GTS had changed, as it had become the Dutch TSO, operating legally independent from Gasunie NV, with its own Council of Commissioners. The network, however, remained an asset owned by Gasunie, while Gasunie Technology and Assets would undertake its maintenance and expansion. Main elements to the statement were the socialization of the variable cost of conversion in the entry tariffs, although there was no conversion capacity available. Moreover, there was an adjustment and a stabilization of the connection fee, which had been calculated on a capacity relative basis until then. Further elements were a reduction of the nomination time to the day-ahead trade and the announcement that there would be a shift in the measurement units from standard cubic meters to kWh. In the meantime, discussions are taking place on the establishment of a spot market, operated by APX, and executed by GTS on the Title Transfer Facility (TTF) (EB, 2004, no. 9, 7).

9 INTERPRETATION AND CONCLUDING REMARKS

It has been shown above that the restructuring of the Dutch gas sector went hand in hand with the growth of an increasingly detailed body of regulation, to implement the broadly formulated provisions of the EU directives of 1998 and 2004, via the Dutch Gas Acts of 2000 and 2004 into the DTe Guidelines and the Gasunie Tariff statements, which set the scene for specific business routines. Each subsequent edition of these sets of rules covered more aspects at a higher degree of fine-tuning than its predecessor, thus providing an increasingly stringent formulation of the regulatory approaches and instruments to be applied. In terms of our theoretical perspective, outlined in section 2, the emergence of this body of regulation can be understood and explained, in part, as a sequence of 'discoveries'.

Using Callon's framework (1998b), we can distinguish the following stylized steps in this process of (re)framing: (1) the identification of external effects, i.e. unframed functions and aspects; (2) identification of actors involved and their roles; (3) the measurement of perceived externalities and their valuation; and (4) negotiations for a revised frame, i.e. the new regulatory approach. Transactions within the new framework, thereupon, yielded new experiences and insights that drove a new round of framing, as the incentives were found to be sufficient.

The essential conclusion is that the process of regulation is not – and cannot be – a one-shot exercise. It will be an ongoing series of sequences. In respect of the *first* step, the identification of unframed functions and aspects, it was argued that in the traditional system, generic functionalities of the gas system, like transport, the provision of hourly, daily and seasonal flexibility and the adjustment of gas quality had been embedded, or framed in Callon's terms, within the overall framework and business routines of the public–private partnership around Gasunie. Yet, once the Dutch government began to dismantle this structure post-1996, step by step, these complex technical, economic and commercial functionalities of the pre-existing gas supply system were unravelled. These functions began to 'escape' from the old framework as external aspects. It became the plight of the actors involved to re-frame these aspects in the newly emerging system, based on the 'competitive' market paradigm, as outlined in the EU Directives and the Gas Acts, supervised by DTe.

Right from the start in 1999, DTe did embark on a journey, to separate the potentially competitive segments from the essential facilities in the gas value chain, in such a way that *shippers*, via transparent contracts, could purchase their *essential* transport and other system needs, on cost-based conditions. The traditional central coordination of the system was to be substituted by commercial transactions, in which shippers would have to contract a portfolio of gas supplies from producers, traders or GT&S, at a specific location and time, and conversion and transport services, in such a way that they would be able to meet both their commercial obligations and the system requirements of GTS. The shippers, thus, would be able to economize on delivery costs, purchasing only those services that were strictly necessary to carry out a transaction, while the gas – as a commodity – was to be provided by competing suppliers. Hence, a 'well-functioning', efficient, self-coordinating gas market was expected to evolve. Reframing in the context of this system occurred only gradually, via the DTe Guidelines, the GTS access regime and via the private storage and other activities by actors in the market, in a continuing discussion between the several actors, as was shown in section 4.

In respect of the *second* step, it was observed in section 4.1 that the new system implicated an expanding set of actors, as compared to the initial situation. With this, came an increasingly complex set of actor perspectives, as regards their roles in the market and their perceptions of the measurement and valuation of the functionalities to be framed. The question of the identification of issues of relevance became highly associated with the evolution of the actors' perspectives – and thus of their investments. Gradually, actors moved from a rather schematic, economic textbook-like, perspective of the market – with all sorts of untested theoretical assumptions – towards a more realistic real world perspective on the operation of the Dutch gas supply system, and their role therein. The several external advisors and consultants played interesting roles in underscoring and gaining acceptance for the principles and attributes of the regulatory concepts advanced by the several parties, or by making the experiences in other markets available to the Dutch scene (see for example Jacobs Consultancy 2001, 2003; Jepma et al. 2001). By means of investing in such studies, DTe, Gasunie and others obviously did influence the process of institution building, *á la* North and Callon.

In respect of the *third* step, the measurement and valuation, the discussion that arose between Gasunie, DTe and the shippers was about the way in which the technical and economic functionalities of the Dutch gas system were identified and given shape institutionally, and about the way the economic costs and rents would be divided over the parties. The public hearings organized by DTe, around the Guidelines and the allegations submitted by the several parties, illustrated that the outcome of the debate on the restructuring – by definition – never could have been satisfying to all, as fundamental conflicts of interest were at stake. Nevertheless, a process of learning and conciliation made the actors aware of the broader perspective. Initially, new entrants' lobbying organizations, independent traders and large consumers chose to depict transport, the provision of flexibility and the adjustment of gas quality as essential facilities controlled by the incumbent, the access to which thus had to be regulated on a cost-plus basis. They shared this perspective with DTc, taking for granted that the current transport, storage and treatment capacity was sufficient. Also the task of technical and long-term economic coordination was considered an unproblematic responsibility of GTS. This implied that long-term system integrity, essentially, did become external to the overall framework of coordination.

So, a complicated discussion arose about the functionality, the divisibility and the valuation of the several services and facilities in the system, like the provision of hourly, daily and seasonal flexibility, the role of the different balancing, storage and blending facilities in the value chain, the procedures to set priorities in transport and capacity allocation, the costing and funding approaches, etc. In this discussion, Gasunie came out with a double-edged sword.

On the one hand, it highlighted the complex, integral character of its operations and the valuable public task it performed. As the Dutch transport system operator, GTS had to maintain the technical and economic integrity of the transport system and its associated functions, like the technical facilitation of the small-fields policy, security of peak delivery in the winter seasons, etc. Traditionally, grid integrity had been maintained through a degree of excess capacity and tight coordination, the separate cost components of which had been internalized in a manner unnoticed and incalculable by outsiders. The way in which a new system of decentralized coordination based on market instruments would develop was a large question. It is evident that the *shippers* by and large lack the necessary overview. The operator, in contrast, is able to manage the system more effectively, also because it can take decisions that are not directly related to specific individual supply contracts, or portfolios. Moreover, it is precisely in a market environment with many short-term transactions that the capacity requirements in specific elements of the system are difficult to estimate, while the use and the cost of these elements cannot be attributed unambiguously to specific gas flows or customers. To secure a sufficient level of supply security, it is necessary to maintain a slight over-dimension of the system and a higher degree of interconnection of its constituting elements, relative to the supply and demand levels at specific locations in the system.

On the other hand, Gasunie hinted at the contestability and potential substitutability of some of the functions – even transport – and demanded negotiated access conditions and tariffs for its services at market-based prices. As was shown above, already in the first round, it had split up its one-size-fits-all tariff, thus 'revealing' the separate elements comprising a gas supply transaction. Indeed, GT&S had its commercial position in selling the lion's share of the indigenously produced Dutch gas at home and abroad at a maximum economic rent, with the challenge to defend its position in the newly emerging context of the liberalizing Dutch and European gas market, with imports from the UK and elsewhere. Of course, the double position of Gasunie, as the incumbent gas supplier and system operator, with a fundamental strategic role as the gatekeeper to the Dutch system, was inherently problematic. Indeed, every argument made on behalf of GTS system integrity could be – and was – interpreted as a strategic move to protect GT&S market share. But, obviously, the positions of the traders and of Gasunie were also exclaimed with an eye towards the *fourth* step in the process, namely the further negotiations on the regulatory framework with DTe and the Ministry of Economic Affairs, possibly the judge's verdict and the accelerating political process in Parliament.

A final factor, although not discussed in detail in this analysis, was that the role of the Dutch Parliament became increasingly important; it added a large number of elements to the regulatory structure, via amendments to the proposed Gas Act and subsequent 'reparations' to the Electricity and the Gas Acts. Often these elements were related to security of supply issues and protection of the position of the captive consumers. It constitutes a clear example of the reintegration of elements of the traditional 'public values', into the newly established market-based system, upon discovering – or just being worried – that this system is unable to take these issues into account adequately.

It goes without saying that the discussions referred to above reflected the interest and the strategy of the parties, defending their perceived economic, strategic and political interests in the evolving system of regulation. But, it is precisely in this struggle for a favorable reframing of elements within the new system that the important role for learning and for experiences comes out. The roles and perspectives of the actors were a mixture of their past and their new – but still undefined – position. What has become abundantly clear is that these several actors had only a very partial idea of what they could expect from each other, and from themselves, in a technical as well as a behavioural sense. Experience and the reflective examination thereof inspired thorough changes in actors' perspectives.

A fascinating aspect constitutes the evolution of the notion of the market as a coordinative device, often depicted as 'the invisible hand'. In the context of the complex Dutch gas system, apparently the expanding requirements of market and system information, to facilitate its coordination, made the coordinative mechanism step-by-step more visible and explicit. This enhanced insight, eventually, brought the rather divergent initial views together, highlighting and framing the newly emerging relationships between the several parties, as can be observed in the more recent stages of the process. It, of course, also inspired new controversies.

In general, this chapter underscores the hypothesis that the major challenge to a government, or regulator, may not be the *ex-ante* choice for an ideal market and ownership structure and a 'superior' regulatory approach that promises voters and customers much choice, low prices and innovation. These rigid derivatives of the *structure–conduct–performance* paradigm take no notice of the processes of discovery and learning that we have highlighted in this chapter. It should be acknowledged explicitly that the industry – including the incumbent – is drawn into a process of learning and discovery in respect of their new business practices and strategies. Those firms that learn, adapt or lobby most effectively will benefit more than others. Customers will have to learn to choose, to express and to value their preferences. Public authorities will have to reformulate and rediscover the content and form of the public values they aim to secure and the way to do that. The regulator, finally, will have to design – and publicly communicate – an effective and efficient *process of regulation*, that allows for the gradual re-framing of systems' functionalities within a gradually developing new system of coordination. Regulation, indeed, will never be 'finished' and the regulator will always be 'too late'...

NOTES

1   An example of such a 'decision model', with some built-in reserves, is found in Aalbers et al. (2002).

2   HTTP://europa.eu.int/comm/energy/gas/madrid/1_en.htm

3   DTe is an acronym for Dienst Toezicht Elektriciteitssector which means
     Supervisory Agency for the Electricity sector. Later it was changed to Dienst
     Toezicht Energiesector.

4.   Already in 1994 on- and off-shore operators – formerly tied by Gasunies right
     of first refusal and its favourable off-take conditions – have been given the
     explicit freedom to sell their gas to customers other than Gasunie, as a
     consequence of the passing of the European Hydrocarbons Directive (RL
     94/22/EG. PB, 1994, L164).

5.   Therewith we deliberately do not focus on the process by which DTe was
     developing its RPI-X regime for the regulation of transmission and distribution
     tariffs. This equally illustrative process is described elsewhere (Nillesen and
     Pollitt 2004; de Jong et al. 2004).

REFERENCES

Aalbers, R., E. Dijkgraaf, M. Varkevisser and H.R.J. Vollebergh (2002), 'Welvaart
     en de regulering van netwerksectoren', 02 ME 12, Den Haag: Ministerie van
     Economische Zaken,
     http://www.few.eur.nl/few/research/pubs/ocfeb/documents/welvaartsam.pdf ,
     14 December 2004.

Agrell, P. and P. Bogetoft (2004), *Evolutionary Regulation: From CPI-X towards
     contestability*, Position paper for ENCORE, The Netherlands Network for
     competition and regulation, delivered 2004-02-16, SUMICSID AB.

BET, Büro für Energiewirtshaft und Technische Planung GmbH (2001), 'Final
     Report Technical Study Gas Storage', www.dte.nl, 16 May.

Baldwin, R. and M. Cave (1999), *Understanding Regulation: Theory, Strategy and
     Practice*, Oxford, UK: Oxford University Press.

Berg, S.V., M.G. Pollitt and M. Tsuji (2002), *Private Initiatives in Infrastructures:
     Priorities, Incentives and Performance,* Cheltenham, UK: Edward Elgar.

Brattle, The, Group (2000), *Dte Implementation of the Gas Act*, London, UK: The
     Brattle Group, Ltd..

Brattle, The, Group (2002), *Access to Storage in The Netherlands,* London, UK: The
     Brattle Group.

Callon, M. (1998a), 'Introduction: The Embeddedness of Economic Markets in
     Economics', *The Laws of the Markets*, The Sociological Review, Oxford, UK:
     Blackwell Publishers.

Callon, M. (1998b), 'An Essay on Framing and Overflowing: Economic Externalities revisted by sociology', In *The Laws of the Markets, The Sociological Review*, Oxford, UK: Blackwell Publishers.

CEC (Commission of the European Communities) (1988), 'De Interne Energiemarkt', *Energie in Europa*, Speciale Uitgave, Brussel: Commissie van de Europese Gemeenschappen, DG XVII (COM(88) 238 def.).

CEC (Commission of the European Communities) (2003), 'Proposal for a Regulation of the European Parliament and of the Council on Conditions for Access to the Gas Transmission Networks' (presented by the Commission), COM(2003), 741 final, 2003/0302 (COD) Brussels, 10 December 2003.

CEC (Commission of the European Communities) (2004), 'Third Benchmarking Report on the Implementation of the Internal Electricity and Gas Market', DG for Transport and Energy, Brussels, 01 March 2004.

Coase, R.H. (1960), 'The Problem of Social Cost', *Journal of Law and Economics*, 3, 1–44.

Correljé, A.F. (1997), 'Naar nieuwe verhoudingen in het energiebeleid', in W. Hout and M. Sie Dhian Ho (eds), *Aanpassing onder druk: Nederland en de gevolgen van de internationalisering*, Assen, NL: Van Gorcum, pp. 165–78.

Correljé, A.F./, J.C. van der Linde and T. Westerwoudt (2003b), *Natural Gas in the Netherlands: From cooperation to competition?* The Hague: Clingendael International Energy Programme/Oranje Nassau.

Correljé, A.F. (2004), 'Markets for Natural Gas', in C. Cleveland (ed.), *Encyclopedia of Energy Volume „* Amsterdam: Academic Press Reference Series, Elsevier Science, pp. 799–808.

Damme, van E. (2004), 'Pragmatic Privatization: The Netherlands 1982–2002' TILEC Discussion Paper DP 2004-007, Tilburg: CentER and TILEC, Tilburg University.

Demsetz, H. (1968), 'Why Regulate Utilities?', *Law and Economics*, 11.

DTe (2000), *Tijdelijke Richtlijnen 2001*, DTe: Den Haag.

DTe (2001a), *Richtlijnen Gaswet Consultatie- en informatiedocument 2001*, Den Haag: Dienst Toezicht Energiesector, juni 2001.

DTe (2001b), *Richtlijnen Gas transport 2002*, Den Haag: Dienst Toezicht Energiesector, augustus 2001.

DTe (2001c), *Richtlijnen Gasopslag 2002*, Den Haag: Dienst Toezicht Energiesector, augustus 2001.

DTe (2002a), *Bindende Aanwijzing 100554/15*, Den Haag: Dienst Toezicht Energiesector.

DTe (2002b), *Ontwerp Richtlijn Gastransport 2003*, Den Haag: Dienst Toezicht Energiesector.

DTe (2002c), *Ontwerp Richtlijnen Gasopslag 2003*, Den Haag: Dienst Toezicht Energiesector.

DTe (2002d), *Richtlijn Gastransport 2003*, Den Haag: Dienst Toezicht Energiesector.

DTe (2002e), *Richtlijn Gasopslag 2003*, Den Haag: Dienst Toezicht Energiesector.

DTe (2004a), *Onderzoek Ontwikkeling Gasmarkt, Informatie- en consultatie document*, Den Haag: Dienst Toezicht Energiesector, Januari 2004.

DTe (2004b), *Toelichting Ontwerp-Richtlijnen Gastransport 2005*, Den Haag: Dienst Toezicht Energiesector.

DTe (2004c), *Ontwerp-Richtlijnen Gastransport 2005*, Den Haag: Dienst Toezicht Energicsector.

DTe (2004d), *Toelichting op Wijziging Richtlijnen Gastransport 2005*, Den Haag: Dienst Toezicht Energiesector.

DTe (2004e), *Richtlijnen Gastransport 2005*, Den Haag: Dienst Toezicht Energiesector.

EB (1996–2004) Energiebeurs Bulletin: onafhankelijk nieuws- en opinieblad over de energiemarkt, F&B, Hilversum.

Foreman-Peck, J. and R. Milward (1994), *Public and Private ownership of British Industry 1820–1990*, Oxford UK: Clarendon Press.

Friedman, M. (1962), *Capitalism and Freedom*, Chicago, US: Chicago University Press.

Ferguson, P.R. (1988), *Industrial Economics: Issues and Perspectives*, London, UK: Macmillan Education Ltd.

GTS (2001), *Indicatieve tarieven en voorwaarden voor transport en noodzakelijkerwijs daarmee verbonden diensten 2002*, Groningen, NL: Gasunie Transport Services.

GTS (2002b), 'Nadere invulling en detaillering Transporttarieven 2003', Groningen: Gasunie Transport Services, http://www.gastransport.nl/_nl/tt/pdf/2002-07-12%20Transporttarieven%202003%20ev%20_ned-website_.pdf, 19 juli.

Haaland Matláry, J. (1997), *Energy Policy in the European Union*, Houndmills, UK: Macmillan.

Harris, D.and C. Lapuerta, (2003), *Wholesale Gas Competition in the Netherlands and Implications for Phase III Customers*, London, UK: The Brattle Group, Ltd.

Helm, D. (2003), *Energy, the State and the Market: British Energy Policy since 1979*, Oxford, UK: Oxford University Press.

Jacobs Consultancy (2001), *(Non-confidential version of) Evaluation of Gasunie Balancing Regime Part 2*, Leiden, NL: The Jacobs Consultancy Nederland, 28 September 2001.

Janssen, M.C.W. (2004), 'De weg naar marktwerking is duister en zelden aangenaam', Paper geschreven ter gelegenheid van de workshop Managing Transition, Den Haag: ENCORE i.s.m. Kenniscentrum voor Ordeningsvraagstukken, Ministerie van Economische Zaken (mimeo) http://www.encore.nl/publications/paper_janssen.pdf, 4 maart.

Jepma, C.J., M ten Hoopen and J. Bandsma (2001), 'Gaslevering onder druk: Invloed van de Richtlijnen van de de DTe op de Nederlandse gasstromen', Groningen, NL: Joint Implementation Network, The Netherlands. http://jiq.wiwo.nl/jepma.pdf 14 December 2004.

Juris, A. (1998), *The Emergence of Markets in the Natural Gas Industry*, Policy Research Working Paper, 1895, Washington, US: The World Bank.

Kirzner, I.M. (1997), 'Entrepreneurial Discovery and the Competitive Market Process: An Austrian Approach', *Journal of Economic Literature*, 35 (1).

Knops, H.P.A., L.J. deVries and A.F. Correljé (2004), *Beleidskeuze(s) belicht: Beleidskeuzes voor de inrichting van de elektriciteits- en de gassector in Nederland*, Den Haag, NL: Wetenschappelijk Instituut voor het CDA.

Köper, N. (2003), *Tegenpolen: de Liberalisering van de Nederlandse Energiemarkt*, Utrecht, NL: Het Spectrum.

Laffont, J.J. and J. Tirole (1993), *A Theory of Incentives in Procurement and Regulation*, Cambridge, US and London, UK: The MIT Press.

Littlechild, S. C. (1983), *Regulation of British Telecommunication's Profitability*, Department of Industry, London, UK: HMSO.

Ministerie van Economische Zaken (MEZ) (1962), *Nota inzake het aardgas* (Kamerstukken II, 1961-1962, nr. 6767): *NOTA DE POUS*.

Ministerie van Economische Zaken (MEZ) (1995), *Derde Energienota 1996*, Kamerstukken II 1995-1996, 24 525, nrs. 1-2.

Ministerie van Economische Zaken (MEZ) (1997), *Gasstromen: discussienota*, Den Haag.

Ministerie van Economische Zaken (MEZ) (2001), *Brief aan de Voorzitter van de Tweede Kamer der Staten Generaal*, 19 November 2001, ME/EP/01059539.

Ministerie van Economische Zaken (MEZ) (2002), *Brief aan de Voorzitter van de Tweede Kamer der Staten Generaal*, 8 April 2002, ME/EP/02018310.

Nelson, R.R. and S.G. Winter (1982), *An Evolutionary Theory of Economic Change*, Cambridge, US: The Belknap Press of Harvard University Press.

Nelson, R.R. and B.N. Sampat (2001), 'Making sense of Institutions as a Factor Shaping Economic Performance', *Journal of Economic Behaviour & Organization*, 44, 31–54.

Newbery, D.M. (2000), *Privatization, Restructuring and Regulation of Network Utilities,* Cambridge, US and London, UK: The MIT Press.

Nillesen, P.H.L. and M. Pollitt (2004), *The Consequences for Consumer Welfare of the 2001–2003 Electricity Distribution Price Review in the Netherlands*, Cambridge Working Papers in Economics CWPE 0446/CMI Working Paper 50, Cambridge, US: University of Cambridge.

North, D.C. (1990), *Institutions, Institutional Change and Economic Performance*, Cambridge, US: Cambridge University Press.

North, D.C. (1994), 'Economic performance Through Time', *The American Economic Review*, 84 (3), 359–68.

Parker, M.J. (2000), *Thatcherism and the Fall of Coal*, Oxford, UK: Oxford University Press.

Robinson C. (2000), 'Energy Economists and Economic Liberalism', *Energy Journal*, 21 (2), 1–22.

Roggenkamp, M.M. and J.A.M. Bos (2001), *Energieliberalisatie in Nederland*, Antwerpen, BE and Groningen, NL: Intersentia Rechtswetenschappen.

Scherer, F.M. (1980), *Industrial Market Structure and Economic Performance* (2nd. ed), Boston, US: Houghton Mifflin Comp.

Shuttleworth, G. (2000), *Opening European Electricity and Gas Markets*, London, UK: National Economic Research Associates.

Stiglitz, J. (1986), *Economics of the Public Sector*, New York, US: W.W. Norton and Company.

Thomas, S. (2002), 'Evaluating the British Model of Electricity Deregulation', *Annals of Public and Cooperative Economics,* 75 (3), 367–98.

Thomas, S. (2004), 'The Seven Brothers', *Energy Policy*, 31, 393–403.

Vogelsang, I. (2003), 'Price Regulation Access to Telecommunications Networks', *Journal of Economic Literature*, 41, 830-62.

Weisman, D.L. and J.P. Pfeifenberger (2003), 'Efficiency as a Discovery Process: Why Enhanced Incentives Outperform Regulatory Mandates', *The Electricity Journal*, January/February 2003, 55–62.

PART TWO

Outcomes

6. Regulated Mixed Firms: Does Continued State Ownership Bias Regulation? The Case of European Telecommunications

Johannes M. Bauer

---

1 INTRODUCTION[1]

Throughout most of the twentieth century, government regulation and public ownership were considered as alternative means of governing network utility industries such as energy and telecommunications. In the US, privately owned public utilities served the majority of customers and were regulated by specialized federal and state agencies. Government owned entities, like the federal power projects or municipal enterprises, were essentially exempted from oversight by the regulatory agencies. Outside of North America, state ownership was dominant. Government oversight was executed through parliament and ministries but no specialized regulatory agencies were established. This started to change during the 1990s, when in many countries liberalization progressed faster than privatization, forcing new market entrants to compete against wholly or partially state-owned incumbents. Where regulation was deemed necessary, the newly created agencies were granted jurisdiction over both privately and publicly owned firms.

This hitherto untested arrangement is now widespread in energy and telecommunications outside of North America. For example, in 2000, regulatory agencies oversaw telecommunications operators with significant public ownership stakes in nine of the fifteen member states of the European Union (EU). In some countries this arrangement was the outcome of deliberate policies to retain direct government control over telecommunications networks. In other nations it emerged as a by-product of stalled privatization, often due to unfavourable conditions in the capital markets. As the privatization process has stagnated in recent years, it is unlikely that regulated public firms will be a transitory phenomenon. The coincidence of state ownership and regulation has created apprehension and support. From a laissez faire ideological perspective, continued state ownership is seen as an anomaly (Yergin and Stanislaw 1998). It is also pointed out that state regulation of public firms is reminiscent of the past, when state monopolies regulated their own markets. Replicating past experience, the dual role of the state as regulator and (part) owner would inevitably lead to regulatory bias against new entrants (Noll 2000). Proponents of both views advocate accelerated privatization. In contrast, recent research in information economics and contract theory insinuates that the combination of government regulation and ownership could mitigate asymmetric information problems hampering the regulation of private firms. The validity of these claims has not yet been tested and is the subject of this chapter.

Although it raises interesting theoretical and practical issues, the behaviour of public and mixed firms under regulation has not been studied systematically. Two aspects are explored in this chapter, using European telecommunications to probe the conceptual arguments. Firstly, the interaction between regulatory agencies and publicly owned enterprises is examined. Does full or partial state ownership bias regulation in favour of these firms? Conversely, do regulators, to avoid the appearance of improper oversight, adopt more stringent measures that potentially disadvantage public and mixed service providers? Or is regulation neutral with regard to ownership? Secondly, the role of continued public ownership in an era of increasing trust in competition and market forces is reviewed. Are regulated public and mixed enterprise used as instruments of government policy to achieve goals unattainable through private enterprise? If so, what are the performance consequences for individual firms and the sector? Or do public and mixed firms behave like private corporations?

The theme is developed as follows. A conceptual framework to study the interaction of ownership, competition, and regulation in regulated public and mixed firms is presented in the next section. The chapter proceeds with a review of the changing role of the state in EU telecommunications. The fifth section examines the practical experience with regulated state-owned firms. In addition to summarizing the main findings the last section presents policy conclusions and questions for further research. In a nutshell, the chapter finds hints but no systematic pattern of favourable or damaging regulatory treatment of public and mixed firms. Thus, overall the new regulatory agencies have demonstrated an astonishing ability to serve as non-partisan referees of the competitive process in the EU. Neither does the chapter find compelling evidence that continued state ownership serves unique public interest goals beyond the reach of regulated private firms. Whereas circumstances are identified in which public ownership could help overcome the limits of markets and regulation, it is unlikely that such policies will be adopted given the present low trust in the public sector. Thus, while there may be no strong reason for accelerated privatization from a competitive point of view, there is also little evidence that further privatization would jeopardize vital public policy goals.

2 REGULATED PUBLIC AND MIXED FIRMS

Compared to the vast literature on ownership, competition, and regulation (e.g., Vickers and Yarrow 1988; Newbery 1999), the published research on partially state-owned ('mixed') firms is slim (Eckel and Vining 1985; Boardman and Vining 1989; Boardman and Vining, 1991). Property rights interact with the competitive setup and the regulatory framework of a market as a system of incentives, affecting decision-making and performance at the firm and sector levels (Vickers and Yarrow 1988). In addition, the courts have an important role in resolving disputes and assuring that all actors follow legal and regulatory provisions. As well, antitrust enforcement affects firm conduct and industry performance. Although the role of the courts and antitrust is important, a detailed treatment would have exceeded the scope of this chapter and was not pursued further. This approach seemed justified by the fact that EU stakeholders have access not only to the national courts but also the European Court of Justice, creating a fairly homogenous system of law enforcement and antitrust supervision throughout the EU.

The interaction of ownership, regulation and competition as a system of incentives in regulated public, mixed and private firms is depicted in Figure 6.1 (see also Sappington and Stiglitz 1987). In regulated private firms, competition and monitoring by private shareholders jointly affect the level of efficiency. Regulation intends to secure the preconditions for effective competition or serves as a substitute for it. Moreover, it attempts to steer private firms toward a desired level of social output (e.g., universality of service). In the case of regulated public and mixed firms, this two-pronged incentive structure is muddled, as both regulation and public ownership may be utilized to enforce social output goals. Because the goals of owners and regulators typically diverge, this arrangement can create considerable strain.

Figure 6.1   Governance relations under regulation

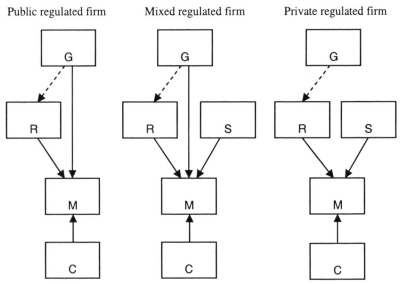

G = government, M = management, R = regulatory agency, S = shareholders, C = competition

However, the combination of regulation and (partial) public ownership could also help overcome structural limits of regulation. For example, regulators can only provide investment incentives but cannot directly decide its level and structure. This lack of control can undermine public policies intended to foster infrastructure expansion and modernization. Public ownership could provide an additional lever to overcome this governance problem.[2] Public ownership may also alleviate the asymmetry of information between the regulatory agency and the firm (Shapiro and Willig 1995).[3] Mixed regulated firms could therefore be seen as an institutional arrangement in which private ownership safeguards efficiency, whereas regulation and partial public ownership assure social output. As regulated public and mixed firms combine incentive mechanisms in unusual and potentially contradictory ways, a brief review of the role of ownership, competition and regulation is useful before their interaction is explored further.

Early theories of public ownership simply assumed that government could utilize state-owned firms as instruments of public policy (Thiemeyer 1993). In practice, managers of public firms operate in a complex political environment. Several government agencies (e.g., legislature, ministries) act as principals, either simultaneously or at different points in time. Their heterogeneous objectives may result in conflicting demands on management (Aharoni; 1986). Strong unionization of state-owned enterprises' employees can further complicate decision-making. Firms operating under public ownership are also shielded from the pressures of the capital and the take-over markets (Vickers and Yarrow 1988). By the same token, as access to the equity market is blocked, they have fewer financing options than private firms. Moreover, managers may be political appointees and therefore indifferent to the reputation effects of poor performance.

The recent literature has demonstrated that the incentive structure of private firms also has serious weaknesses (Nelson 1981; Laffont and Tirole 1993; Willner 2001). Nevertheless, given the organizational set-up of public firms, the utility of state-owned firms' managers will likely be more influenced by 'staff' e than profit π. The recent survey by Megginson and Netter (2001), who find that private firms are more efficient than publicly owned firms, corroborates this conjecture. Empirical observations show a great variance, however: some state-owned firms exhibit extraordinary performance (e.g., Telia, the Swedish telecommunications operator, until recently fully state-owned) and many outperform private rivals (Willner 2001; Kwoka 2002). Moreover, where government officials work in a pragmatic environment, they may succeed in negotiating social objectives with a public firm's management without distorting its performance (Nowotny;1982, Willner 2001).

In contrast to the diversity of findings on ownership, there is consensus that effective competition is a powerful efficiency incentive. Nonetheless, there is a wide range of theories on how competition achieves its beneficial effects (Vickers 1994). Under conditions of stable technology and slow technological change, effective competition prevails if the conditions for actual or potential competition are met (Shepherd 1996; Baumol, Panzar and Willig 1982). The conditions for efficiency are more complicated if technology is dynamic. Schumpeter (1942) pointed out that dynamic efficiency gains frequently can only be achieved at the sacrifice of static efficiency (see also von Weizsäcker 1980). Competition is generally considered a more powerful mechanism than the specification of property rights (Vickers and Yarrow 1988; Newbery 1999).

Regulation was traditionally conceptualized as enforcement of market-like discipline in situations where competition was not effective (e.g., Phillips 1993). With the move to more open market environments, its role has been redefined to secure the preconditions for competition in industries where monopolistic and competitive market segments coexist (Laffont and Tirole 2000). Like monitoring by owners, public regulation has to overcome asymmetric information. Efficient regulation therefore needs to design a system of incentives that induces the desired behaviour (Laffont and Tirole 1993). Effective regulation will shift the outcome toward a higher level of social output and possibly toward a higher level of efficiency.

For the purposes of this chapter, the interplay of these component incentive mechanisms needs to be examined. This question has attracted growing interest and recent empirical studies of telecommunications deserve brief mentioning.[4] In a panel study of the effects of privatization and competition on network expansion and efficiency, Ros (1999) found that in high-income nations private ownership was correlated with significantly wider diffusion of telephone service, faster growth in the number of access lines per capita, and higher labour productivity. However,

Ros did not find any influence of private ownership in countries with a gross domestic product per capita below US$10,000. Boylaud and Nicolctti (2001) combined cluster analysis and panel data to examine telecommunications markets in the OECD. They found that privatization had weakly enhanced efficiency, but that competition had a more decisive influence. In a study of 31 privatised telecommunications firms in 25 countries, Bortolotti, et al. (2002) observed significant increases in post-privatization performance, and that a significant part of the gains was attributable to regulatory change and the introduction of competition. Wallsten (2001) found for a group of 30 African and South American nations that competition was the main source of efficiency improvements. Privatization alone yielded only limited benefits; however, privatization combined with regulation was positively correlated with better performance. Li and Xu (2002) detected that efficiency improvements were highest when privatization and competition were combined. Gutierrez and Berg (2000), Levy and Spiller (1996) and Henisz (2002) emphasize the importance of regulatory commitment and a stable institutional framework for investment as preconditions for good performance. The general tenor emerging from these studies is that the configuration of property rights, competition and regulation is crucial. However, as most of these studies model ownership as a dichotomous dummy variable, they do not directly explore the effects of mixed ownership on performance.

From this brief review – abstracting for a moment from regulation – we would expect that mixed enterprises fall between the public and private cases. Compared to fully private enterprise, we would expect lower efficiency but higher levels of social output. Compared to fully public enterprise, we would expect higher efficiency but no clear ranking with regard to social output. However, these potential advantages may be neutralized by inherent conflicts of interest once regulation is added. For example, the state as an owner may want to delay competition to increase the profitability of the firm or its market value prior to privatization.[5] As the regulated public and mixed firms originated from the monopolies of the past, management may attempt to get protection from competition, perhaps in exchange for social output promises. This is not fundamentally different from private firms seeking protection from a regulatory agency. However, in the case of public and mixed firms, management may have more effective access, as the government-owner is also the principal of the regulator.[6] This risk may be counterbalanced by the fact that national regulatory agencies (NRAs) are relatively new organizations, subject to review by the courts and close scrutiny by the public. Under pressure to show tangible improvements, regulators may adopt a stringent and even vindictive attitude towards public and mixed firms. Given these concerns, the clearer incentive structure created by the regulation of private firms may, after all, constitute a superior arrangement to achieve efficiency and social output goals. An answer to these questions can only be given empirically and will be pursued in section 4 after a synopsis of the telecommunications reform process in Europe.

3   PRIVATIZATION AND REGULATORY REFORM IN EU TELCOMMUNICATIONS

Since the 1980s, the European Commission, Council, Parliament, and Court of Justice have accelerated and harmonized national policies to open markets and introduce transparent regulation. Shaped by nearly 30 directives from the European Commission and the Council since 1988, terminal equipment, value-added services, mobile services, cable services, and satellite services were liberalized. In 1998, restrictions to enter the remaining non-competitive areas – basic services and network infrastructure – were eliminated (Hulsink 1999; Jordana 2002).[7] In contrast to its liberalization measures, the EU did not stipulate any particular ownership regime but left the choice to national governments. This position was the outcome of two considerations. Given different national preferences, it could avoid a heated debate on state ownership issues and secure agreement on the basic liberalization blueprint. Moreover, it reflected the pragmatic stance that competition was more important than ownership for sector efficiency.

Different patterns emerged from national struggles between proponents and opponents of privatization. During the 1990s, all European nations but Luxembourg sold shares of Public Telecommunications Operators (PTOs) to private investors. To avoid stressing the stock market and to bolster sales revenues, privatization typically occurred in slices. By the end of 2000, EU member states had conducted 33 partial sales. Britain, which had begun privatization in 1984, and Denmark had fully relinquished ownership rights; Portugal and Spain had only retained a 'golden' share. In Ireland and Italy the public sector had reduced its holdings to a minute 1.1 per cent and 3.5 per cent of equity capital, respectively.[8] In some countries, for example Germany and France, tentative plans for the privatization of further slices of the PTO were announced but delayed by political developments and the unpredictability of the stock market. Austria, Belgium, and Ireland sold minority stakes to publicly owned or partially privatized PTOs from other EU countries (Elixmann and Wörter 2001).

Figure 6.2 illustrates the expansion of private ownership in European telecommunications between 1990 and 2000. It depicts the number of fixed access lines supplied by fully state-owned, mixed, and private PTOs. Mixed ownership is further differentiated into 'mixed—public' for firms with a majority public ownership stake and 'mixed–private' for firms with a minority public ownership stake. In 1990, state-owned PTOs provided 62 per cent and mixed PTOs 38 per cent of all fixed access lines (there were no private PTOs). Ten years later, this picture had clearly shifted. Fully state-owned PTOs supplied only 2 per cent of the access lines. Despite the decline in full state ownership, mixed PTOs supplied 68 per cent, and fully private PTOs 27 per cent of all fixed access lines. In addition, new entrants had captured a small fraction of 3 per cent of the access lines.[9]

Figure 6.2   Shifting boundaries of the state (percent of fixed access lines by ownership form)

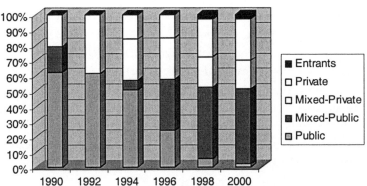

Source: OECD Communications Outlooks (various years), own calculations.

To safeguard liberalization, the EU mandated the separation of operation and regulation that had historically been vested in the state-owned PTOs. In 1990, only the UK had established an independent regulatory agency. As a precondition for the full liberalization of the telecommunications markets in 1998, all member states were required to set up regulators. These national regulatory authorities (NRAs) differ with respect to their degree of independence and therefore their susceptibility to pressure from government, an issue that will be examined in more detail below.

4   METHOD AND FINDINGS

Several approaches are possible to study the two questions posed in this chapter, including case studies of the interaction of regulators and public firms, an examination of complaint records, or an investigation of regulatory and court decisions. However, as capture can happen tacitly or even unknowingly, it may be difficult to uncover with case-oriented methods. Moreover, complaints and court decisions could be seen as instances of working institutional safeguards, unless there is a systematic pattern in favour of the incumbent. To avoid these problems, we adopted an alternative, indirect route of reviewing actual conduct and performance indicators. Case information, complaint records and interviews were used in a supplementary way.[10] Empirical tests can be constructed in three ways: using time series data reflecting periods of public, mixed and private ownership (a 'before-and-after approach'); cross-sectional data; or panel data. As longitudinal data were only available for some of the variables, the chapter relies on a cross-national design. Data for all fifteen incumbent European PTOs (one for each EU member state) were collected for the year 2000, the most recent year for which all relevant data was available on a consistent basis. The harmonization of the legal and regulatory framework in the EU reduces national diversity in relevant conditions, easing some of the challenges of cross-national research. Our observations can either be interpreted as reflecting the population of regulated incumbent PTOs in the EU or as a convenience sample of regulated PTOs.

To examine the interaction of regulation and public ownership, it was necessary to establish how an abuse would manifest itself. In a monopolistic environment, capture would likely result in prices above cost or forms of X-inefficiency. In a competitive framework, price increases are limited by actual and potential entry, but incumbents can benefit from regulator-sanctioned entry barriers. Therefore, we collected information on interconnection prices, which are a critical variable affecting entry opportunities. Interconnection allows new entrants to link their networks with existing service providers, thus overcoming the disadvantages created by network externalities, economies of scale, and reputation effects (Brock and Katz 1997). In addition, we reviewed the number of new competitors. Controlling for other factors, an observation that regulated public or mixed firms were allowed to charge higher interconnection rates than private regulated firms or were otherwise shielded from new entrants was interpreted as a distortion of regulation in their favour. Searching for answers to the second question, indicators of government influence on management decisions in pursuit of social output goals had to be identified. Historically, such intervention typically resulted in demands to maintain or expand employment and to provide universal service by using some form of internal subsidy. It could also become visible in demands to keep prices low and offer unified prices across the entire service territory. Either observation was interpreted as a sign of continued government influence in favour of social output goals.

Tables 6.1 and 6.2 summarize descriptive statistics by ownership form. PTOs were classified as 'public' if the state held $x \geq 75$ per cent of the shares; as 'mixed' if the public share was $25\% \leq x < 75\%$; and as 'private' if $x < 25\%$.[11] These thresholds were used as they correspond to business law, which typically empowers owners of more than 25 per cent of the stock with veto rights, giving them considerable clout over management decisions.[12] Population-weighted averages were calculated to correct for varying country size. In addition, the range of observations was determined. Prices for three types of interconnection – double transit, single transit, and local termination, all at peak – were distinguished. Double transit interconnection allows access to all customers on an incumbent's national network. Single transit interconnection allows access to all customers in a metropolitan area. Local termination grants access at a point close to the customer (e.g. a local exchange) (CEC 2001). For this reason, double transit usually incurs the highest and local termination the lowest charge. We found that interconnection price levels were lowest for privately owned and highest for publicly owned PTOs.

Table 6.1   Ownership, interconnection and competition (2000)

	Public	Mixed	Private
PTOs in category	Austria, Luxembourg	Belgium, Finland, France, Germany, Greece, Netherlands, Sweden	Denmark, Ireland, Italy, Portugal, Spain, UK
Interconnection (Euro cents)			
–Double transit	2.53 (1.69–2.58)	2.11 (1.70–2.63)	1.92 (1.54–2.28)
–Single transit	1.63 (1.63–1.69)	1.62 (1.24–1.89)	1.22 (0.90–1.53)
–Local termination	1.05 (1.02–1.69)	0.86 (0.63–1.43)	0.76 (0.62–0.99)
Number of competitors	40 (13–41)	99 (7–167)	137 (24–203)
Number of competitors per million population	6.3 (5–30)	2.3 (1–12)	3.0 (2–10)
PTO market share (%)			
–Local	90 (89–100)	85 (70–100)	85 (68–100)
–Long distance	86 (85–100)	76 (70–99)	73 (59–100)

Note: (Population-weighted averages, range in parentheses)

Sources: CEC (2000), CEC (2001), OECD (2000), OECD (2001), own calculations.

With the exception of single transit, interconnection charges of mixed PTOs fell in between these two cases. The levels of all interconnection prices of public PTOs exceeded the benchmarks established by the Commission of the European Communities (CEC 2000).[13] In the case of mixed PTOs, local termination charges were within the EU limits but single and double transit prices exceeded them. However, the margin by which double transit charges exceeded the benchmark was lower than that of regulated public PTOs. The interconnection prices of privately owned PTOs for local termination and single transit were within the EU limits; however, the charges for double transit exceeded the upper bound by 6.7 per cent.

Whereas these differences can be seen as signs of a strategic use of interconnection charges, they do not represent unequivocal proof. As the debate between proponents and opponents of the Efficient Component Pricing Rule (ECPR) indicates, there is considerable discrepancy among scholars as to the most efficient pricing of interconnection (see Laffont and Tirole 2000 for an overview). Even if there is agreement that long-run incremental cost (LRIC) is the appropriate concept, as is the case in the EU, there are different methods of calculating the charges. Moreover, while higher interconnection prices slow down the entry of new competitors in the short run, they increase new entrants' incentives to invest in substitute facilities. Some authors have argued that EU interconnection prices are so low that they have slowed down facilities-based entry (Cave and Prosperetti 2001). Therefore, while public and mixed PTOs (and to a very limited degree private PTOs) may have been able to get temporary protection from competition, it comes at the cost of more intense facilities-based competition in the medium and long run. Thus, we cautiously interpret the findings as weak proof for a more favourable treatment of public and mixed PTOs.

Table 6.1 also indicates that the absolute number of new licensees was highest in countries with a fully private operator and lowest in nations with a publicly owned operator. However, after correcting for the differing population sizes, nations with publicly owned operators attracted a larger number of new entrants. New competitors were able to gain higher market shares in nations with fully private and mixed ownership of the incumbent PTO, as would be expected given the level of interconnection prices and the number of entrants. They were least successful in penetrating local or long distance markets in nations with a publicly owned operator.

Retail price levels were measured using the standardized OECD baskets for residential and business voice services. The basket methodology includes prorated fixed charges and variable charges representing average calling patterns. It includes important forms of discounts and reflects the overall price level of each PTO (Cherry and Bauer 2002). Prices were lowest for mixed and highest for privately owned PTOs, with public PTOs in between

(Table 6.2). Comparable price data were available for earlier periods. Prices for all PTOs declined between 1997 (the year before full liberalization) and 2000. The prices charged by publicly owned PTOs fell most (22.9 per cent for residential, 40.2 per cent for business) and those for privately owned PTOs the least (19.1 per cent for residential, 25.3 per cent for business). Mixed PTOs were positioned in between, with a decline of 22.2 per cent for residential and 32.7 per cent for business customers.

Table 6.2   Ownership and performance (2000)

	Public	Mixed	Private
Retail prices (US$ PPP)			
– Residential	362	324	375
	(246–368)	(240–396)	(275–491)
– Business	710	676	869
	(444–724)	(456–738)	(467–923)
Profitability (operating	12.1[2]	16.7	20.5
income/revenue, in %)[1]	(n/a)	(9.0–32.7)	(15.8–8.4)
Labor productivity (access	335	297	326
lines per employee)	(325-516)	(280–340)	(221–392)
Teledensity			
– Fixed access lines	49	59	50
	(47–76)	(50–68)	(42–75)
– Access paths (fixed	125	116	120
plus mobile)	(123–161)	(102–140)	(103–135)
% of PTOs under universal			
service policy			
– Explicit funding	0	14	33
– Funding planned	100	29	50
– Unfunded	0	43	17
– No plan	0	14	0
Index of regulatory	6.0	5.6	5.8
Independence	(6.0–6.0)	(4.0–6.0)	(4.0–6.0)

Notes: (1) Data for 1999. (2) Only Austria.
            Population-weighted averages, range in parentheses

Sources: Cherry and Bauer (2002), CEC (2000), CEC (2001), ITU (2002), OECD
            (2000), OECD (2001), own calculations.

This pattern indicates that prices fell more sharply in the more competitive business market and that the differences between public and mixed PTOs have decreased whereas those between PTOs with public ownership and private ones have relatively increased. The lower prices of mixed firms reflect more stringent regulatory regimes and a willingness to grant more downward pricing flexibility.[14]

Teledensity was highest in countries with a mixed PTO and lowest in countries with a public PTO. When mobile phones are taken into account, countries with a public PTO are ahead of those with private and mixed PTOs. This indicates consumers' use of mobiles as substitutes to the fixed voice service and is confirmed by the cancellation of fixed service in nations with high mobile penetration, such as Austria. Nations with public or mixed PTOs relied less on explicit funding mechanisms than nations with private PTOs to finance universal service. This could indicate that public ownership rather than a transparent mechanism was used to enforce a public service goal. However, policy makers consider the net cost low compared to total revenues (CEC 2001).[15] There is also indirect evidence that public and mixed PTOs have reduced their workforce less than private PTOs. Between 1997 and 1999, independently of ownership, PTOs experienced strong and comparable output growth. However, employment data show divergent patterns: public PTOs increased employment by 14.5 per cent, mixed PTOs expanded employment by 5.6 per cent, and private PTOs reduced their workforce by 4.8 per cent. This divergence could indicate a continued concern with high employment levels in PTOs with public and – to a lesser degree mixed – ownership.

To examine the relations between government and regulatory agencies, we constructed a measure of the degree of regulatory independence from an OECD (2000) report. Using a dichotomous coding scheme, regulatory agencies were evaluated based on eight criteria: the independence from the executive branch, the procedure for appointing regulators, financing sources, the ability of the government to overrule regulatory decisions, reporting duties, and three tasks of the agency. Each national regulatory agency received one point if the degree of independence was high and a zero if it was low. NRAs could therefore receive a low score of zero and a high score of eight in case of a highly independent set-up. We hypothesized that the risk of capture by managers of publicly owned firms (or their public owner) would be higher, the less independent an agency. Interestingly, regulatory agencies in nations with publicly owned PTOs enjoyed a slightly higher degree of independence than in nations with fully private PTOs. The score was lowest in nations with mixed PTOs. Although the differences were small, this might indicate that in efforts to maintain a non-partisan reputation of regulatory agencies, a higher degree of independence was chosen in countries pursuing slower privatization. The low score in the case of regulated mixed firms may reflect attempts of the government to secure continued control through ownership and regulation channels.[16]

A descriptive study of the data provides first insights, but it does not unveil multivariate patterns. To this end, the data was also scrutinized with econometric methods. While space constraints prohibit a detailed discussion in this chapter, the results overall corroborated the picture presented so far. All but two of the patterns described in section 4 remained visible after other independent variables were taken into account. Only in the models for double transit interconnection prices and teledensity did ownership not have detectable effects and we could not reject the null hypothesis. However, these effects could only be found when ownership was specified as a continuous variable. No direct evidence of the organization of regulatory agencies or of interaction terms could be found.

5   CONCLUSIONS

This chapter analysed the phenomenon of regulated public and mixed firms through conceptual and empirical lenses. The coexistence of regulation and state ownership emerged from a mismatch in the timing of liberalization and privatization and is now widespread outside the US Two aspects of the new phenomenon were explored. Firstly, we examined potential conflicts of interest between the state as a regulator and owner. Secondly, we explored whether the combination of public ownership and regulation reduced shortcomings of the regulation of private firms. To tackle these questions empirically, data for the incumbent telecommunications operators of the fifteen EU member states were analysed.

With regard to the first question, comparative statistics revealed that interconnection prices by regulated public and mixed PTOs were above those of privately owned PTOs. The interconnection prices of public firms exceeded the EU benchmarks more often and by a higher margin than those of mixed and private firms. Adjusted for population, the number of newly licensed competitors was highest in countries with a publicly owned PTO and lowest in countries with a mixed PTO. The market shares of new competitors in countries with mixed and private PTOs were very similar but they were lower where the incumbent was a regulated public PTO. With regard to the second question, we found that retail prices were lowest for mixed PTOs and highest for privately owned PTOs. Profitability was lowest for public and highest for private PTOs. With regard to a simple partial productivity measure, public PTOs scored better than private and mixed PTOs. Countries with a mixed PTO had the highest teledensity and countries with a public PTO the lowest. However, this result was strongly influenced by the income level of a nation. Regulated public and mixed firms were more often than their private counterparts asked to finance universal service obligations without explicit compensation. However, compared to overall revenues the net costs of these services were considered low by policy-makers. Lastly, although the differences were small, we found that an index of regulatory independence was highest in countries with a publicly owned and lowest in the case of mixed PTOs. In line with the expectations from the conceptual discussion, we found that mixed PTOs outperformed public PTOs with respect to key performance indicators such as prices, profitability and teledensity. Interestingly, mixed PTOs offered their services at lower prices than private PTOs.

These findings amount to a mixed picture. On the one hand, we found hints that regulated public and mixed PTOs derived advantages from the dual roles of the government as owner and regulator, especially with regard to interconnection and downward pricing flexibility. However, there is considerable theoretical disagreement about the correct level of interconnection charges and so far no successful legal challenge has been won against high-price PTOs. We also found counteracting forces and even potential disadvantages. PTOs were generally not shielded from new entrants and they were sometimes constrained in their flexibility (for example, the lay-off of staff). We also found clues that regulated public and mixed PTOs were utilized to pursue universal service goals without explicit compensation, although most countries had plans to move to such a scheme. The empirical observations point to potential tensions between government regulation and ownership, but not a systematic pattern of abuse. This surprising 'ownership neutrality' of regulation is an outcome of the mature legal and institutional framework in the EU, with its high degree of regulatory pragmatism and enforcement by a stable court system.

In line with the findings of other studies, competition was found to be an important aspect of the institutional matrix with respect to prices and teledensity. In an open market framework, only limited room is left to utilize public ownership to pursue policy goals. Rather, regulation becomes the main incentive mechanism to foster social output. Therefore, the ability to use government ownership to overcome some of the limits of regulation is probably limited to monopolistic market segments where public policy retains more degrees of freedom. In principle, and under ideal conditions, public ownership could be used to pursue public policy goals without harming competition, but in the EU this is an unlikely choice given the diminished trust in the ability of government to steer industries. Thus, while we found no compelling reason for accelerated privatization from a competitive point of view, we also found little evidence that further privatization would jeopardize vital public policy goals. However, it would likely reduce the appearance of inappropriateness of the dual role of the state as owner and regulator.

The empirical observations in this chapter represent the universe of regulated incumbent PTOs in the EU. Given its unique institutional setup, especially the integrated approach to communications infrastructure regulation and a stable and capable institutional endowment, care is required when drawing lessons for other countries. In countries with less stable institutional endowments, regulated public and mixed firms may outperform unregulated public and mixed firms, but they may be afflicted with serious disadvantages, combining the worst of the worlds of state ownership and regulation. It would be interesting to expand the research in several directions. As more information becomes available, additional insights could be gained from panel data. Case studies could reveal details of the decision-making process in regulated public and mixed firms. Lastly, the set of observations could be extended to include other nations and industries.

NOTES

1. The author wishes to thank Carol Ting for research assistance. Douglas N. Jones and Jeffrey H. Rohlfs provided helpful comments on an earlier version of the chapter.
2. For example, during the past few years, several US states (e.g., Iowa, Colorado) and cities (e.g., Blacksburg, Virginia or Ashland, Oregon) established public or mixed organizations to accelerate the development of advanced telecommunications infrastructure.
3. This potential advantage is likely weakened in a competitive environment in which the management of publicly owned firms – like managers of private firms – may be reluctant to reveal proprietary information to the regulator.
4. An early detailed survey of other industries was conducted by Borcherding, Pommerehne and Schneider (1982). Boardman and Vining (1989) review 500 competitive manufacturing and mining corporations and find that private firms outperform mixed and public enterprise. Willner (2001), reviewing 68 studies of competitive and non-competitive industries, emphasizes the wide range of results, especially in monopolistic industries. See also Megginson and Netter (2001).
5. This happened, for example in the UK where in the interest of successful privatization the introduction of competition was postponed.
6. A strong overlap exists in Belgium. The Minister of Telecommunications, who represents the state as majority owner of the PTO (Belgacom), is also the head of the regulatory authority. In 2002, to alleviate conflicts, independent task forces were established to deal with unbundling and interconnection issues.
7. In recognition of the weaker economic situations of Greece, Ireland, Portugal, and Spain most liberalization deadlines were staggered.
8. In Spain and Italy the PTOs had historically been mixed enterprises. In 1990, the Italian state directly and indirectly owned 40 per cent of the predecessor companies of Telecom Italia and the Spanish government held 32 per cent of Telefónicas shares.
9. State ownership is less important in the fast growing mobile communications sector, where newly licensed private service providers in most countries captured more than half of the total market (Curwen 2002).
10. Selected interviews were conducted with representatives of the Austrian, Dutch and German regulatory agencies.
11. Only the PTOs of Austria and Luxembourg fell into the 'public' category, together representing only 2 per cent of the EU's fixed access lines. Austria is nearly twenty times as populous as Luxembourg and thus dominates the observations.

12. Strategic investors may be given managing power even though they only hold a minority of the shares. However, this issue was not relevant in our cases.
13. The ranges set by the European Commission are 1.5–1.8 euro cents for dual transit, 0.8–1.5 euro cents for single transit, and 0.5–0.9 euro cents per minute of local termination (CEC 2000).
14. Of the fifteen incumbents, three can set their prices freely, nine operate under price caps and enjoy downward flexibility, and three need prior approval by the NRA for price changes (CEC 2002, Annex II, p 5–6). In Belgium, Greece, Spain and the Netherlands, there are recurrent complaints that incumbents use retail prices to exert price squeezes on new entrants (CEC 2002). Sappington and Sidak (2002) maintain that state-owned enterprise have a stronger incentive than private firms to choose prices below an acceptable cost standard.
15. Based on the determination of negligible universal service obligation costs, Germany chose not to develop a universal service plan at all. The coincidence of higher interconnection rates and unfunded universal service obligations could point to a form of cross subsidization. However, note the caveat regarding interconnection charges above.
16. We were not able to measure differences in enforcement that may exist among EU NRAs. The annual reports of the European Commission (CEC 2000, 2001, 2002) reflect concerns about such variations.

REFERENCES

Aharoni Y. (1986), *The Evolution and Management of State-owned Enterprises*, Cambridge, US: Ballinger.

Baumol W.J., J.C. Panzar and R.D. Willig (1982), *Contestable Markets and the Theory of Industrial Structure*, New York, US: Harcourt Brace Jovanovich.

Boardman A.E. and A.R. Vining (1989), 'Ownership and Performance in Competitive Environments: a Comparison of the Performance of Private, Mixed, and State-owned Enterprises', *Journal of Law and Economics*, 1–33.

Boardman A.E. and A.R. Vining (1991), 'The Behaviour of Mixed Enterprises', *Research in Law and Economics*, 223–50.

Borcherding T.E., W.W. Pommerehne and F.F. Schneider (1982), 'Comparing the Efficiency of Private and Public Production: the Evidence from Five Countries', *Zeitschrift für Nationalökonomie*, 2, 127–56.

Bortolotti B, J. D'Souza, M. Fantini and W.L. Megginson (2001), 'Privatization and the sources of performance improvement in the Global Telecommunications Industry', *Telecommunications Policy*, 243–68.

Boylaud O. and G. Nicoletti (2001), 'Regulation, Market Structure and Performance in Telecommunications', *OECD Economic Studies*, 99–142.

Brock G.W. and M.L. Katz (1997), 'Regulation to Promote Competition: A First Look at the FCC's Implementation of the Local Competition Provisions of the Telecommunications Act of 1996', *Information Economics and Policy*, 103 (17).

Cave M. and L. Prosperetti (2001), 'European Telecommunications Infrastructures', *Oxford Review of Economic Policy*, 416 (31).

CEC, Commission of the European Communities (2000), Sixth Report on the Implementation of the Telecommunications Regulatory Package, COM 814, Brussels BE.

CEC, Commission of the European Communities (2001), Seventh Report on the Implementation of the Telecommunications Regulatory Package, COM 706, Brussels BE.

CEC, Commission of the European Communities (2002), Eight Report on the Implementation of the Telecommunications Regulatory Package, COM 695, Brussels BE.

Cherry B.A. and J.M. Bauer (2002), 'Institutional Arrangements and Price Rebalancing: Evidence from the United States and Europe', *Information Economics and Policy*, 495–517.

Curwen P.J. (2002), *The Future of Mobile Communications: Awaiting the Third Generation*, New York, US: Palgrave MacMillan.

Eckel C.C. and A.R. Vining (1985), 'Elements of a Theory of Mixed Enterprise', *Scottish Journal of Political Economy*, 82–94.

Elixmann D. and M. Wörter (2001), *Strategien der Internationalisierung im Telekommunikationsmarkt*, Diskussionsbeitrag Nr. 220, Wissenschaftliches Institut für Kommunikationsdienste, Bad Honnef, GER.

Gutierrez L.H. and S.V. Berg (2000), 'Telecommunications Liberalization and Regulatory Governance: Lessons from Latin America', *Telecommunications Policy*, 865 (84).

Henisz W.J. (2002), 'The Institutional Environment for Infrastructure Investment', *Industrial and Corporate Change*, 355–89.

Hulsink W. (1999), *Privatization and Liberalization in European Telecommunications: Comparing Britain, the Netherlands, and France*, London, UK and New York, US: Routledge.

ITU (2002), *World Telecommunications Development Report*, International Telecommunication Union, Geneva.

Jordana J. (2002), *Governing Telecommunications and the New Information Society in Europe*, Cheltenham, UK and Northampton, MA, USA Edward Elgar.

Kwoka J.E. (2002), 'The Comparative Advantage of Public Ownership: Evidence from Electric Utilities', paper presented at the 29th Annual Conference of the European Association for Research in Industrial Economics (EARIE), September 5–8, Madrid, Spain.

Laffont J.-J. and J. Tirole (1993), *A Theory of Incentives in Public Procurement and Regulation*, Cambridge, US: MIT Press.

Laffont J.-J. and J. Tirole (2000), *Competition in Telecommunications*, Cambridge, US: MIT Press.

Levy B. and P.T. Spiller (1996), *Regulations, Institutions, and Commitments: Comparative Studies of Telecommunications*, Cambridge, US: Cambridge University Press.

Li W. and L.C. Xu (2002), *The Impact of Privatization and Competition in the Telecommunications Sector around the World*, Working Paper, University of Virginia, Richmond, World Bank, Washington. DC http://www.idlo.int/texts/IDLO/mis6365.pdf, 14 December 2004.

Megginson W.L. and J.M. Netter (2001), 'From State to Market: a Survey of Empirical Studies of Privatization', *Journal of Economic Literature*, 321 (89).

Nelson R.R. (1981), 'Assessing Private Enterprise: an Exegesis of Tangled Doctrine', *Bell Journal of Economics*, 93–111.

Newbery D.M.G. (1999), *Privatization, Restructuring, and Regulation of Network Utilities*, Cambridge, US: MIT Press.

Noll M.A. (2000), 'Telecommunication Privatization: Mixed Progress', *Info*, 21–3.

Nowotny E. (1982), 'Nationalized Industries as an Instrument of Stabilization Policy: the Case of Austria', *Annals of Public and Cooperative Economics*, 41–57.

OECD (2000), *Telecommunications Regulations: Institutional Structures and Responsibilities*, DSTI/ICCP/TISP(99)15/FINAL, Organization for Economic Co-operation and Development, Paris, France.

OECD (2001), *Communications Outlook*, Organization for Economic Co-operation and Development, Paris.

Phillips C.F., Jr. (1993), *The Regulation of Public Utilities: Theory and Practice*, Public Utilities Reports, Arlington, VA.

Ros A.J. (1999), 'Does Ownership or Competition Matter? The Effects of Telecommunications Reform on Network Expansion and Efficiency', *Journal of Regulatory Economics*, 15 (1), 65–92.

Sappington D.E.M. and J.E. Stiglitz (1987), 'Information and Regulation', in E.E. Bailey (ed.), *Public Regulation: New Perspectives on Institutions and Policies*, Cambridge, US: MIT Press, pp. 1–43.

Sappington D.E.M. and J.G. Sidak (2002), 'Competition Law for State-owned Enterprises', Working Paper, University of Florida, Gainesville, American Enterprise Institute, Washington, US.

Schumpeter J.A. (1942), *Capitalism, Socialism and Democracy*, New York, US: Harper.

Shapiro C. and R.D. Willig (1995), 'Economic Rationales for the Scope of Privatization', in E.E. Bailey and J. Rothenberg Pack (eds), *The Political Economy of Privatization and Deregulation*, Aldershot, UK and Brookfield, US: Edward Elgar.

Shepherd W. (1996), *The Economics of Industrial Organization*, Upper Saddle River, US: Prentice Hall, pp. 95–127.

Thiemeyer T. (1993), 'Deregulation in the Perspective of the German Gemeinwirtschaftslehre', *Journal of Institutional and Theoretical Economics*, 405 (18).

Vickers, J. (1994), *Concepts of Competition*, Oxford, UK: Clarendon Press.

Vickers J. and G. Yarrow (1988), *Privatization: An Economic Analysis*, Cambridge, US: MIT Press.

Wallsten S.J. (2001), 'An Econometric Analysis of Telecom Competition, Privatization, and Regulation in Africa and Latin America', *Journal of Industrial Economics*, 1–19.

Weizsäcker C.C. von (1980), *Barriers to Entry: A Theoretical Treatment*, Berlin. Springer.

Willner J. (2001), 'Ownership, Efficiency, and Political Interference', *European Journal of Political Economy*, 723 (48).

Yergin D. and J. Stanislaw (1998), *The Commanding Heights: The Battle Between Government and the Marketplace that is Remaking the Modern World*, New York, US: Simon and Schuster.

7. Limits of Law as a Planning Mechanism in Infrastructure Industries

Tony Prosser

1 INTRODUCTION

Looking back at over fifteen years of experience of privatized infrastructure industries in the UK, we face an apparent paradox. On the one hand, dire warnings as to the adverse social effects of privatization have not been realized in practice. We still have universal utilities services; the network of telephone call boxes has not collapsed in rural areas, we still have rural rail services and the introduction of competitive markets for services has not led to wholesale cream-skimming (Prosser, 2000). On the other hand, we are now experiencing a major overhaul of the electricity trading arrangements because those introduced after privatization had serious anti-competitive effects, and a fundamental review of energy policy, an issue neglected since privatization, has been commissioned. More seriously the privatization of rail is widely perceived to have been disastrous. The key date for this was the Hatfield rail crash of 17 October 2000, the first fatal accident which could directly be attributed to problems in the design for privatization. Partly as a result of this, but also for reasons of economic mismanagement, Railtrack, the rail infrastructure company, became insolvent after the refusal of the Government to provide additional funds. It was taken into court administration on 7 October 2001; it is likely to be replaced by a non-profit making company in which rail stakeholders are represented. I write as a lawyer, not an economist, and I shall argue in this chapter that the contrast between the successes and failures of privatization is partly due to the different ways in which law has been used as part of the privatization of network industries in the UK. Of course, planning, the theme of this collection, involves the use of law but in a variety of different forms. What I shall argue is that the use of public law, predominantly by independent regulators, has been broadly successful in protecting public service. However, the use of the private law of contract to reorganize network industries, replacing administration through internal hierarchy, has been much less successful. Rail, in which the previously unified British Rail was split into over one hundred separate companies linked by contract, is the most striking example of this.

2   PRIVATIZATION AND PUBLIC SERVICE

To start with the successful use of law to protect public service, this represents a new departure for the UK (in contrast with Continental countries such as France and Italy). By public service law I mean law designed to make basic public services available to all citizens without discrimination.[1] Our common law once had a rather weak tradition of law of this kind, however this effectively ended with nationalization. Recourse against the nationalized enterprises was to be political rather than legal. This was remarkably ineffective (Prosser, 1986). For example, in some respects the pricing policies of the energy and postal industries were more regressive than those of an ordinary capitalist enterprise in that they were used as surrogate tax-gatherers for government through the latter imposing price increases, the proceeds from which were to be paid to the Treasury. Nor did they adopt liberal policies on the disconnection of supply where bills were not paid on time, one of the most important social issues relating to the public utilities. The UK public enterprises did have great success in establishing the network for universal service through, for example, schemes for rural electrification, but their record of running services was not a good one.

At the time of privatization, many of its critics suggested that it would end the relevance of public service to the public utilities; indeed the Thatcher Government which pioneered privatization did not have public service as a central goal (Foster, 1992). However, somewhat reluctantly, regulators were established for each sector of the public utilities; political compromises had to be made and the legislation setting out their duties and those of ministers included social duties, including those of universal service (Prosser, 1997). For example, in all cases the privatized utility enterprises were obliged to meet all reasonable demands, and their regulators were obliged to pay special regard to the interests of consumers, especially those in rural areas, the elderly and the disabled. Further requirements were incorporated into the licences under which the enterprises operated, for example limiting the ability of the enterprises to disconnect supply in the event of non-payment of bills. There was thus a body of law which required the meeting of certain public service goals, responsibility for enforcement lying with the regulators rather than with the courts, although the occasional dispute did reach the latter.[2]

Initially, the regulators stressed their role as primarily an economic one of promoting or mimicking competition. However, all of them treated some elements of social regulation as within their powers (Prosser, 2000). For example, at the time of the privatization of British Telecom, strong fears had been expressed that it would mean the end of unprofitable public call-boxes, especially in rural areas. In fact complex provisions in British Telecom's licence restricted the circumstances in which public call-boxes could be closed, and the number has increased considerably since privatization, although the rapid growth of mobile telephony has stopped further increases and led to higher charges. The regulator also required special tariffs for low users, and this culminated in successive reviews of universal service now strongly influenced by European Union developments.[3]

In the energy utilities, the first major concern was disconnection of supply for non-payment. In the case of gas and electricity, disconnections rose dramatically immediately after privatization. However, regulatory action to restrict disconnection and to require alternative modes of payment to be offered resulted in large drops in disconnection rates to below pre-privatization levels. In the case of electricity the number of disconnections declined from 70 000 per year before privatization to only 400 in 1998, though for gas the record was less impressive, rising from 36 000 before privatization to 61 000 in the year after it, and running at almost 30 000 in 1998. A more recent concern is that after privatization prices for the connection of new premises to gas supplies rose considerably, thereby threatening the further development of rural supplies; once more, regulatory action is promised to counter this.

More recently, the most important development in relation to gas and electricity has been the opening up to competition of supply markets. The process of liberalization was completed in May 1998 for gas and May 1999 for electricity. A number of fears had been expressed during the process about the effects of liberalization, especially for households. The major fear was that it would result in 'cream skimming' by which new entrants would be interested only in the most profitable customers, broadly those with high consumption and who pay bills quickly directly from bank accounts. This would leave the less profitable customers, generally poorer consumers, with the former monopoly suppliers who would be forced to increase prices with the loss of their most profitable business. As a result public service concerns about equal access to the benefits of competition were expressed. There was some evidence that this was happening early on; the National Audit Office published reports on both gas and electricity liberalization claiming that, although all customers had benefited from liberalization, poor households had benefited least.[4] Regulatory action was taken to limit the effect of this problem. Initially price controls were maintained on the former monopoly suppliers, preventing them from imposing price increases on domestic consumers to counteract their loss of business. At the request of the Government, the regulator prepared a 'Social Action Plan' requiring certain social obligations to be met by all suppliers.[5] Supply companies were also encouraged to promote new tariffs aimed at those on low incomes, for example providing energy at a fixed price rather than on the basis of consumption. Recent evidence suggests that low-income groups have been switching supplier at the same rate as others, although some problems remain in relation to those dependent on prepayment meters by which energy is purchased before consumption by the insertion of a token into the meter.

In the case of water, the story is rather similar and legislation in 1999 went so far as to ban disconnections for non-payment for domestic premises; government has also used legislation to limit charges for households paying a metered charge with large numbers of children or people with specified medical conditions requiring heavy water consumption.[6] Finally, in the case of rail, privatization was predicted to lead to substantial route closures, especially in rural areas, and the end of unprofitable services such as late evening trains. In fact the complex procedures for the withdrawal of passenger services were strengthened at the time of privatization and there have been no closures of importance since.[7] Minimum service requirements also protect unprofitable services with a social role, such as evening and rural services.

What we saw, then, was a change from consumer protection being based on the goodwill of an industry, or on very ineffective political controls, to rules enforceable by regulators in the form of statute or licence conditions. Some systematization has been carried out since the 1997 change of government. The new government undertook a review of utilities regulation which proposed that the regulators be subject to a new overriding duty to promote the interests of consumers, wherever appropriate by promoting competition.[8] New statutory duties to pay particular regard to the interests of low-income customers and the chronically sick were to be added. In addition, ministers were to be given the power to issue non-binding guidance to regulators on social and environmental matters, though these would not be able to be used to impose new financial obligations on the industries. These reforms were implemented by the Utilities Act 2000, though regrettably at a late stage the scope of the Act was limited to the energy utilities; telecommunications and water were to wait for future reform of those utilities in the future.

These reforms in the regulation of the utilities in the UK in some senses mirror developments within the European Union which reflect a greater concern with guaranteeing universal service in telecommunications and a recognition that the public utilities may be required to respect social, distributive objectives. These have been reinforced by decisions from the European Court of Justice, most notably the *Corbeau* case[9] and now the new Article 16 of the Treaty. The latter is of extraordinary vagueness, but does require recognition by the Community and Member States of the special role of services of general economic interest.[10]

The conclusion to be reached is that privatization of infrastructure industries in the UK has not resulted in the adoption of socially regressive policies; indeed, it can be argued that public service goals are better protected through the legal means I have described after privatization than they were by political means before privatization. This is not through any attempt to engage in comprehensive state planning in the command economy sense or even in the French sense; the UK has anyway never known any serious attempt to plan in this way, though compare the energy review to be discussed below. Rather public service has been left to individual, decentralized interventions by the utility regulators on the basis of a mixture of widely-drawn legal duties in the statutes. It has been the regulators themselves who have been responsible for making most of this law, notably in the forms of licence amendments. This may have led to an unsystematic and inconsistent body of law; however the reforms to the regulatory duties in the Utilities Act and the power to issue ministerial guidance may do something to remedy this, at least in the energy field. In addition, one argument which has been used in the past is that it is illegitimate for regulators to pursue social (as opposed to economic) goals when they are not democratically responsible to the electorate; the new ministerial powers to issue guidance to regulators may also be an answer to this. In conclusion, then, the development of public law to protect social goals in the British utilities has been a success.

3   COMPETITION AND PUBLIC POLICY: THE ELECTRICITY INDUSTRY

Of course the major goals of privatization have been economic rather than social; in particular, increasing competition. In some areas this has been successful; notably in telecommunications and, as noted above, in the supply of electricity and gas where by mid-2001 almost one in three domestic gas customers had changed supplier, as had almost one in four electricity consumers. The average domestic electricity bill fell by 11 per cent in real terms between 1998 and 2001, and that for gas by 18 per cent between 1996 and 2001.[16]

In other areas the development of competition has been less successful, notably in electricity generation. On privatization, this was where competition was supposed to be most important, and no price controls were imposed on the generating companies (although the regulator had later to introduce them for a limited period); new entry, including generation by the regional distribution and supply companies, was to be encouraged. Electricity was traded through a complex system known as the 'pool', a form of spot market. However, it had a number of peculiar characteristics, notably through the fact that the actual price paid to a generator was not the price it had bid but the 'system marginal price', representing the highest bid necessary to make supplies available. This worked so as to benefit the large privatized generating companies; although there was extensive new entry, this did not operate to reduce prices in the pool.

Apart from a temporary price control for two years from 1994, the strategy adopted was to require the dominant generators to reduce generating capacity as a condition for approving their acquisition of other electricity companies; by 1998 the market share of the two largest generators had fallen from 80 per cent to 40 per cent, and to 25 per cent by the year 2000. However, this did not fully resolve the problems, and the pool has now been replaced by the New Electricity Trading Arrangements for England and Wales which were introduced in March 2001.[11] This is a new wholesale market between generators and suppliers, based on bilateral contracts supplemented by central mechanisms to ensure that demand meets supply. It is as yet unclear how effective the new arrangements will be, although there have already been complaints from small, environmentally-friendly producers that they are disadvantaged by them to the benefit of the larger generators. These attempts to create a more competitive market have been supplemented by measures to increase the powers of the regulatory authorities to prevent unfair competition.[12]

What the problems of introducing competition into electricity generation suggest is that strong regulatory steps must be taken to ensure that competition is effective; creating surrogate markets in the form of the pool is not enough to ensure such competition if reform of market structure is neglected. A further set of problems relates to electricity generation and public policy, in particular the achievement of goals such as security of supply, diversity of energy sources and environmental goals. At the time of privatization, little was done to address these longer-term issues, the assumption being that the market would provide optimal solutions (although extensive powers of governmental regulation were retained in the legislation). In electricity, in particular, the results of privatization were of considerable importance and were not entirely anticipated. The most striking example was the so-called 'rush for gas'. There was a major shift from coal generation to the use of new, small gas generators. This had potential environmental advantages in relation to carbon emissions and in the short term it increased diversity of fuel sources; however, it had devastating effects on the already severely contracted domestic coal industry; coal's share of total UK energy use fell from 36 per cent in 1980 to 17 per cent in 2000, whilst that of gas rose from 22 per cent to 41 per cent. This raised questions of security of supply and potential overdependence on gas; the UK is likely to be importing up to 15 per cent of its gas by 2006, much of it from unstable regimes such as Russia and Algeria. The position has been exacerbated by the Government's commitment in its 1997 election manifesto not to build new nuclear power stations; existing stations are being progressively decommissioned as they reach the end of their lives so the share of nuclear generation is likely to decline further. The earlier solution of putting pressure on the large generators to buy British coal became difficult to use after markets had been liberalized.

The initial response of the Labour Government elected in 1997 was to undertake a review of security of supply and fuel diversity in the granting of consents for new power stations; a moratorium was imposed on the construction of new gas stations.[13] The moratorium was lifted in 2000, accompanied by the direct granting of aid to the coal industry to assist it through a period of transition. However, the Prime Minister took the view that the earlier review of energy policy was too limited, and in June 2001 a more far-reaching Energy Policy Review was announced, to be carried out by the Performance and Innovation Unit of the Cabinet Office. The Prime Minister stated that 'the aim of the review will be to set out the objectives of energy policy and to develop a strategy that ensures current policy commitments are consistent with longer-term goals'; it will examine energy policy for the period up to 2050.[14] This marks a fundamental change of approach towards the adoption of a strategy for meeting energy needs rather than relying on the market, subject only to minor adjustments to limit anti-competitive behaviour. The review's advisory committee is chaired by the Minister for Industry and Energy, one of the few remaining advocates of nuclear generation, leading to press speculation that it may result in a future development of more nuclear capacity.[15]

What is most striking here is that it is now accepted that the future of energy in the UK cannot be left to the decentralized contracting between private parties in the marketplace; government has a legitimate long-term planning role. Indeed, one commentator discussing the announcement of the Review considered that 'the review not only has a longer and wider scope than any previous one, but is also a rather un-British exercise. ... [It] smacks more of the French *planification* ... than the traditional British short-term policy review designed to deal with problems as they arise.'[16]

4   THE RAIL INFRASTRUCTURE AND THE FAILURE OF PRIVATE LAW

In the rest of this chapter I shall concentrate on a radically different form of privatization of an infrastructure industry, that of rail, where things have gone dramatically wrong, culminating in the insolvency of the infrastructure company, Railtrack. I shall suggest that an attempt to set up an industry which is organized through contractual relations between the participants instead of the previous administrative hierarchy disastrously overestimated the ability of such relations to provide a self-regulating structure for co-ordination of the different actors involved.

The privatization of the rail system involved fragmenting it into over one hundred companies. Passenger services are provided by twenty-five train operating companies, broadly regionally-based, operating under franchises issued by a franchising director, specifying service requirements and subsidy or payment levels. The franchising director has since been merged into a new Strategic Rail Authority.[18] Rolling stock was transferred to three leasing companies. Infrastructure and signalling was put into the hands of Railtrack; initially it was to remain under public ownership but was in fact privatized at a late stage to assist government finances. However, it was not intended that Railtrack would engage in maintenance, renewal and development of the rail infrastructure itself; rather it would contract this work out. Railtrack thus took the form of a procurement company with the actual work being performed by a large number of private contractors. The overall system is regulated by the Office of the Rail

Regulator, who is particularly concerned with fair access to the network for operators.[19]

Despite the monopoly nature of Railtrack and the very limited extent of competition between operating companies, in the case of rail the structure of privatization was more clearly designed to incentivize the participants in the system than in other cases; indeed, the special adviser to the minister was an economist, Sir Christopher Foster, who has also published widely about the economic justification for this approach.(Foster, 1994). The incentivization was to take place through contracts. Whereas British Rail had been a vertically-integrated enterprise build around an administrative hierarchy (though with increasing devolution to businesses centres within it) and employing only eight solicitors, efficiency gains would result through specifying in contracts the relationships between the different firms involved. As a result, an enormous body of work went to lawyers in writing and administering the contracts; for example in 1993–1994 £4 million was paid by government for legal consultancy, by far the largest category of consultancy work.

The system was problematic from the start.[20] For example, it became clear that the major justification for privatization, that of permitting vastly increased investment through access to the private markets, was not working and government has had to continue to provide extensive investment funding, whilst the subsidy costs for the franchise holders doubled at the time of privatization; the hope was that there would then be a substantial decrease as efficiency gains took place, but that has not happened. The incentives in the contracts were not well thought out; for example, in the contracts between Railtrack and the operating companies, penalties and bonuses applied based on Railtrack's performance in avoiding delays, yet in 1998–99 Railtrack received a £25 million bonus when it remained responsible for a third of delays and the Regulator was considering action against it because it had missed its target for reducing them. Crucially, the contracts involved the payment of penalties where lines were occupied for maintenance, thereby creating an incentive to skimp on it. The arrangements for safety regulation, through which Railtrack itself became responsible for overseeing the safety of the network and validating the safety cases of users, was also strongly criticized; as a detailed study put it 'prominent here are concerns about the independence of the industry-based regulator. This is especially so when the company vested with major regulatory responsibilities is in a contractual relationship with the regulated concerning access to the industry (in this case via the rail network) and the financial arrangements for this' (Hutter, 2001).

Concern was increased by two major accidents in 1997 and 1999 leading to considerable loss of life; the official inquiry into the accidents was highly critical of a number of aspects of the industry structure; for example, the overall fragmentation of the system which had made it difficult to provide overall leadership and to take united action on safety, and the inadequate monitoring and supervision of contractors. Moreover, '[t]he disparity in sanctions between those for failures in performance and those for failures in safety may well have conveyed to the industry that performance was of top priority' (Hutter, 2001). The key date was discrediting the system was, however, 17 October 2000 when four passengers were killed and over seventy injured in the Hatfield accident.[21] Other more serious accidents had occurred before and after privatization, but this was directly attributable to a broken rail which had not been replaced due to failure of contractual monitoring. Moreover, the rail system descended into chaos due to the decision of Railtrack to impose hundreds of speed restrictions to permit the inspection of other sites where similar dangers might arise. Between 17 October and 11 December there was no published rail timetable; the final target for lifting the restrictions of last Easter was not met, and some are still in place in late 2001. By January over 260 miles of rail had had to be replaced. Communication of restrictions was limited; for example, it was announced at 5pm that the main line to Scotland was to be closed for three days from 8am the following morning. The operating companies then sought compensation from Railtrack for the severe loss of revenues which resulted; settlement of these disputes imposed additional financial burdens on the company. This in turn contributed to a severe financial crisis (already serious due to an inability to control costs) for Railtrack which demanded greatly increased government funding and a lifting of regulatory constraints on its charges. Although more funding was granted, with £1.5 billion agreed in April 2001, the Government refused to agree to continuing requests for additional finance (for £2.6 billion in May and a further £1 billion in July) and in October 2001 Railtrack was taken into administration as insolvent. It is planned to replace it with a not-for-profit company limited by guarantee and with no shareholders; its board will include appointments made after consultation with operating companies and other stakeholders, such as representatives of passengers.[22]

What caused this disastrous chain of events? The immediate answer was the ineffective arrangements for monitoring maintenance when it was contracted out. The contractors had inspected the Hatfield section of track in 1998 and had decided it should be re-railed; no action had been taken. It was tested again in June but using equipment which did not work; this was not picked up by Railtrack. Some work was undertaken in September but this was inadequate; no speed restrictions were imposed and the short closure of the tracks necessary to replace them was postponed due to the fear of incurring financial penalties as a result of delays to traffic. The Parliamentary Committee investigating the accident concluded that Railtrack's management of the contractor was 'totally inadequate', and that 'Railtrack has failed to ensure that the culture of safety now espoused by its senior management is not [*sic*] always shared by its contractors, sub-contractors and the front line workers on the railway'.[23] In a separate inquiry into renewal, maintenance and development of the rail network, it found that management of contractors had been 'woeful' and strongly recommended that Railtrack take over direct responsibility for inspecting the network and for directly employing those who work on maintenance and renewal.[24]

I have concentrated on Hatfield and its aftermath because it has been important in the public eye in discrediting one particular type of privatization; that which relies on contracts to incentivize within a fragmented industry. It has shown repeated defects in arrangements for contractual monitoring and an inability of contract to co-ordinate the many actors now involved in delivering safe rail services. This is partly due to the defects of the contracts themselves; the incentives were badly designed, and it seems that there was too much pressure for efficiency savings at the expense of safety, leading, for example, to the casualization of staff. Thus since 1994 the number of permanent maintenance staff has fallen from 31000 to between 15000 and 19000 but there are 84 000 holders of certificates to work on the track, mainly casual staff.[25]

Those are contingent pressures not directly related to the inherent role of contract. However, contract has some inherent disadvantages. The transaction costs are high in the form of legal fees, etc., and the assumption that these will be compensated for by increased efficiency may not be realistic. In addition, contracts do not encourage a sharing of responsibility, rather they are a means for passing responsibility on to someone else; indeed this seems to have been the intention of those who drafted the rail contracts. In that sense contracts are a substitute for trust. Finally, contractualization encourages adversary relationships resulting in litigation.[26] The intention in the planning of rail privatization was that parties would act rationally to create other forms of dispute resolution. This has to some extent happened in the case of rail, but when disputes of the seriousness of those resulting from Hatfield occur, in a fragmented industry they will end up in the courts, increasing transaction costs further and souring relations further. The conclusion is that rather than attempting to create incentives through contractual specification, it should be accepted that sometimes hierarchical organizations will work better through having cultures of co-operation embedded in them; indeed, this is one of the major themes of the Cullen inquiry into the two major pre-Hatfield rail accidents in the UK.[27] These cultures may facilitate the achievement of safety goals, for example, through an acceptance that some types of conduct are simply unacceptable thus simplifying monitoring. They may reduce transaction costs through keeping lawyers out and providing simpler means of resolving disputes than litigation. The challenge is to combine such cultural expectations with a degree of transparency which is similar to that which may be required by independent regulation.

5   CONCLUSIONS

The privatization of infrastructure industries has not in general resulted in the regressive social consequences forecast at the time of privatization. This is largely due to the creation of specialist regulatory authorities for each sector which have developed a body of public service law to protect essential services. In some areas, notably energy supply, there has been considerable success in creating competitive markets; once more, it has usually involved the necessity of strong action by regulators to reduce the dominance of incumbent enterprises. In the field of electricity generation, regulation for competition has had less success through the initial mis-design of the pool trading arrangements; new structures have now been introduced, again through regulatory and government intervention, but it is too early to assess the extent to which they will represent an improvement. The Government, through the commissioning of its energy review, has also acknowledged that there are issues of energy policy which cannot be left to markets but which require longer-term planning and public intervention.

The most striking failure of privatization has been in the case of rail, and this is to a large extent due to the fragmented structure adopted for the industry and the inadequacy of the private law of contact as a co-ordinating mechanism. This was partly due to the mis-design of contractual and regulatory incentives, but I have suggested that it also reflects some problems inherent in the use of contract in this way, for example high transaction costs and the destruction of cultures of co-operation. It remains to be seen whether the new arrangements to be adopted for the rail industry go some way towards resolving these problems; in the meantime, the lesson seems to be that the absence of planning and the use of mechanisms which do not secure co-operation has proved far worse than decentralized planning through the work of the regulatory authorities.

NOTES

1. For further details see Prosser, *ibid.* The concept of public service is a key one in French administrative law, for which see e.g. Conseil d'Etat, *Etudes et Documents No 46, Rapport Public 1994* (La Documentation Française, Paris, 1995).
2. See '*R v Director of Water Services*, ex parte Lancashire County Council and Others', *The Times*, 6 March 1998.
3. See most recently Office of Telecommunications, 'Universal Service Obligation, A Statement Issued by the Director General of Telecommunications' (OFTEL, London, 2001).
4. National Audit Office, *Giving Customers a Choice: The Introduction of Competition into the Domestic Gas Market*, HC 403 (1998–9) and *Giving Domestic Customers a Choice of Electricity Supplier*, HC 403 (1998–9).
5. Office of Gas and Electricity Markets, *The Social Action Plan* (OFGEM, London, 2000).

6. Water Industry Act 1999, ss. 1-5; The Water Industry (Charges) (Vulnerable Groups) Regulations, SI 1999/3441.
7. Railways Act 1993 sec. 43; Transport Act 2000 ss. 234-239.
8. Department of Trade and Industry, *A Fair Deal for Consumers: Modernising the Framework for Utility Regulation*, Cm 3898 (1998); the final proposals are in Department of Trade and Industry, *A Fair Deal for Consumers: The Response to Consultation* (Department of Trade and Industry), London, 1998.
9. Case C-320/91, *Regie des Postes v Corbeau* 1993 ECR 1-2533; [1993] 4 CMLR 621.
10. These figures are obtained from the Office of Gas and Electricity Markets, *Annual Report 2000–2001*, HC 78 (2001-2), ch. 4.
11. For details see Office of Electricity Regulation, *Review of Electricity Trading Arrangements: Proposals* (OFFER, Birmingham, 1998); Office of Gas and Electricity Markets, *The New Electricity Trading Arrangements* (OFGEM, London, 1999) and the Utilities Act 2000, s. 68.
12. Competition Act 1998, s. 54 and sch. 10.
13. Department of Trade and Industry, Conclusions of the Review of Energy Sources for Power Generation and the Government's Response to the Fourth and Fifth Reports of the Trade and Industry Committee, Cm 4071 (1998).
14. Cabinet Office News Release, CAB 124/01, 25 June 2001.
15. See 'Nuclear Power Back on Agenda', *The Financial Times*, 26 June 2001
16. 'More Than One Master', *The Financial Times*, 6 August 2001.
17. For the Government's plans see Department of Transport, *New Opportunities for the Railways*, Cm 2012 (1992) and the Railways Act 1993.
18. Transport Act 2000, ss. 201–22.
19. For the regulatory system, see Prosser, *Law and the Regulators*, op. cit., 181–200.
20. For characteristic earlier criticism see, e.g., Environment, Transport and Regional Affairs Committee, *The Proposed Strategic Rail Authority and Railway Regulation*, HC 286, 1997–8.
21. For the background see the Environment, Transport and Regional Affairs Committee, *Recent Events on the Railway*, HC 17, 2000–2001 and *Rail Investment: Renewal, Maintenance and Development of the National Rail Network*, HC 18, 2000–2001.
22. See HC Debs, 23 October 2001, col. 195W (written answers).
23. *Recent Events on the Railway*, op. cit., para. 12.
24. *Rail Investment*, op. cit.
25. *Rail Investment*, ibid., para. 45.
26. For the situation in New Zealand, where specialist utility regulators were not established and interconnection arrangements between telecommunications

officers left to private contract, see e.g. *Telecom Corporation of New Zealand Ltd. v Clear Communications Ltd* (1994) 5 NZBLC 103 (PC).
27. *The Ladbroke Grove Rail Inquiry, Part 2 Report*, op. cit., ch. 5.

REFERENCES

Foster C.D. (1992), *Privatization, Public Ownership and The Regulation of Natural Monopoly*, Oxford, UK: Blackwell.

Foster C.D. (1994), *The Economics of Rail Privatization*, Bath, UK: Centre for the Study of Regulated Industries.

Hutter B. (2001), *Regulation and Risk: Occupational Health and Safety on the Railways*, Oxford, UK: Oxford University Press.

Prosser T. (1986), *Nationalised Industries and Public Control*, Oxford, UK: Blackwell.

Prosser T. (1997), *Law and the Regulators*, Oxford, UK: Oxford University Press.

Prosser T. (2000), 'Public Service Law: Privatization's Unexpected Offspring', *Law and Contemporary Problems*, 63–82.

Ross M. (2000), 'Article 16 EC and Services of General Interest: From Derogation to Obligation?', *European Law Review*, 25 (22).

The Rt. Hon. Lord Cullen PC (2001), *The Ladbroke Grove Rail Inquiry, Part 2 Report*, London, UK: HSE Books, http://www.hse.gov.uk/railways/paddrail/lgri2.pdf, 14 December 2004.

8. The Economic Regulation of the Essential Facilities in the Oil and Electricity Industries in Spain

Pablo Arocena Garro and Ignacio Contín Pilart

1 INTRODUCTION[1]

In the process of restructuring and deregulation that has taken place in network industries over the last decade, the challenge for public policy has been to deregulate the competitive activities, while maintaining adequate antitrust and regulatory safeguards over the remaining natural monopoly elements or essential facilities (Lyon and Hackett, 1993).[3]

This process often involves regulatory policies requiring the essential facility to provide 'open access' to its transport facilities and vertical divestiture or separation of vertically integrated activities of incumbents (Sidack and Spulber, 1998).

In many cases, regulatory policies clearly specify the prices and conditions under which the essential facility shall grant its users access. To this end, the economic regulation of the essential facilities is established with a twofold objective: first, to secure coverage of their costs and financial viability, while encouraging their modernization (long-term innovation); and second, to prevent a potential abuse of their market powers.

As in many other countries, infrastructure-based industries in Spain were involved in an ongoing process of fundamental reorganization and modernization over the last decade. With respect to the energy industries, the 1990s were witness to a large number of mergers and acquisitions that led to the building of 'nation champions', through protections in their domestic markets, capable of competing with foreign multinationals. As a result, highly concentrated oligopolies emerged in the Spanish energy industries (Sánchez, 1997; Contín et al., 2000). This process was also pursued to expand the national electric transmission network and the oil products and gas pipeline transport systems, which are currently operated by *Red Eléctrica de España* (REE), *La Compañía Logística de Hidrocarburos* (CLH), and *Enagas*, respectively. Parallel to their restructuring, Spanish energy industries have undergone major regulatory reforms (OECD, 2000; IEA, 1999) in order to promote the liberalization of the oil, electricity and gas markets.

Thus, liberalization was undertaken together with decisions aimed at building leading Spanish energy firms (the national champions). A high degree of concentration persists years after liberalization and reflects the slow progress of competition in these sector (Arocena, 2004)

This chapter focuses on the analysis of CLH and REE,[4] which are the essential facilities of the oil and electricity industries. In making decisions over the access charges of the essential facilities, the regulator faces a clash of interests: an increase in access charges simultaneously implies a decrease in the users' surplus and an increase in the regulated firm's revenues. We compare the evolution of the average tariffs of CLH and REE, as well as the productivity and input price differentials between these companies and competitive industries. We explore whether access price regulation has served to protect CLH and REE's users and to share cost reductions with shareholders, or whether the essential facilities have been systematically allowed to internalize such productivity gains as profits. In other words, the research question is to what extent CLH and REE's access prices have resulted in a pro-users or pro-companies bias. This chapter analyses how these situations occurred.

Three price benchmarks are constructed to that effect. The first benchmark represents the best reference from the point of view of the users. This would be the case of a competitive price adjustment, which assumes that the regulatory objective is to set prices so as to maintain breakeven operations over time. The second benchmark represents an evolution of tariffs that includes the input price variation while essential facilities absorb the total amount of productivity changes. The third alternative may be considered the most attractive from the perspective of the essential facility: price increases allow it to keep all cost reductions and pass all the cost increases of inputs on to the users. We use the benchmarks to provide a taxonomy of access price increases in order to assess the potential biases of the pricing policies in distributing the rents between CLH, REE and their customers.

The chapter is organized as follows. The next section discusses the dynamics and consequences of the regulation of prices for essential facilities. Section 3 outlines the main features of the regulation of the transport of oil products and electricity in Spain. Section 4 presents our data and the main results for each company. A conclusions section completes the chapter.

2   PRICING POLICIES FOR REGULATED COMPANIES

Following Crew and Kleindorfer (1987) and Bernstein and Sappington (1999), let us imagine one firm producing $y_1,...,y_m$ outputs, with respective output prices $p_1,...,p_m$. The firm uses $x_1,..., x_n$ inputs which it purchases at prices $w_1,...,w_n$. The firm's profit (Π) as the difference of total revenue (R) and total cost (C) is given by

$$\Pi = R - C = \sum_{j=1}^{m} p_j y_j - \sum_{i=1}^{n} w_i x_i \qquad (8.1)$$

Assuming that the firm is operating in a competitive industry, free entry dissipates economic profits and the firm exactly breaks even,[5] so that

$$\sum_{j=1}^{m} p_j y_j = \sum_{i=1}^{n} w_i x_i \qquad (8.2)$$

Since zero extraordinary profits persist in the long run, the identity (8.2) holds true over time, so that taking differentials provides:

$$\sum_{j=1}^{m} p_j y_j \frac{dy_j}{y_j} + \sum_{j=1}^{m} p_j y_j \frac{dp_j}{p_j} = \sum_{i=1}^{n} w_i x_i \frac{dx_i}{x_i} + \sum_{i=1}^{n} w_i x_i \frac{dw_i}{w_i}$$

(8.3)

Dividing both sides of this expression by the left- and right-hand side of equation (8.2), we have the following identity:

$$\sum_{j=1}^{m} \alpha_j \dot{p}_j + \sum_{j=1}^{m} \alpha_j \dot{y}_j = \sum_{i=1}^{n} \beta_i \dot{x}_i + \sum_{l=1}^{n} \beta_i \dot{w}_i$$

(8.4)

where:

$$\alpha_j = \frac{p_j y_j}{\sum_{j=1}^{m} p_j y_j} \quad \text{is the revenue share for product } j$$

$$\beta_i = \frac{w_i x_i}{\sum_{i=1}^{n} w_i x_i} \quad \text{is the cost share for input } i.$$

$\dot{p}_j, \dot{y}_j, \dot{x}_i, \dot{w}_i$ denote the rate of change of output price, output quantity, input quantity and input price respectively.

Expression (8.4) can be rewritten as

$$\dot{P}_C - \dot{W}_C + (\dot{Y}_C - \dot{X}_C) = 0$$

(8.5)

where:

$$\dot{P}_C = \sum_{j}^{m} \alpha_j \dot{p}_j$$

$$\dot{Y}_C = \sum_{j}^{m} \alpha_j \dot{y}_j$$

$$\dot{X}_C = \sum_{i=1}^{n} \beta_i \dot{x}_i$$

$$\dot{W}_C = \sum_{i=1}^{n} \beta_i \dot{w}_i$$

Subscript c is included here to indicate we are considering a competitive industry.

The expression in parenthesis in (8.5) represents the difference between the growth rates of units of output Y and units of input X, i.e. it is equal to the total factor productivity $(T\dot{F}P)$ growth. Therefore,

$$\dot{P}_C = \dot{W}_C - T\dot{F}P_C \qquad (8.6)$$

Expression (8.6) indicates that in a competitive industry, output price change in each period $(\dot{P}_c)$ is equal to input price change $(\dot{W}_c)$ less the variation in total factor productivity $(T\dot{F}P_c)$. Therefore, the decrease (increase) of input prices and productivity gains (losses) result in lower (higher) output prices for consumers. In other words, the dynamic of competition transfers any efficiency improvement (deterioration) to consumers.

Let us now consider a monopoly where an economic authority (hereafter the regulator) has been assigned the task of setting output prices. Let us also assume that the regulator has the objective of replicating the results achieved in an industry that operates under perfectly competitive conditions, as summarized in expression (8.6). Accordingly, the regulator should adjust output prices in such a way that

$$\dot{P}_R = \dot{W}_R - T\dot{F}P_R \qquad (8.7)$$

where subscript R is included this time to denote a regulated sector is under consideration.

Following Bernstein and Sappington (1999), subtracting expression (8.7) from expression (8.6) and rearranging terms provides:

$$\dot{P}_R = \dot{P}_C + (\dot{W}_R - \dot{W}_C) - (T\dot{F}P_R - T\dot{F}P_C) \qquad (8.8)]$$

Expression (8.8) establishes that the regulator should allow output prices to rise at a rate equal to the rate of change of output prices in the competitive industry; plus the difference in the rate of growth in input prices between the regulated monopoly and the rest of the industry; less the difference in productivity growth rates between the regulated and the competitive firm.

Otherwise, a rate of growth above $\dot{P}_R$ would generate positive profits for the monopoly.

Therefore, by fulfilling the condition (8.8) the regulator replicates the evolution of competitive prices, by automatically adjusting prices to reflect any cost variation. However, the regulator actually observes the costs incurred *ex post*; he is not *ex ante* able to know the firm's costs and the real effort required to improve the productivity. Moreover, he cannot verify *ex post* whether the firm had cost-minimizing behaviour. Therefore, the regulator makes its pricing decisions under asymmetry of information: Regulated firms have better information than the regulator about their costs and about the efforts required to be efficient.

In this respect, if the regulator uses the information on a firms costs to update output prices *ex post* according to (8.8), the firm's managers have not *ex ante* any incentive to cut costs, since they know in advance that every potential cost reduction only benefits consumers (see Laffont and Tirole, 1993; Armstrong et al., 1994). The firm could strategically exploit the asymmetry of information by declaring higher costs than those actually needed to supply the service and by relaxing its effort to cost cutting. Alternatively, if the regulation of output prices allows the firm to retain any profit generated by cost reduction, the regulator provides the firm with maximum incentives to increase its productive efficiency.

Therefore, the design of the price regulatory regime must cope with the trade-off between the provision of incentives for cost reduction and the concern for setting cost-reflecting prices. Assuming that variations in input prices are largely beyond the firm's control, which seems to be quite realistic since interest rates, wages and fluctuations in the acquisition prices of primary fuels (i.e. coal and crude oil) depend essentially on exogenous factors, one regulator seeking to balance both criteria would allow output prices to increase at a rate P such that

$$\dot{P}_R < \dot{P} < \dot{P}_W, \quad \text{if } T\dot{F}P_R > T\dot{F}P_C$$

or

$$\dot{P}_W < \dot{P} < \dot{P}_R, \quad \text{if } T\dot{F}P_R < T\dot{F}P_C \qquad (8.9)$$

where $\dot{P}_W = \dot{P}_C + (\dot{W}_R - \dot{W}_C)$

That is, in the event of higher $T\dot{F}P$ growth of the regulated firm than that of the competitive one, the cost-reflecting rate $\dot{P}_R$ may be interpreted as beneficial for consumers, in the sense that it reflects a major concern for delivering all the productivity gains achieved in the regulated firm to the consumers. On the contrary, a rate of $\dot{P}_W$ allows the monopoly to retain any profit generated from productivity improvement, so that such an increase may reflect some industry bias. A rate of growth of prices in between, may then reflect an attempt to counterbalance the firm's and consumers' interests.

Finally, we compute the potentially most favourable evolution of prices from the point of view of the company. Such a benchmark captures the maximal increase of output prices attainable by using the registered change in relative cost variation. Particularly, this rate is constructed in the event that price review only had reflected relative input price increases and productivity declines, without accounting for input price reductions and productivity improvement. We denote this rate as $\dot{P}_{max}$ and by construction, it is obvious that $\dot{P}_{max} \geq \dot{P}_R$ given that:

$$\dot{P}_{max} = \dot{P}_C + \begin{vmatrix} (\dot{W}_R - \dot{W}_C) & only\ if & \dot{W}_R \geq \dot{W}_C \\ (T\dot{F}P_C - T\dot{F}P_R) & only\ if & T\dot{F}P_R \leq T\dot{F}P_C \end{vmatrix} \quad (8.10)$$

Therefore, $\dot{P}_{max}$ may be interpreted as a reference against which measure the degree of the consumers' protection from an excessive increase of prices. In this regard, a rate of growth of prices higher than $\dot{P}_{max}$ indicates a very lax and ineffective regulation for consumers or, alternatively, an excessive inclination to the monopoly.

Table 8.1 summarizes the previous discussion and provides a taxonomy of the inclination of the pricing policies according to the magnitude of output price increases observed ex post.

Table 8.1   Taxonomy of price reviews

Output price increase	Inclination
$\dot{P} \leq \dot{P}_R$ ($\dot{P} \leq \dot{P}_W$)	Pro-consumer bias
$\dot{P}_R < \dot{P} < \dot{P}_W$ ($\dot{P}_W < \dot{P} < \dot{P}_R$)	Rents sharing
$\dot{P}_{MAX} > \dot{P} \geq \dot{P}_W$ ($\dot{P}_{MAX} > \dot{P} \geq \dot{P}_R$)	Pro-Industry bias
$\dot{P} \geq \dot{P}_{MAX}$	Ineffective/lax control

Note: Conditions in parenthesis apply when the productivity growth in the competitive industry exceeds the corresponding rate of the regulated firm, i.e. when $T\dot{F}P_R < T\dot{F}P_C$.

3   THE REGULATION OF THE TRANSPORT OF OIL PRODUCTS AND OF ELECTRICITY IN SPAIN

As stated, this chapter focuses on the analysis of the essential facilities of the Spanish oil and electricity industries; CLH and REE, respectively. Given that the evolution of CLH and REE's regulatory policies have been rather different, next we analyse them separately.

3.1 Compañía Logística de Hidrocarburos (CLH)

The Spanish oil monopoly was operated by the *Compañía Arrendataria del Monopolio de Petróleos Sociedad Anónima* (hereafter CAMPSA) between 1927 and 1993. However, in 1986, the Spanish government initiated a process of progressive liberalization of the oil sector, which culminated with the dismantling of the legal monopoly of CAMPSA by the early 1993.

Parallel to this process of liberalization, through mergers, the number of refining companies was reduced from eight in the early 1970s to only three by the early 1990s. Subsequently, the two private Spanish refiners, Cepsa and Petromed, were integrated into the production systems of large foreign oil companies, Elf-Aquitaine and BP, respectively. The several public refining and crude-producing companies were merged into one 'national champion', Repsol, which was privatized tranche by tranche.

In 1984, CAMPSA was sold to the existing refiners, in proportion to their share in total Spanish refining capacity. By mid-1992, the commercial assets (i.e. service stations) were separated from CAMPSA's distribution facilities and divided up among the shareholding refiners in proportion to their respective shareholdings in CAMPSA, while a new company was created to carry on CAMPSA's distribution activities: *Compañía Logística de Hidrocarburos* (CLH). The three Spanish-based refining companies plus Shell became the joint owners of CLH as reported in Table 8.2.

Table 8.2   Shareholders of CLH (1993-2000)

Shareholder	%
Repsol	61.46
Cepsa-Elf	25.1
BP	7.61
Sell	5
Others	0.83

By 1990, the three Spanish-based refiners controlled virtually 100 per cent of the market for oil products. The gradual entry of relatively small independent operators in the successive years had little effect in reducing their market dominance (Contín et al., 1999).[6]

In the mid-1980s, CAMPSA – then owned by the refiners – undertook a radical modernization of its distribution system, to improve the overall efficiency and to adjust it to the shifting composition of demand, towards lighter fuels. Over the 1980s and early 1990s, some 22 local depots were closed. All 37 remaining depots were either located in a seaport and/or connected to the pipeline grid. So, with exception of the Cepsa-Elf refinery on the Canary Islands, all Spanish refineries were connected through pipelines with distribution depots in the main consumption areas or near seaports from which they supply their outlets inland. Storage capacity for fuel oil was reduced, while that for light products, in particular for gas oil, was expanded. Large investments were made in modernizing the remaining depots and in the construction of automatic loading facilities for trucks. Around 1.600 kilometres of new pipeline were constructed, while optimal use of the pipeline system was facilitated through a satellite-based control system (Correljé, 1994).

The Spanish state, through its control over retail, ex-refinery prices, and CAMPSA's oil products transport and storage tariffs, enabled the refiners to generate the income necessary to, respectively, finance the acquisition of CAMPSA and its subsequent modernization (Correljé, 1994; Contín et al., 2001). This whole operation, at the time motivated by the objective to 'prepare the Spanish oil industry for operations in a competitive market', thus deliberately rendered the refiners the current financial and operative control over a modernized distribution system.

Because of its large economies of scale, the first-mover advantage involved and its technological superiority, the CLH pipeline system is to be considered as the essential facility of the Spanish inland market for oil products. Indeed, the rather unstable situation of the new entrants in the Spanish market, the small scale of their operations and the dispersion of their outlets render the construction of alternative pipeline systems by independent operators unprofitable and unlikely. Whereas low cost intra-modal distribution systems, using for example river barges, might have offered effective competition to a potential natural monopoly (Hillman, 1991), these alternatives are not feasible for inland transport in Spain.

Until the abolishment of the monopoly in 1992, the government set CAMPSA's oil products transport and storage tariffs and conditions. Thereafter, CLH did determine them on a contractual basis. In the mid-1990s, the *Tribunal de Defensa de la Competencia* (TDC), the Spanish Antitrust Authority, examined the degree of competition in the Spanish oil industry (TDC, 1995). It suggested the government should regulate CLH, so that it would provide its services and set its fees on a non-discriminatory basis for all shippers, regardless of whether they were owners or not, to allow the entry of new firms. In June 1996, the government followed this advice, required CLH to provide transportation and storage services on a '*non-discriminatory, transparent and clear*' basis and stated that only technical circumstances and lack of capacity would be accepted as conditions under which CLH was exempted from providing its services. Both the contracts between CLH and the shippers and the exemptions to supply were subject to the approval of the Ministry of Industry (Contín et al., 2001).

Eventually, the Law on the Oil Sector, of October 1998, introduced *negotiated access*, under which CLH and the shippers had to negotiate over access fees and conditions, with tariffs agreed upon to be published. The law also provided the government with the discretion to set storage and transport tariffs in areas without adequate alternatives to CLH's distribution system. In June 2000, the government forced a restructuring of CLH's ownership share. It restricted the maximum stake in CLH to 25 per cent per firm. Moreover, cumulatively, the (in)direct stake of the Spanish-based refiners shall not surpass 45 per cent, while independent operators will be offered to acquire CLH shares.

3.2 Red Eléctrica de España (REE)

Since its creation in 1985, Red Eléctrica de España (hereafter REE) has been in charge of the Spanish transmission grid and operation of the electricity system. It owns most of the Spanish high-voltage transmission grid and it is the only company in Spain which specializes in the transmission of electrical power. Indeed, REE was the first company in the world to specialize exclusively on the transmission of electricity and the operation of electricity systems. In this respect, it anticipated further international trends leading to the separation of such activities and showed that transmission is an independent activity, separate from generation and distribution.

In the mid-1980s, the Spanish electricity industry was made up of eleven vertically integrated companies operating in generation, transmission and distribution, and one state-owned company (Endesa) exclusively involved in generation. As a result of a process of mergers and acquisitions over the 1990s, in 2001 these firms clustered into four private groups: Endesa, Iberdrola, Unión Fenosa and Hidroeléctrica del Cantábrico. Endesa (privatized by the end of 1997) and Iberdrola have a dominant position (80 per cent market share) both in generation as well as in distribution. Though these four companies have a significant number of high-voltage lines (mostly 220 KV lines) they dos not conduct business in Spain in the transport of electricity. They also jointly have a 40 per cent share in REE, as shown in Table 8.3.

Today, REE is a private firm whose shares can be held by any individual or corporation provided that their total direct or indirect stake in the company's share capital is no greater than 10 per cent. Likewise, the cumulative direct or indirect stakes of agents carrying out activities in the electricity sector must be no greater than 40 per cent and these shareholdings may not be syndicated.

Table 8.3   Shareholders of Red Eléctrica de España (2001)

Shareholder	%
SEPI	28.5
Endesa Group	10
Iberdrola	10
Unión Fenosa	10
Hidroeléctrica del Cantábrico	10
Free float	31.5

From 1988 to 1998 the Spanish electricity industry was governed by the so-called 'Marco Legal Estable' (hereafter MLE) or Stable Legal Framework, established by Royal Decree 1538/1987 of 11 December 1987. Under the MLE the Spanish electricity industry operated as an integrated system with respect to key decision-making, both long term and short term. Thus, decisions on investments in generation were made through the National Energy Plan (PEN) and approved by Parliament. REE was created in 1985 as a publicly controlled stand-alone company responsible for the design and maintenance of the high-voltage system capacity and for the national central dispatch.

The MLE introduced a system of remuneration of the companies based on the so-called 'standard costs'. Each input necessary to supply electrical power was assigned a standard cost allowance. These 'standard' costs were established separately for generation, transmission and distribution, and included some fair rate of return linked to the prime rate. The firms' revenues were then essentially determined by their aggregate standard costs, irrespective of the actual costs incurred. Hence the system essentially worked as a type of revenue-cap regulation giving strong incentives to reduce actual costs (see Rodríguez and Castro, 1994; Crampes and Laffont, 1995; Arocena and Waddams-Price, 2002). Accordingly, REE was allowed revenue based on the total cost of transport recognized for each year.

The MLE was in force until the approval of the Electricity Law 54/1997, which liberalized the sector as of 1 January 1998 (see Arocena et al., 1999). The act ratifies REE as responsible for the operation, maintenance, development and management of the electricity lines, entrusting to it the functions of System Operator, which is of ensuring a proper coordination of the system of production and transport of electricity, to ensure continuity and safety in its transport.

The legislative development of the Electricity Act, particularly the Royal Decree 2017/1997 and the Royal Decree 2819/1998, established a system of RPI-X for the regulation of the electric power transmission and distribution activities. In other words, it introduced some adjustments in the standard costs for potential productivity improvements. The Ministry of Industry and Energy sets the value of X for a maximum period of four years, at the end of which it shall publish new values for the said index, if any. The X factor was established at 1 per cent for the period 1998–2001.

4 DATA, METHODOLOGY AND RESULTS

In this section we assess the evolution of the charges of CLH and REE during the decade 1990–2000. To this end, we first estimate expression (8.8) stated above and its components. The actual change of output prices for REE and CLH ($\dot{P}_E$, $\dot{P}_o$) is computed as the rate of variation of average transport charges per kWh of electricity and per ton of oil products respectively. The Spanish manufacturing sector is the competitive benchmark industry for which we construct our price references. The rate of variation of the prices experienced by manufacturing products ($\dot{P}_c$) is provided by the National Institute of Statistics. The rate of change in Total Factor Productivity, both for manufacturing ($\dot{TFP}_c$). and regulated sectors ($\dot{TFP}_R$) is estimated through the well known Tornqvist index:

$$ TFP = \left(ln \ y^{t+1} - ln \ y^t \right) - \left[\sum_{i=1}^{n} 1/2 \left(\beta_i^t + \beta_i^{t+1} \right) \left(ln \ x^{t+1} - ln \ x^t \right) \right] $$

where β_i^t represents the cost share of input i in period t.[7]

All the variables and their corresponding definitions are shown in Table 8.4. We use data from all companies in each industry. Data for manufacturing were provided by the National Statistics Institute and by the Fundación BBV. We use data from the annual reports of CLH and REE, as well as from the electricity association UNESA.

Tables 8.5 and 8.6 display the results for each company. Columns (1) to (7) in each panel show the annual price variation benchmarks ($\dot{P}_R$, $\dot{P}_W$, $\dot{P}_{max}$) as well its components according to expressions (8.8), (8.9) and (8.10). Columns (8) to (11) summarize the cumulative results up to the period in question. Additionally, Figures 8.1 and 8.2 illustrate the temporal pattern of actual average transport charges ($\dot{P}_E$, $\dot{P}_o$), as well as the price variation benchmarks ($\dot{P}_R$, $\dot{P}_W$, $\dot{P}_{max}$) in cumulatively terms for REE and CLH respectively, constructed from columns (8) to (11) of Tables 8.5 and 8.6.

Let us start with the results for REE in Table 8.5. As the first row in column (3) shows, manufacturing prices ($\dot{P}_c$) increased by 1.3 per cent in 1991. At the same time, column (4) reveals that the rise of input prices for REE was 2.0 per cent points lower than that in the manufacturing industry. Further, the productivity growth rate of REE exceeds by 2.2 per cent points the corresponding growth rate in the manufacturing sector – column (5) Therefore, if transport charges would have updated according to expression (8.8) ($\dot{P}_R$), in 1991 tariffs should have decreased by 2.9 per cent, as shown in column (2).[8]

Table 8.4   Definition of variables

	Variable	Definition
$T\dot{F}P$	Total Factor Productivity Change	$\left(lny^{t+1} - lny^{t}\right) - \left[\displaystyle\sum_{j=1}^{n} 1/2\left(\beta_{i}^{t} + \beta_{i}^{t+1}\right)\left(lnx^{t+1} - lnx^{t}\right)\right]$
y^{t}	Value Added in period t (1995 prices)	Value Added = Sales − Cost of sales and other external and operating costs (Value Added = Personnel Costs + Gross Operating Profit)
x_{1}^{t}	Labour in period t	Average number of employees
x_{2}^{t}	Capital in period t (1995 prices)	Tangible fixed assets
β_{1}^{t}	Labour share	Personnel Costs/Value Added
β_{2}^{t}	Capital share	Gross Operating Profit/Value Added
$\dot{W}$	Change in input prices	$\left(\dfrac{\beta_{1}^{t} + \beta_{1}^{t+1}}{2}\right)\dot{w}_{1} + \left(\dfrac{\beta_{2}^{t} + \beta_{2}^{t+1}}{2}\right)\dot{w}_{2}$
$\dot{w}_{1}$	Labour price variation	Annual variation in labour costs per employee
$\dot{w}_{2}$	Capital price variation	Deflator of Gross Fixed Capital Formation

Table 8.5   Price variation benchmarks for REE

	Annual growth rate								Cumulative growth			
	(1)	(2)	(3)	(4)*	(5)*	(6)	(7)		(8)	(9)	(10)	(11)
	$\dot{P}_E$	$\dot{P}_R$	$\dot{P}_C$	$\dot{W}$	$T\dot{F}P$	$\dot{P}_W$	$\dot{P}_{max}$		$\dot{P}_E$	$\dot{P}_R$	$\dot{P}_W$	$\dot{P}_{max}$
								1990	100	100	100	100
90–91	7.4	-2.9	1.3	-2.0	2.2	-0.7	1.3	1991	107	97	99	101
91–92	8.9	0.7	1.2	-2.4	-1.9	-1.2	3.1	1992	117	98	98	104
92–93	7.4	-4.4	2.4	-0.5	6.2	1.9	2.4	1993	126	94	100	107
93–94	6.0	4.5	4.5	-0.7	-0.7	3.8	5.2	1994	133	98	104	113
94–95	1.3	1.4	6.8	-0.6	4.7	6.2	6.8	1995	135	99	110	120
95–96	1.8	-0.9	1.8	-0.5	2.2	1.3	1.8	1996	137	98	112	122
96–97	-8.4	5.9	1.2	-0.2	-4.9	1.0	6.1	1997	126	104	113	130
97–98	-2.8	-11.8	-0.7	0.3	11.4	-0.4	-0.4	1998	122	92	112	129
98–99	-3.6	-4.1	0.7	1.2	5.9	1.8	1.8	1999	118	88	114	132
99–00	-2.0	-2.9	2.7	1.7	7.3	4.4	4.4	2000	116	85	119	137

Table 8.6   Price variation benchmarks for CLH

	Annual growth rate								Cumulative growth			
	(1)	(2)	(3)	(4)*	(5)*	(6)	(7)		(8)	(9)	(10)	(11)
	$\dot{P}_O$	$\dot{P}_R$	$\dot{P}_C$	$\dot{W}$	$T\dot{F}P$	$\dot{P}_W$	$\dot{P}_{max}$		$\dot{P}_O$	$\dot{P}_R$	$\dot{P}_W$	$\dot{P}_{max}$
								1993	100	100	100	100
93–94	-7.0	-1.7	4.5	-9.1	-2.9	-4.6	7.4	1994	93	98	95	107
94–95	-3.6	1.8	6.8	-4.4	0.6	2.4	1.8	1995	90	100	98	109
95–96	-8.6	4.2	1.8	3.7	1.3	5.5	5.5	1996	82	104	103	115
96–97	-1.8	-1.1	1.2	-1.2	1.1	0.0	1.2	1997	81	103	103	117
97–98	-	-8.3	-0.7	-3.2	4.4	-3.9	-0.7	1998	72	95	99	116
98–99	9.1	-6.4	0.7	0.4	7.5	1.1	1.1	1999	79	89	100	117
99–00	11.7	-0.8	2.7	3.0	6.6	5.7	5.7	2000	88	88	106	124

Figure 8.1   The evolution of REE charges

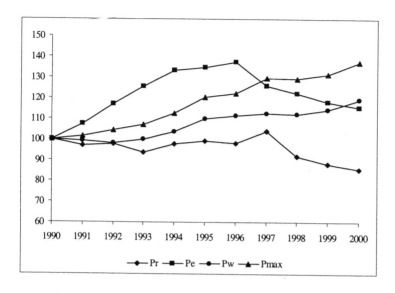

Figure 8.2   The evolution of CLH charges

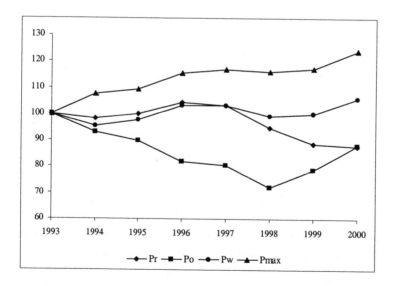

Nevertheless, as column (1) indicates, REE average tariffs ($\dot{P}_E$) actually increased by 7.4 per cent that year. Consequently, according to expression (8.9) the price increase allowed REE to keep all productivity gains since the sum of columns (3) and (4) results in a lower rate $\dot{P}_W = \dot{P}_C + (\dot{W}_R - \dot{W}_C) =$ minus 0.7 per cent. Moreover, as stated in expression (8.10, P_{max} would have increased by 1.3 per cent, which, according to our classification in Table 8.1, reflects a virtually ineffective price control from the point of view of the REE's users.

Looking at the cumulative results, the last row of column (8) confirms that the growth of the average REE charges was 16 per cent over 1990–2000. In the event of competitive adjustment of prices, they would have been reduced by 15 per cent – column (9) –. Column (10) shows the expected price increases when only relative input price changes are accounted for ($\dot{P}_W$). In such a case, prices would have increased by 19 per cent. Finally, column (11) shows that if prices had adjusted according to $\dot{P}_{max}$, they would have increased by 37 per cent.

As can be observed in Figure 8.1, REE charges increased more rapidly over the first half of the period considered (1990–96) than over the second half. As a result of this pricing policy, the cumulative growth of tariffs was even higher that the 'best of the worlds' for REE ($\dot{P}_{max}$). In summary, it is patent that pricing policy was very favourable to REE, allowing it keeping the totality of productivity gains achieved over time. Only during the second half of the decade did it apply some effective price restraint.

Table 8.6 summarizes the results for CLH. By focusing exclusively on the cumulative results – columns (8) to (11) – CLH average charges ($\dot{P}_G$) decreased by 12 per cent over the 1993–2000 period, which is the same reduction that a competitive price adjustment would have led to. The control of prices has effectively limited the maximal surplus that CLH could potentially extract from its customers ($\dot{P}_{max} = 124$).

Figure 8.2 plots the evolution of transport charges. As for the REE case, it is also possible to distinguish two different patterns. Up to 1998, the evolution of prices was below ($\dot{P}_R$), reflecting a pro-consumer bias in price updating. On the contrary, from 1998 onwards tariffs rose rapidly, parallel to the rate of growth most favourable to firms ($\dot{P}_{max}$).

In order to contrast the evolution of price variation and firms' profitability Figure 8.3 plots the evolution of the Return on Equity of the manufacturing sector and that of CLH and REE. A comparison of Figure 8.3 with Figures 8.1 and 8.2 shows that, as expected, the evolution of firms' profits is consistent with the temporal pattern of the average transport charges discussed earlier. Unsurprisingly, both companies exhibit higher and more stable returns than that of the manufacturers. The profitability of REE remains fairly constant around 15 per cent over the decade, whereas the profitability of CLH is the highest, above 20 per cent during the whole period.

Figure 8.3   Return on equity (profit from ordinary operations/equity)

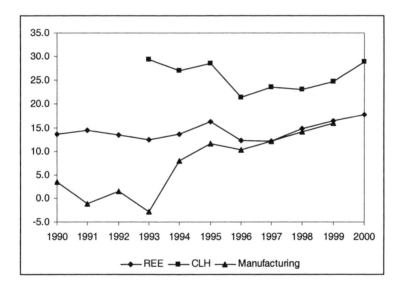

5   CONCLUSIONS

This chapter has analysed the regulation of the companies in charge of the transport of oil products and electricity in Spain (CLH and REE respectively). Particularly, this chapter suggests an approach to determine whether regulators set prices that either yield an advantage to those companies or to the consumers.

To accomplish this objective we have constructed three alternate evolutions of prices as benchmarks. One represents the best reference from the point of view of the consumers and corresponds to competitive price adjusting, on the assumption that the regulatory objective is to set prices so as to maintain breakeven operation over time. A second alternative may be considered the most attractive from the perspective of the companies, since the resulting price increases allow firms to keep all cost reductions and pass all cost increases on to the consumer. The third benchmark may represent a bias in either direction. By taking into account the input price variation while allowing companies to absorb the total amount of productivity changes, it lets the sign of the changes suggest the direction of the bias - pro-consumer if negative; pro-industry otherwise. We use those benchmarks to provide a taxonomy of price increases to assess the inclination of pricing policies in distributing the rents between consumers and firms.

Unsurprisingly, our results show that CLH average charges decreased by the same proportion that competitive price adjusting would have led to during the period 1993–2000. The high transport and storage tariffs that the regulator allowed CAMPSA to charge over the second part of the 1980s and early 1990s (Correljé, 1994 Contín et al.;. 2001), enable it to generate the income necessary to finance the expansion and modernization of its oil pipeline and storage system. This, in turn, allows CLH to reduce its average charges, on cumulative terms, by 12 per cent over the period 1993-2000 while maintaining higher returns than those of the manufacturers and REE.

Likewise, our results show that the successive price adjustments over time of transport charges of REE have protected consumers from an excessive monopolistic abuse. This has not, however, precluded REE from maintaining higher and more stable profitability rates than those achieved in the manufacturing sector. This suggests that REE's restraint of prices was not very tight.

To sum up, although our results show that the successive price adjustments over time of the tariffs of the Spanish oil and electricity's essential facilities have protected consumers from an excessive monopolistic abuse, they have allowed REE and CLH to maintain high and stable profitability rates.

NOTES

1. The authors gratefully acknowledge financial support from the Spanish Ministry of Science and Technology under the project SEC2001-2793-C03-12.
2. *Universidad Pública de Navarra*, Departamento de Gestión de Empresas, Campus de Arrosadia. 31006 Pamplona, Spain. Fax +34 948169404. Emails: pablo@unavarra.es, contin@unavarra.es
3. Within an industry, the essential facility is monopolized because of large economies of scale, of first-mover advantages or of technological superiority (Laffont and Tirole, 1996).
4. Because of lack of data for the gas industry, this chapter only focuses on the analysis of REE and CLH.
5. That is, expression (8.2) assumes that *total* revenue covers *total* costs, including the costs of the financial capital that the owners have provided to the firm.
6. Thus, in 1997 the joint market share of Repsol, Cepsa-Elf and BP Spain was around 86–80 per cent in 2000 for automotive fuels (gasoline and gas oil) and still close to 100 per cent for fuel oil in 2000.
7. See Diewert and Nakamura (1993) and Balk (1998), for comprehensive studies of the nature and the properties of this index number.
8. We should recall that we are considering a *post factum* price adjustment, with the purpose of analysing the rent sharing between firms and consumers actually registered. As explained in section 2, an *ex ante* commitment with such a competitive adjustment would modify substantially the firms' incentives to efficient behaviour.

REFERENCES

Armstrong, M., S. Cowan and J. Vickers (1994), *Regulatory Reform: Economic Analysis and British Experience,* Cambridge, US: MIT Press.
Arocena, P. (2004), 'Privatization policy in Spain: Stuck between liberalization and the protection of national's interests', Cesifo Working Papers, N. 1187.
Arocena, P. and C. Waddams-Price (2002), 'Generating efficiency: economic and environmental regulation of public and private electricity generators in Spain', *International Journal of Industrial Organization*, 20(1), 41–69.
Arocena, P, K–U. Khün and P. Regibeau (1999), 'Regulatory reform in the Spanish electricity industry: a missed opportunity for competition', *Energy Policy*, 27, 387–99.

Balk, B. (1998), *Industrial Price, Quantity, and Productivity Indices*, Boston, US: Kluwer Academic Publishers.

Bernstein, J.I. and D. Sappington (1999), 'Setting the X Factor in price-cap regulation plans', *Journal of Regulatory Economics*, 16, 5–25.

CBBE (1999), *Resultados anuales de las empresas no financieras*, Banco de España, Central de Balances, Madrid, Spain.

Contín, I., A. Correljé and E. Huerta (1999), 'The Spanish gasoline market: From ceiling regulation to open market pricing', *The Energy Journal*, 20 (4), 1–14.

Contín, I., A. Correljé and E. Huerta (2000), 'Integración vertical en el refino de petróleo: El caso español', *Boletín de Estudios Económicos*, 55, 169, 39–60.

Contín, I., A. Correljé and E. Huerta (2001), 'The Spanish distribution for oil products: An obstacle to competition?, *Energy Policy*, 29, 103–11.

Correljé, A. (1994), *The Spanish Oil Industry*, Tinbergen Institute Research Series, 84. Amsterdam.

Crampes, C. and J.J. Laffont (1995), 'Transfers and incentives in the Spanish electricity sector', *Revista Española de Economía, Monográfico* 'Regulación', 117–40.

Crew, M.A. and P.R. Kleindorfer (1987), 'Productivity Incentives and Rate-of-Return Regulation', in M.A., Crew: *Deregulating Utilities in an Era of Deregulation*, London, UK: MacMillan Press.

Diewert, W.E. and A.O. Nakamura (1993), *Essays in Index Number Theory, Volume I*, Amsterdam, NL: Elsevier Science Publishers.

Hillman, J.J. (1991), 'Oil Pipeline Rate: A Case for Yardstick Regulation', in M.A. Crew, *Competition and the Regulation of Utilities*, London, UK: Kluwer Academic Publishers.

IEA (1999), *Energy Policies of IEA Countries, 1999 Review*, Paris: OECD/International Energy Agency.

Laffont, J. and J. Tirole (1996), 'Creating competition through interconnection: theory and practice', *Journal of Regulatory Economics*, 10, 227–56.

Laffont, J. and J. Tirole (1993), *A Theory of Incentives in Procurement and Regulation*, Cambridge, US: MIT Press.

Lyon, T. and S. Hackett (1993), 'Bottlenecks and government structures: Open access and long-term contracting in natural gas', *Journal of Law and Economics and Organization*, 9 (2), 380–98.

OECD (2000), *Regulatory Reform in Spain*, Paris: OECD.

Rodríguez, L. and F. Castro (1994), 'Aspectos económicos de la configuración del sector eléctrico en España: ¿una falsa competencia referencial?, *Cuadernos Económicos de Información Comercial Española*, 57(2), 161–83.

Sánchez P. (1997), 'Los modelos de regulación de los sectores energéticos en España', *Economía Industrial*, 318, 77–86.

Sidack, J.G. and D.F. Spulber (1998), Deregulatory Taking and the Regulatory Contract. The Competitive Transformation of Network Industries in the United States, Cambridge, US: Cambridge University Press.

TDC (1995), 'Distribución de productos petrolíferos', in *La competencia en España: Balance y nuevas propuesta*, Madrid, Spain. http://www.globalcompetitionforum.org/regions/europe/Spain/informa.pdf, 14 December 2004.

9. Privatization of Amsterdam Airport: Schiphol and the Public Interest

Jacco R. Hakfoort

---

1 INTRODUCTION

Aviation is a large industry that has experienced rapid growth over the past decades. Airliners transport more than 1,350 passenger kilometres per annum, while freight transport makes up more than 1/3 of the total value of exports. Since 1960, passenger traffic has shown a stunning average growth of 9 per cent per annum, while cargo traffic has grown at an even higher rate: 11 per cent.

One important trend affecting air traffic worldwide has been the deregulation of the industry. Deregulation has created the possibility for entry of new players on routes traditionally governed by (national) airlines through bilateral agreements between individual governments, and has introduced competition between the incumbent carriers. The business strategies of the airlines following deregulation (including the channelling of flights through hub airports and the formation of global alliances) have affected the relative position of airports in the aviation network. While some airports have emerged as central airports of one of the global airline alliances, others have been reduced to airports of only secondary importance.

Partly as a result of the increased competition among airlines in the deregulated environment, airports have been reluctant or unable (because of regulation) to raise airport charges and have sought other sources of revenues. Over time, almost all larger airports have seen an increase in the share of non-aviation revenues in total revenues. These revenues consist of retail concessions, parking fees, real estate development and so on. Airports have a natural incentive to keep airport charges low given the demand complementarities between aviation revenues and non-aviation revenues.

A third trend in international aviation has been the redefinition of the role of the government towards the ownership and control of airports. In a number of cases, this has resulted in various forms of private sector participation in airports ranging from outright asset sales through initial public offering to the awarding of management contracts to commercial operators. While this seems a natural step after the deregulation of the airline market, it also raises the question whether a privatized airport will have the same incentives as a publicly owned airport. If there is a large gap between the social and private optimum, clearly additional regulation is necessary or the government might decide against private ownership and/or operation at all.

This chapter looks at the economic trade-offs between the privatization of an airport, inspired by the proposed public flotation of the stocks of Amsterdam Airport Schiphol. To provide some background to the debate, section 2 first discusses the deregulation of the European aviation market. Section 3 discusses the increased importance of non-aviation revenues for airports such as Amsterdam Airport Schiphol. Section 4 identifies market failures that might provide a rationale for government intervention, and the government failures that might mitigate the beneficial impact of any public intervention. Section 5 then applies these insights to the debate on the privatization of Amsterdam Airport Schiphol. Section 6 concludes.

2   DEREGULATION OF AIR TRANSPORT MARKETS

The origin of bilateral agreements that ruled air traffic for so long goes back to the Paris Convention of 1919. During this Convention, the political independence and territorial immunity of the participating member states was asserted. For the air transport market, this meant that countries were awarded sovereignty over their own airspace (Burghouwt and Hakfoort, 1998; Zacher and Sutton, 1996 91). According to Nijkamp (1996 5) 'direct government intervention in air transport became inevitable, so that the free trade laissez faire approach during the first years of aviation was gradually replaced by an incomplete pattern of bilateral agreements between countries to or over which those airlines wished to fly'.

At the end of the Second World War, an attempt was made at the Chicago Convention to replace the patchwork of bilateral agreements with one multilateral agreement. The Chicago Convention was only a partial success. The participating member states could not agree on the majority of so-called 'freedoms of the air'. Sixty percent of the participating countries accepted the freedom to fly through the air space of other countries (first freedom) or the freedom to land in another country for non-commercial reasons (second freedom). However, there was no agreement on the freedom to operate flights to another country (third and fourth freedom) or the freedom to transport passengers on to a third country (fifth freedom) (see also Button and Swann, 1992).

From the Chicago Convention on, the jurisdiction on the airspace was arranged through a system of bilateral agreements between national governments. These agreements set the terms for the freedoms for the 'flag carriers' of the individual countries, the airports that could be used for landings and take-offs and the number of carriers on the route. In almost all cases, the two national airlines were the only airlines that could benefit from the bilateral agreements. Market shares and revenues on the routes between the two countries were arranged in so-called 'inter-airline pooling agreements' while prices were regulated through the International Air Traffic Association (IATA) which operated as a price cartel. The whole system of bilateral agreements therefore resulted in an aviation market that was more guided by the need for political control over airspace by member states and equality between countries than by the need for efficiency through competition (Zacher and Sutton, 1996).

The 1970s saw a change of regime in the United States. Until 1978 entry and exit on the US aviation market as well as prices and market shares were determined by the Civil Aviation Board. As was the case for countries with bilateral agreements, competition was absent in this system. As a result of a changing political climate, scientific research on the contestability of the aviation market and lobbies of consumers and airliners, President Carter signed the Airline Deregulation Act in 1978 that allowed competition in the US aviation market. In the 1980s other countries such as Australia, New

Zealand and the United Kingdom also decided to deregulate their internal market (Button and Swann, 1989a; 1989b).

The United States also tried to open up the existing bilateral agreements with other countries. Over the period 1977–80 a number of bilateral agreements between the United States and other countries were opened up to competition. An example is the 'open sky agreement' between the US and the Netherlands in 1978 that amongst others allowed multiple designation, freed up the existing capacity and frequency restrictions and prices on the routes between the two countries. During the 1980s a number of bilateral agreements between European countries were also liberalized such as between the United Kingdom and the Netherlands (1984), the United Kingdom and Belgium (1985) and the United Kingdom and Ireland (1988) (Button et al., 1998).

In 1988, the European Council of Ministers finally decided to deregulate the European aviation market completely in three 'packages' starting in 1990, 1992 and 1997 respectively. Each of the packages introduced more freedom for the airlines to set ticket prices, frequencies and so on and allowed third parties access to the internal European routes. In 1997 the aviation markets *within* the European Union were completely liberalized. However, for access to intercontinental routes European airlines are still dependent on the bilateral agreements of their national governments within non-European governments. The national airlines are therefore 'tied' to their country of registration. Former European Commissioner Neil Kinnock has therefore argued for an extension of the multilateral agreement within the European Union in the direction of the United States, a Common Transatlantic Aviation Area (Kinnock, 1999). Deregulation has also taken place in other regions such as Asia and between Australia and New Zealand.

The deregulation of the aviation market as described above has affected the possibilities for national governments to control the outcomes on the deregulated aviation market (Hakfoort and Schaafsma, 2000). Entry, prices and market shares are no longer determined by bilateral agreements and a price cartel but are the result of the profit-maximizing behaviour of airlines. As a result of deregulation, airlines have adopted various business strategies to improve or at least consolidate their level of profitability.

One of the most noticeable strategies of airlines has been the reconfiguration of their route networks after deregulation. After deregulation of the internal US aviation market the growth of air transport was concentrated on a small number of large airports or hubs where passengers could transfer to a connecting flight (Goetz and Sutton, 1997; Reynolds-Feighan, 1998; Viscusi et al., 1998). Hub-and-spoke networks have a number of potential advantages over the point-to-point networks that existed before deregulation.

Airlines can offer more destinations at higher frequencies by combining point-to-point traffic with transfer passengers at a central hub. Hub-and-spoke route systems offer the opportunity of cost savings, particularly for those passengers with a high marginal cost per passenger (Brueckner and Spiller, 1994; Graham, 1995; Pels, 2001; Williams, 1994). Finally, hub airports can act as a barrier to entry for new airlines because the dominant, incumbent airlines already have an advantage over new airlines in terms of the number of direct and indirect connections they can offer from the hub, higher frequencies, loyalty programmes and the possibility of cross-subsidization of flights (Borenstein, 1992; Zhang, 1996).

Another important business strategy of airlines after deregulation has been the formation of global airline alliances. Alliances are co-operative agreements between airlines that can vary from code-sharing on individual flights to a complete integration of networks and marketing services (EURAFOR, 2000; Hanlon, 1996). The formation of alliances can be seen as a response to the hybrid system of limited competition. On the one hand, co-operation offers an opportunity to increase the cost and revenue advantages of hub-and-spoke systems and to limit competition by integrating networks and marketing programmes (such as frequent flyer programmes) (Oum et al., 2001; Pels, 2001). On the other hand, alliances are 'second best solutions' (Kinnock, 1998) to mergers between airlines from different countries of registration. Alliances allow access to foreign markets through the networks of alliance partners. Changes in alliances can have a big influence on the position of individual airports in the aviation network (Burghouwt and Hakfoort, 2001). Alliances therefore more and more take control over the worldwide aviation flows and the future of individual airports, where national governments used to control these flows before deregulation.

Table 8.1 provides some insight into the evolution of the European aviation network after deregulation over the period 1990–98. In theory, deregulation will lead to shorter routes, higher frequencies, the use of larger aircraft, higher levels of congestion at hub airports and increased price discrimination. Can we observe the same evidence of hub-and-spoke formation as in the United States? According to Table 9.1, there is indeed evidence of the increased concentration of intercontinental traffic on the major airports on Europe. However, we find no evidence for the concentration of intra-European traffic on a small number of hubs.

Table 9.1   *Convergence or divergence in the European aviation*
               network? Percentage share in total seat capacity of top 5 and
               10 airports in intercontinental and intra-European traffic in
               1990, 1994 and 1998

	1990	1994	1998
Intercontinental			
Top 5 airports	52.5	56.0	58.6
Top 10 airports	73.1	74.6	76.6
Intra-European			
Top 5 airports	22.6	21.9	19.9
Top 10 airports	32.5	35.1	33.4

Source: Burghouwt and Hakfoort (2001).

3   GROWING IMPORTANCE OF NON-AVIATION REVENUES

The deregulation of the European aviation market has not been without its consequences for the operation of airports. Before deregulation, airports were more or less assured of a certain number of flights as a result of the bilateral agreements. The most important non-aviation activities consisted of the handling of cargo and luggage. Airports were almost by definition owned and operated by national, regional or municipal governments.

The liberalization of the European aviation market that is accompanied in many cases by the incorporation or privatization of national airlines and/or airports has increased the incentive for airports to operate efficiently. For certain segments of passengers, airports now have to compete for passengers (Barret, 2000), although in many cases the link with the (former) national carrier is still strong.

Besides the competition on the market for passengers, the slow process of incorporation and privatization of airports has been important for the changing role of passengers. The most important and well-known example of privatization within the European Union is the privatization of seven BAA airports in the United Kingdom in 1987. These included London Heathrow, London Gatwick and London Stansted. Examples of (partial) privatization include the airports of Vienna, Copenhagen and Athens (see Schneiderbauer and Feldman, 1999 for a survey).

The more competitive environment and the changing ownership structures have had implications for the strategies of airports. Through the competitive situation on the airport market and the regulation of airport charges by the government or an independent regulator there is not much growth to be expected in the profits on aviation revenues. Traditionally, these aviation revenues formed the bulk of total revenues. Increasingly, however, airports have turned to non-aviation revenues. These include revenues from property development, retail concessions, parking fees and so on. Table 9.2 shows the percentage of these 'commercial revenues' in total revenues as well as the retail revenues in US$ per passenger for the four largest European airports.

BAA and Schiphol are dependent for more than half of their revenue on non-aviation activities. Within the non-aviation revenues, more than half is based on retail revenues on both airports. More recent data from the Airports Council International (ACI) shows that European airports had almost as much revenue from aviation activities as from non-aviation activities in 1997, similar to airports in North America. The non-aviation revenues on average consisted of parking fees (12.8 per cent), retail concessions (44.4 per cent), other property (20.7 per cent) and other income (19.4 per cent). European airports are on average more dependent on retail concessions than airports in the United States where this type of real estate makes up only 13.3 per cent of total revenues. (The abolishment of duty-free sales from July 1, 1999 has reduced the income from retail activities somewhat.)

Table 9.2   *Airports as shopping malls with a runway. Commercial revenues as a percenaget of total revenues and commercial and rental revenues in US$ per passenger, 1995*

	Commercial revenues as a % of total revenues, 1995	Commercial revenues in US$ per passenger, 1995	Retail revenues in US$ per passenger, 1995
BAA	65 %	13.05	9.44
Amsterdam	55 %	12.06	6.23
Paris	45 %	12.00	3.85
Frankfurt	30 %	13.58	8.72

Source: Natwest Markets (1999).

4   PRIVATIZATION OF AIRPORTS

A third trend (after the deregulation of aviation markets and the increase in non-aviation revenues of airports) has been the changing ownership patterns of individual airports (see Kapur, 1995). Traditionally owned and operated by national or regional governments, in the last two decades there is more and more private sector participation in airports although the form this takes is very diverse. Table 9.3 gives an overview of the total investment in airport projects by the private sector in billion US$, based on data collected by the World Bank.

Table 9.3 shows that private sector participation has been particularly strong in Latin America and the Caribbean. This is partly due to the complete privatization of the Argentinean airport system during the 1980s. Private sector participation is also strong in Europe, Asia and the Pacific.

Table 9.3   *Total investment in airport projects with private*
                   participation in billion US$, 1990–1998

East Asia/Pacific	1,243
Europe and Central Asia	1,154
Latin America and Carribean	2,450
Middle East and North Africa	198
South Asia	138
Sub-Saharan Africa	263
Total	5,445

Source: World Bank (1999).

Private investment in airport infrastructure can range from joint ventures, majority or partial divestures, management contracts to build-operate-transfer (BOT), build-own-operate-transfer (BOOT), lease-develop-operate (LDO) and wraparound addition schemes. The experience so far (see Kapur, 1995) shows that efficient airport corporations will become global operators and that the awarding and monitoring of private concessions generally lacks transparency.

5   IDENTIFYING POTENTIAL MARKET FAILURES

Amsterdam Airport Schiphol is the fourth largest airport in Europe, both in terms of passengers and in terms of connectivity (CPB, 2000). The airport operator, the Schiphol Group, is incorporated, but the control of the shares is still in the hands of the central government (which owns a majority share) and the municipalities of Amsterdam and Rotterdam. Schiphol Group considers it essential to have a public float of its shares, 'to continue playing a role in this highly dynamic aviation market' (Schiphol Group, 2000). In particular, Schiphol Group wants to use the revenues of a public float to expand its non-aviation activities and to participate in airport(s) alliances abroad. The conditions of the public float are currently under discussion with the Dutch (aviation and competition) authorities.

The case of the privatization of Amsterdam Airport Schiphol raises the question whether a privatized airport will act in the public interest. Is there any need to review the government involvement with the airport as a result of privatization?

In a number of cases, the commercial interest of Amsterdam Airport Schiphol coincides with the public interest. Take, for example, an investment needed for a further expansion of the airport. Through an expansion of the airport, the operator is able to increase both aviation and non-aviation revenues. Society as a whole profits through direct and (possibly) indirect economic effects from this expansion. Direct effects are based on the quality of the airport for business and leisure travellers. This quality consists of the prices of the flights from the airport, the number of destinations that can be reached directly and indirectly from the airport, taking into account the travel time and frequency of these flights. Indirect effects might also occur in the form of clustering activities on and around the airport (although a substantial part of the literature typically overestimates the welfare gains from indirect activity around an airport).

We can point, however, to a number of potential cases in which the interest of the airport does not coincide with the public interest. These provide cases for government intervention (see also CPB, 2000).

A good example is the existence of negative externalities such as noise or pollution that are not acknowledged by the airport when considering expansion. The government can intervene in a number of ways to protect the public interest in that case. In each case, the benefits and costs (which include the distortionary effects that public intervention might have) of public intervention must be weighed. The possibilities for public intervention are further restricted by decisions made on the European level (see above).

The public float of an airport does not substantially change the policy agenda. With or without privatization, the government still has certain matters to regulate: noise levels, for example, and safety or spatial planning. On the positive side, regulation is likely to become more transparent after privatization. Indeed, improving the current situation, where the government is stakeholder, owner, policymaker and regulator may the most important reason to privatize in the first place! However, a number of specific issues require special attention. In the four cases we discuss below, there might be a difference between the commercial interest of the privatized airport and the public interest. The nature of the discussion is to set a policy and/or research agenda, not necessarily to provide all the answers.

5.1 Investments: Positive and Negative Externalities

Investment decisions by private firms are made on the basis of their profitability. This can lead to situations in which investments are either to high (negative externalities), too low (positive externalities) or at a location where total welfare is not maximized. Possible (often partial) solutions include the following:

(1) Use market-based regulation such as shadow prices in the case of negative externalities;
(2) Subsidize in the case of positive externalities (if internalizing the effects is too difficult for the airport operator);
(3) Do a cost-benefit analysis if location choices are at stake.

These options are more or less in line with current practice – with the exception of noise regulation where the Dutch government opted for a policy based on an absolute maximum noise level (which does not yield optimal incentives to invest in noise efficiency).

5.2 Market Power

The most obvious way in which airports can deviate from the public interest is by exploiting their market power. Airports such as Amsterdam Airport Schiphol have market power because many customers cannot substitute between suppliers and are therefore 'captured'. This provides the basis for regulation of aviation and non-aviation charges (Prices Surveillance Authority, 1993). There are basically three issues here.

First, does it make sense to regulate aviation and non-aviation activities in one basket (the so-called 'single till') (Starkie, 1999)? In general, non-aviation activities are quite profitable. To keep non-aviation activities in check, the UK regulates the major London airports and Manchester according to the single till. This leads to cross-subsidization of airport charges, with the potential that those charges are lower than marginal costs. This clearly affects competition. A complicating issue here is the fact that regulatory principles are often based on bilateral agreements, and therefore hard to synchronize across Europe.

Second (and related to the first issue): how fierce is competition in air charges? It is true that the major European hubs compete to a certain extent on charges. But to what extent? If one hub is regulated by a single till (Heathrow) and another is not, then competition is distorted. To assess the importance of this distortion, we need more research on airport charge competition (Kunz, 1999).

Third, should market power be checked by ex ante regulation (i.e. via an independent aviation regulator) or can we solely rely on competition law (ex post regulation)? Because of the complexity of the exploration possibilities of market power, and the importance of quick decision making and clarity, there is a lot to say in favour of an independent authority. This holds for regulation of aviation activities. What about non-aviation activities? Suppose that one decides not to employ the single till. Non-aviation activities are quite similar to other types of activities in the economy – so that the competition law seems to be sufficient here.

5.3 Ownership

The mere fact that the ownership of assets changes hands can lead to undesirable situations. It should, therefore, first of all be clarified which part of Schiphol is to be privatized. Should the land remain in the hands of the government? And what about the slots? In each case, there exists a trade-off between the possibilities of market abuse or undesirable distribution effects and government failure (i.e. necessary intervention in private activities).

5.4 Managerial Incentives: Myopia

Managers can behave myopically, i.e. pursue short-term interests at the expense of long-term interests. In other sectors, this could lead to takeovers or even bankruptcy. Both these market corrections seem either unfeasible or undesirable in the case of Schiphol. The research question is how big this problem is, and how it can be corrected.

Changes in market and government failure after privatization have consequences for the process of privatization. Anticipating potential problems is a vital success factor of any privatization. We see four areas calling for such anticipation.

5.4.1 Regulation principles in place before privatization

This process refers to the potential benefits of privatization: a reduction of government failure. These benefits can only be reaped if future principles are clarified ex ante. The value of privatization depends, among other things, on the willingness of a privatized Schiphol to invest. This willingness can be hampered by regulatory uncertainty as well as by 'hold-up problems', in which Schiphol anticipates a bailout by the government – which can lead to moral hazard and under-investment. The willingness to invest can be enhanced by reducing regulatory uncertainty, i.e. being clear on regulatory principles before privatization. Clarity about future regulatory principles is advantageous not only for cost–benefit analysis of possible extensions, but also because it enhances the transparency of policy and allows some check on political decision making.

5.4.2 Organization of regulation before privatization

The current regulatory set-up involves the Ministry that is at the same time stakeholder, policymaker and regulator. In a privatized environment, it is preferable to split up the roles of policymaker and supervisor. For practical reasons, the independent supervisor is better installed before privatization. This enables the supervisor to obtain a reputation and find good people in time.

One possible advantage (perhaps the biggest advantage) of privatization of the airport is the division of labour between the airport, the regulator and government makes regulation more transparent than in the case of public ownership of the airport (CPB, 2000).

5.4.3 Ownership of slots

Under current law and bilateral agreements, slots are not tradable, nor is it possible to auction slots. Possible future changes of these constraints might lead to a situation in which the airport owns a scarce asset that can be auctioned to the highest bidder, leading to substantial windfall profits. Similar to radio and ether frequencies, for example, the slots can be considered as property of the public. It may not be efficient, however, to let them be exploited publicly. Therefore, auctions can be organized and one can argue that the returns from these auctions should go to the taxpayers rather than to the shareholders of the airport. However, there are also reasons for internalizing slot allocation within the airport. There can be knowledge advantages and better incentives to combine noise with slot allocation. The literature is quite silent on these matters. Optimal future slot allocation seems to be a promising topic for a research agenda.

5.4.4   Temporary concessions
For private goods, unlimited property rights are normal. As argued above, however, it is unclear whether it is logical to consider Schiphol as a private good. If the government were to keep the land, and give a concession to exploit the airport to a private party, it seems inappropriate to give such a concession to a certain party forever. A temporary concession keeps open the possibility that in the future other parties may be more efficient to exploit the airport. A reason for having unlimited concessions that is sometimes mentioned is that private parties are not prepared to invest if their concession is temporary. This reasoning is flawed. Private parties invest if they think the investment is profitable. If the profits can be reaped only after the termination of the concession period, then this point can be dealt with separately and does not justify irreversible decisions.

6   CONCLUDING REMARKS

Changes in European aviation policy and the proposed privatization of Amsterdam Airport Schiphol affect the trade-offs behind government intervention to address the various market failures that are present. In this article, we have described these trends and discussed their implications for the policy debate – in particular with respect to the regulation of a privatised airport and the process of privatization. Our analysis suggests that the policy debate should be concerned with positive and negative externalities, market power, management control and incentives after privatization. With regard to the privatization process, we argue that the regulatory regime should be in place before the privatization process, the government should think of the possibility of auctioning slots in the future, the term of concession for the airport operator should not be unlimited, and an independent regulator should be set up before the privatization process.

REFERENCES

Barret, S.D. (2000), 'Airport competition in the deregulated European aviation market', *Journal of Air Transport Management*, 6, 13–27.

Borenstein, S. (1992), 'The evolution of US airline competition', *Journal of Economic Perspectives*, 2, 45–73.

Brueckner, J.K. and P.T. Spiller (1994), 'Economics of traffic density in the deregulated airline industry', *Journal of Law and Economics*, 37 (2), 379–415.

Burghouwt, G. and J.R. Hakfoort (1998), 'Deregulering van de luchtvaart. Concurrentie en concentratie', *Economisch Statistische Berichten*, 11 September 1998, 936–9.

Burghouwt, G. and J. Hakfoort (2001), 'The evolution of the European aviation network, 1990–1998', *Journal of Air Transport Management*, 7, 311–8.

Button, K. and D. Swann (1989a), 'The deregulation of US interstate aviation: an assessment of causes and consequences (Part 1)', *Transport Reviews*, 2, 99–118.

Button, K. and D. Swann (1989b), 'The deregulation of US interstate aviation: an assessment of causes and consequences (Part 2)', *Transport Reviews*, 2, 189–215.

Button, K. and D. Swann (1992), 'Transatlantic lessons in aviation deregulation. EEC and US experiences', *The Antitrust Bulletin*, Spring 1992, 207–55.

Button, K., K. Haynes and R. Stough (1998), *Flying into the Future Air Transport Policy in the European Union*, Cheltenham, UK and Lyme, USA Edward Elgar Publishing.

CPB (2000), 'Schiphol: een normaal bedrijf?', CPB Working Paper 126, June.

EURAFOR (2000), *Airline Alliances*, draft, European Civil Aviation Conference.

Goetz, A.R. and C.J. Sutton (1997), 'The geography of deregulation in the US airline industry', *Journal of the Association of American Geographers*, 2, 238–263.

Graham, B. (1995), *Geography and Air Transport*, Chichester, UK: John Wiley and Sons.

Hakfoort, J.R. and M. Schaafsma (2000), 'Planning AirportCity Schiphol. Een heroriëntatie op de toekomst van de luchthaven', in L. Boelens (ed.), *Nederland Netwerkland. Een inventarisatie van de nieuwe condities van planologie en stedenbouw*, Rotterdam: NAi Uitgevers, pp. 79–98.

Hanlon, P. (1996), *Global Airlines. Competition in a Transnational Industry*, Oxford, UK: Butterworth-Heineman Ltd.

Kapur, A. (1995), 'Airport infrastructure. The emerging role of the private sector', World Bank Technical Paper, 313, Washington, US: The World Bank.

Kinnock, N. (1998), Speech to the Association of European Airlines President's Assembly, Hotel Adlon, Berlin, Speech 98/224, 30 October.

Kinnock, N. (1999), 'European Air Transport Policy: All our tomorrows or all our yesterdays replayed', Speech at the European Aviation Club, 12 May.

Kunz, M. (1999), 'Airport regulation: the policy framework', in W. Pfähler, H.-M. Niemeier and O.G. Mayer (eds), *Airports and Air Traffic: Regulation, Privatization and Competition*, Frankfurt, GE: Peter Lang Verlag, pp. 11–55.

Nijkamp, P. (1996), 'Liberalization of air transport in Europe. The survival of the fittest?' Research Memorandum, 1996-11.

Oum, T.H., C. Yu and A. Zhang (2001),' Global airline alliances. International regulatory issues', *Journal of Air Transport Management*, 7, 57–62.

Pels. E. (2001), 'A note on airline alliances', *Journal of Air Transport Management*, 7, 3–7.

Prices Surveillance Authority (1993), *Inquiry into the aeronautical and non-aeronautical charges of the Federal Airports Corporation*, Melbourne, AUS: PSA.

Reynolds-Feighan, A. (1998), 'The impact of US airline deregulation on airport traffic patterns', *Geographical Analysis*, 234–53.

Schiphol Group (2000), 'Preparations for Schiphol Group's flotation on schedule', Schiphol Group, www.schiphol.nl, 14 December 2004.

Schneiderbauer, D. and D. Feldman (1999), 'Global airport management: strategic challenges in an emerging industry', Mercer Management Consulting.

Starkie, D. (1999), 'A new deal for airports, IEA Regulation Lectures', www.iea.org.uk/wpapers/regstarkie.htm, 16 November.

Viscusi, W.K., J.M. Vernon and J.E. Harrington (1998), *Economics of Regulation and Antitrust*, second edition, Cambridge, US: The MIT Press.

Williams, J. (1994), *The Airline Industry and the Impact of Deregulation*, Cambridge, US: Cambridge University Press.

Zacher, M.W. and C.J. Sutton (1996), Governing Global Networks. International Regimes for Transportation and Communication, Cambridge, US: Cambridge University Press.

Zhang, A. (1996), 'An analysis of fortress hubs in airline networks', *Journal of Transport Economics and Policy*, September 1996.

Index

Stanislaw, J. 154
Starkie, D. 227
state
    intervention of 123–4
    omnipresence of 119
    see also public ownership of firms
Stiglitz, J. 123, 156
Stoft, S. 103, 107
Summers, L. 70
Sutton, C. 218, 219, 221
Svindland, E. 42
Swann, D. 219, 220

TDC 202
Teece, D. 79, 80
telecommunications industry
    employment 167
    interconnection prices 164–5, 168–9
    new market entrants 165, 169
    ownership forms 161
        effect of 164, 165, 166, 167, 168,
            169–70
    predicted consequences of regulatory
        reform 67, 68
    privatization 160–61, 170
        effects of 158–9
    productivity 169
    profitability 169
    regulation of 153–4, 162–3, 170
        independence of regulatory
            authorities 162, 167–8, 169
    retail prices 165, 166, 167, 169
    teledensity 167, 169
    see also British Telecom
Thatcher, M. 124
Thiemeyer, T. 157
Thomas, S. 116
Tirole, J. 124, 157, 158, 165, 198
transaction costs 4, 5, 119
Tribunal de Defensa de la Competencia
    (TDC) 202

tying 73

Union of Concerned Scientists 90
Utterback, J. 61

Varian, H. 84
Vickers, J. 155, 157, 158
Vining, A. 155
Virtanen, M. 70
Viscusi, W. 221
Vogelsang, I. 116
Vollaard, B. 67

Waddams-Price, C. 205
Wallsten, S. 159
water industry
    legislation on social issues 180–81
Weisman, D. 121
Weizsäcker, C. von 158
welfare consequences of regulatory
    reform 68, 69
Wene, C. 57
White, L. 70
Whitley, R. 48, 64
Williams, J. 221
Williamson, O. 2, 3, 4, 5, 6, 7
Willig, R. 157, 158
Willner, J. 157, 158
Winter, S. 121
Woolfolk, J. 91, 95
World Bank 225
Wörter, M. 161

Xu, L. 159

Yardley, J. 103
Yarrow, G. 155, 157, 158
Yergin, D. 154

Zacher, M. 218, 219
Zhang, A. 221